Anxiety & Depression Workbook

FOR DUMMIES®

by Charles H. Elliott, PhD and Laura L. Smith, PhD

Foreword by Aaron T. Beck, MD
University Professor of Psychiatry, University of Pennsylvania

Wiley Publishing, Inc.

Anxiety & Depression Workbook For Dummies®

Published by
Wiley Publishing, Inc.
111 River St.
Hoboken, NJ 07030-5774
www.wiley.com

For general information on our other products and services, please contact our Customer Care Department within the U.S. at 877-762-2974, outside the U.S. at 317-572-3993, or fax 317-572-4002.

For technical support, please visit www.wiley.com/techsupport.

Wiley also publishes its books in a variety of electronic formats. Some content that appears in print may not be available in electronic books.

ISBN-13: 978-0-7645-9793-0

Manufactured in the United States of America

10 9 8

1B/RX/RQ/QV/IN

WILEY

About the Authors

Charles H. Elliott, PhD, is a clinical psychologist and a member of the faculty at Fielding Graduate University. He is a Founding Fellow in the Academy of Cognitive Therapy, an international organization that certifies cognitive therapists. He has a part-time private practice in Albuquerque, New Mexico, that specializes in the treatment of anxiety and depression. In addition, he has written many articles and book chapters in the area of cognitive behavior therapies. He has made numerous presentations nationally and internationally on new developments in assessment and therapy of emotional disorders. He is coauthor of *Depression For Dummies* (Wiley), *Overcoming Anxiety For Dummies* (Wiley), *Why Can't I Get What I Want?* (Davies-Black, 1998; A Behavioral Science Book Club Selection), *Why Can't I Be the Parent I Want to Be?* (New Harbinger Publications, 1999), and *Hollow Kids: Recapturing the Soul of a Generation Lost to the Self-Esteem Myth,* (Prima, 2001).

Laura L. Smith, PhD, is a clinical psychologist at the Presbyterian Medical Group, Behavioral Medicine Outpatient Clinic in Albuquerque, New Mexico. She specializes in the assessment and treatment of both adults and children with depression, anxiety, and other emotional disorders. In addition, she has presented on cognitive therapy and mental health issues to both national and international audiences. Dr. Smith is coauthor of *Depression For Dummies* (Wiley), *Overcoming Anxiety For Dummies* (Wiley), *Hollow Kids: Recapturing the Soul of a Generation Lost to the Self-Esteem Myth,* (Prima, 2001) and *Why Can't I Be the Parent I Want to Be?* (New Harbinger Publications,1999).

Drs. Elliott and Smith are available for speaking engagements and workshops. You can visit their Web site at www.PsychAuthors.com.

Dedication

We dedicate this book to our kids: Alli, Brian, Grant, Nathan, Sara, and Trevor. And to our granddaughter: Lauren Melodie. And finally to our parents: Edna Louise Smith, Joe Bond Elliott, Tea Elliott, William Thomas Smith (1914-1999), and Suzanne Wieder Elliott (1923–2004).

Acknowledgments

We're no longer in denial. We're hopelessly addicted to this writing business. We no longer need to apologize to our family and friends for our neglect; they're used to it by now!

We appreciate the efforts of our agents, Ed and Elizabeth Knappman who have encouraged our pursuits. Thanks to our editors at Wiley: Mikal Belicove, Tim Gallan, and Elizabeth Rea.

We would not be able to function without help from Audrey Hite. Special thanks to Scott Love at Softekllc.com, who designed our Web site and keeps our computers happy. Thanks also to Elizabeth Deardorf for making our dogs smile in our authors' picture.

Finally, we have been privileged to hear the many stories of suffering, hurt, trauma, hope, recovery, and resilience from our clients over the years. We respect and appreciate what they have taught us. This book would not be possible without their collective wisdom.

Publisher's Acknowledgments

We're proud of this book; please send us your comments through our Dummies online registration form located at www.dummies.com/register/.

Some of the people who helped bring this book to market include the following:

Acquisitions, Editorial, and Media Development

Senior Project Editor: Tim Gallan

Acquisitions Editors: Mikal Belicove, Mike Lewis

Copy Editor: Elizabeth Rea

Editorial Program Assistant: Courtney Allen

Technical Editor: Linda Ames

Editorial Manager: Christine Meloy Beck

Editorial Assistants: Nadine Bell, David Lutton, Hanna Scott

Cover Photos: © Tim Brown, Stone, Getty Images

Cartoons: Rich Tennant (www.the5thwave.com)

Composition Services

Project Coordinator: Adrienne Martinez

Layout and Graphics: Lauren Goddard, Denny Hager

Proofreaders: Leeann Harney, Sandra Profant

Indexer: Naomi Linzer

Publishing and Editorial for Consumer Dummies

Diane Graves Steele, Vice President and Publisher, Consumer Dummies

Joyce Pepple, Acquisitions Director, Consumer Dummies

Kristin A. Cocks, Product Development Director, Consumer Dummies

Michael Spring, Vice President and Publisher, Travel

Kelly Regan, Editorial Director, Travel

Publishing for Technology Dummies

Andy Cummings, Vice President and Publisher, Dummies Technology/General User

Composition Services

Gerry Fahey, Vice President of Production Services

Debbie Stailey, Director of Composition Services

Contents at a Glance

Table of Contents

Foreword

Not long ago I wrote the following foreword for the book, *Depression For Dummies*. As the current *Anxiety & Depression Workbook For Dummies* is a companion to that book as well as *Overcoming Anxiety For Dummies,* I believe the previous foreword is both germane and worth repeating, followed by some specific comments about the current work.

"I am very pleased that Drs. Charles Elliott and Laura Smith have reviewed and distilled the scientific literature on the treatment of depression for the general public. This book is uniquely comprehensive in that it thoroughly covers the scientifically validated treatments for depression, including behavior therapy, medications, interpersonal therapy, and cognitive therapy. The authors have also included promising ideas based on mindfulness and positive psychology. However, they have chosen to emphasize the importance of cognitive therapy because no other therapy has received as much support as cognitive therapy for the treatment of depression.

Thus, Drs. Elliott and Smith have woven important cognitive therapy principles into their presentation of the other validated approaches to depression. This decision is appropriate since research has suggested that some of these other therapies may in fact work due in part to the cognitive therapy strategies embedded within them.

I believe a word about cognitive therapy is in order. In the late 1950s, I began developing cognitive therapy. At the time, I was dissatisfied with the lack of evidence supporting the value of the prevailing psychotherapy — Freudian psychoanalysis — in treating depression. Cognitive therapy quickly became established as a highly effective treatment for depression, a finding that has been verified in numerous subsequent clinical trials. Over the ensuing decades, cognitive therapy has also demonstrated excellent outcomes in the treatment of problems with anger, anxiety, panic disorder, stress, relationship problems, substance abuse, eating disorders, and most recently, even schizophrenia. To date, no other psychotherapy has demonstrated such consistent effectiveness across a broad swath of problems. *Depression For Dummies* does a marvelous job of providing readers with the core techniques and principles of cognitive therapy as applied to depression.

I feel it's important to note that *Depression For Dummies* is not a book for dummies! Rather, this book lays out the principles of cognitive therapy, as well as other validated psychotherapies, in exceptionally clear terms. Drs. Elliott and Smith include fascinating clinical examples and effective exercises within the most reader-friendly, entertaining format I've seen in a book of this genre. I have no doubt it will prove to be a powerful self-help resource as well as an adjunct to psychotherapy.

I have known Dr. Elliott since the early 1980s, when he was a highly skillful cognitive therapist serving in a major psychotherapy outcome study. I recall last encountering Drs. Elliott and Smith just a few years ago at an international conference on cognitive therapy in Catania, Italy. They presented at this conference as part of their honeymoon. Such dedication to cognitive therapy!

If you struggle with depression, I strongly recommend *Depression For Dummies.* These authors convey considerable compassion, empathy, and insight in addition to unusual clarity."

At this time, I am especially pleased to see that Drs. Elliott and Smith have written a companion workbook called *Anxiety & Depression Workbook For Dummies.* This workbook gives you the basic essentials of each therapeutic strategy. After providing the rudimentary understanding you need, it quickly shows ways to put that information to work in your own life. You won't have to spend hours reading about technical jargon and irrelevant material. Almost everything in this book can be immediately applied to improving the way you feel, behave, and think. In addition, the authors have made the process amazingly painless. The exercises are highly engaging, and Drs. Elliott and Smith weave humor throughout that manages not to demean or condescend. You might just have a good time with this workbook!

Aaron T. Beck, MD
University Professor of Psychiatry
University of Pennsylvania

Introduction

Do you worry too much? Are you often sad or down in the dumps? Do you have to drag yourself out of bed in the morning? Or maybe you avoid people more than you should. If so, you're probably dealing with some type of anxiety or depression. Depression and anxiety are serious problems — they darken vision and distort thinking while draining joy and pleasure from life.

Everyone feels sad or worried from time to time. Unpleasant feelings are a normal part of life. But when depression or anxiety interferes with your work, play, and/or relationships, it's time to take action.

Good news! You can conquer these problems. And the *Anxiety & Depression Workbook For Dummies* will help. You can use this workbook on its own or as a supplement to counseling. In either case, numerous studies show that self-help efforts work.

Experts estimate that almost a quarter of the people in the world will experience significant problems with anxiety at some point in their lives. And between 15 and 20 percent will succumb to the ravages of depression at one point or another. Unfortunately, many people suffer from both of these maladies. Over the years, we've known many clients, friends, and family members who have anguished over anxiety or depression, but most of them have found significant relief.

So if you struggle with anxiety, depression, or both, you're not alone. We join you in your battle by giving you research-based strategies and plenty of practice opportunities to help you defeat depression and overcome anxiety.

About This Book

Our purpose in writing this book is to give you a wide range of skills and tools for managing anxiety and depression. Although we touch on essential concepts about depression and anxiety, this book is action-oriented — in other words, you have the opportunity to actively apply our professional ideas to your life in meaningful ways.

No doubt you used workbooks in school. A math workbook may have helped you apply math concepts to everyday problems. Or a reading workbook may have improved your ability to comprehend stories. Today, you can find workbooks on almost any topic, from selling your home and succeeding on tests to preparing your taxes and improving your memory.

The purpose of any workbook is to lay out the basics of a topic and then provide numerous opportunities to apply and practice the concepts at hand. Typically, books *explain* issues, and workbooks help you *master* new skills. In other words, the *Anxiety & Depression Workbook For Dummies* is "less talk — more action."

Did you notice the "work" part of workbook? Don't put this book back on the shelf quite yet! You'll be well paid for your work in the form of increased life satisfaction and reduced emotional distress. And the work is actually rather interesting because you discover new ways to live your life and get what you want.

A Note to Our Depressed and Anxious Readers

Feeling depressed or anxious certainly isn't funny. In fact, when you're feeling this way, you may find it quite difficult to see the humor in anything. Nevertheless, we've chosen to include a little humor throughout this workbook. We understand that you may be offended that we appear to make light of what is a dark, difficult subject, but humor is an important coping tool. Our intention is to cheer you up a bit.

How to Use This Book

Unlike most workbooks, you don't necessarily have to read and use the chapters of this book in order, beginning to end. You can pick and choose what chapters to read and what exercises to do, and you can also choose where to start and stop. We give you just enough information to carry out the exercises and improve your moods.

This book is meant to be written in. Writing enhances skills and commits you to taking action, so we strongly encourage you to do the work required for your recovery by writing out your answers in the forms and worksheets. Don't worry about your handwriting or spelling — nobody's grading your work.

Throughout this book, you'll see sections labeled My Reflections. When you come across a reflection space, we recommend that you take a little time to ponder what you're feeling, what you've discovered, and/or any new insights you've achieved. But hey, this is your workbook — write down anything you want in My Reflections.

What Not to Read

Workbooks may conjure up memories of boredom and drudgery for you. Do you recall endless hours of mindless homework? Your teacher probably told you to fill out every single page of each and every assignment, whether you'd mastered the skills or not.

Not in this book! We don't tell you what you have to do. You can pick and choose which sections to read and which exercises to complete. Although we believe all our suggestions have value, we encourage you to judge for yourself which exercises offer maximum benefit to you.

What We Assume About You

By the sheer fact that you've picked up this book, we assume, perhaps foolishly, that you want to do something about depression and/or anxiety. We hope you already know a little about these topics, but if you want to know more, we suggest you read either or both of the companion books to this workbook: *Overcoming Anxiety For Dummies* (Wiley) and *Depression For Dummies* (Wiley). Of course, we're slightly biased toward these books because we wrote them, but honestly, they'll broaden your understanding of working through emotional distress.

How This Book Is Organized

The *Anxiety & Depression Workbook For Dummies* is organized into seven parts, which we outline in the following sections.

Part 1: Analyzing Angst and Preparing a Plan

This part is all about helping you identify your problem and take the first small steps toward recovery. Chapter 1 helps you discover whether you have a problem with anxiety or depression. The quizzes in this chapter help you see where these problems show up in your world and what they do to your thoughts, behaviors, feelings, and relationships. In Chapter 2, you go on a journey to the origins of your problems with anxiety and depression because knowing where it all began helps you realize that you're not to blame. Because change sometimes feels overwhelming, Chapter 3 addresses self-sabotage and helps you keep moving forward. Chapter 4 provides you with ways for keeping track of your moods and becoming more aware of your thoughts.

Part 11: Thinking About Thinking: Thought Therapy

The chapters in this part help you become a thought detective. In Chapter 5, you find out how to examine your thoughts for distortions; then, in Chapter 6, you prosecute those distorted thoughts and rehabilitate them.

Chapter 7 shows you how certain core beliefs darken and distort your view of yourself, your world, and your future as surely as eyeglasses with the wrong prescription muddle normal sight. We include tools for regrinding your life-lenses so you see things more clearly. Finally, in Chapter 8, you have the opportunity to practice mindfulness and acceptance — more techniques for handling troubling thoughts.

Part 111: Actions Against Angst: Behavior Therapy

Chapter 9 spells out how you take direct action against the natural tendency to avoid what makes you depressed or anxious. In Chapter 10, we get you up and moving by providing workbook-type exercises that encourage physical exercise. When you're depressed or anxious, few activities sound like fun, so Chapter 11 has worksheets for reintroducing pleasure into your life. Finally, Chapter 12 helps you tackle life problems that grow out of your emotional distress.

Part 1V: Phocus on Physical Pheelings

Addressing the physical side of distress is as important as addressing the mental or emotional side. Excessive stress associated with anxiety and depression produces hormones that ravage the body by increasing blood pressure and contributing to stomach problems, weight gain, and heart disease. Therefore, relaxation techniques play an important role in alleviating anxiety and depression. In Chapter 13, you find a variety of exercises for reducing tension and stress. Because medication is an additional option for many people who are depressed or anxious, Chapter 14 guides you through the decision of whether or not medications are the right choice for you.

Part V: Relationship Therapy

Depression and anxiety can spill over and contaminate your relationships like sewage dumped into a river. Good relationships offer support in dealing with emotional distress, whereas spoiled relationships just make things worse. Chapter 15 helps you figure out if your relationships are suffering, and the worksheets and exercises in Chapter 16 guide you in improving the quality of your relationships.

Part VI: Looking Beyond Anxiety and Depression

After people overcome their anxiety and depression, naturally they prefer to go on with their lives as though they'd never had a problem. Unfortunately, like the flu, you can catch depression or anxiety more than once. Chapter 17 tells you how to prepare for and deal with any setbacks in your condition, and Chapter 18 helps you develop positive habits that lead to a more joyful, meaningful, and connected life.

Part VII: The Part of Tens

This part contains a couple of our top ten lists when it comes to the subject of anxiety and depression. Chapter 19 recommends ten resources for getting help in dealing with your depression and anxiety. If you're looking for a quick way out of a bad mood, Chapter 20 is for you — it lists ten remedies that don't take a whole lot of effort.

Characters in This Book

Throughout this workbook, we use fictional characters to illustrate how you can complete the various worksheets and exercises. Although these characters aren't real people, they represent composites of various clients and others we've known and worked with over the years. Any resemblance to an actual individual, whether alive or deceased, is unintended and coincidental. Nonetheless, we believe you'll find yourself relating to these characters and find their experiences useful.

Icons Used in This Book

Throughout the book, icons in the margins alert you to important types of information:

This icon marks particularly noteworthy information that we hope you'll remember long after you read this workbook.

This icon tells you it's time to roll up your sleeves and get to work! It denotes a worksheet, form, or exercise for you to fill out.

This icon points to specific examples that show you the way through worksheets or exercises.

This icon appears when you need to take care; you may need professional help or should be on the lookout for possible trouble.

This icon alerts you to especially useful insights and explanations.

Where to Go from Here

The *Anxiety & Depression Workbook For Dummies* can help you deal with your depression and anxiety. It's pragmatic, concrete, and goes straight to the point. As such, this workbook doesn't devote a lot of text to lengthy explanations or embellishments of basic concepts, so you may wish to find out more about specific types of depression and anxiety, available medications, and alternative treatments. For that purpose, we strongly recommend that you consider reading one or both of the companion books, *Depression For Dummies* (Wiley) and *Overcoming Anxiety For Dummies* (Wiley).

Part I
Analyzing Angst and Preparing a Plan

The 5th Wave   By Rich Tennant

"We've tried adjusting your diet, and prescribing medication for your anxiety. Now let's try loosening some of those bolts and see if that does anything."

In this part . . .

We help you figure out how anxiety or depression affects your thinking, behaving, feeling, and bodily sensations. You discover how your problems began and work toward accepting that you're not to blame for having them. In case you feel stuck or unable to move forward, we give you strategies for overcoming obstacles. Finally, you see how to keep track of both your moods and the thoughts that accompany distressing feelings.

Chapter 1

Sorting Out Signs of Anxiety and Depression

In This Chapter

▶ Figuring out how depression and anxiety affect you

▶ Finding your personal starting point

▶ Knowing when to get more help

*E*veryone feels sad or worried from time to time. Such emotions are both natural and unavoidable. People worry about their children, bills, aging parents, jobs, and health. And most people have shed a tear or two watching a sad movie or a news story about a poignant tragedy. That's normal. A little bit of anxiety and depression is part of everyday life.

But when sadness fills most of your days or worries saturate your mind, that's not so normal. You may be experiencing a real problem with depression or anxiety. Anxiety and depression can affect how you think, behave, feel, and relate to others. The discussion and quizzes in this chapter help you figure out how depression and anxiety affect your life. When you understand what's going on, you can start doing something about it.

Don't freak out if the quizzes in this chapter reveal that you have a few symptoms of anxiety or depression. Most people do. We let you know if you should be concerned.

If your symptoms are numerous and severe or your life seems out of control, you should consult your primary care physician or a mental health professional. These quizzes aren't meant to replace trained mental health professionals — they're the only people who can really diagnose your problem.

Dwelling on Dismal and Worried Thoughts

If you were able to listen in on the thoughts that reverberate through a depressed person's head, you might hear "I'm a failure," "My future looks bleak," "Things just keep on getting worse," or "I regret so many things in my life."

On the other hand, the thoughts of an anxious person might sound like "I'm going to make a fool out of myself when I give that speech," "I never know what to say at parties," "The freeway scares me to death," "I know that the odds of a plane crash are small, but flying scares me," or "I'm going have a nervous breakdown if my editor doesn't like what I write."

Thoughts influence the way you feel. The very darkest thoughts usually lead to depression, whereas anxiety usually stems from thoughts about being judged or hurt. And, of course, people often have both types of thoughts.

Do your thoughts dwell on the dark, dismal, or the scary aspects of life? Take the quiz in Worksheet 1-1 to determine if your thoughts reflect a problem with anxiety or depression. Put a check mark next to an item if you feel the statement applies to you.

Worksheet 1-1	The Negative Thinking Quiz

- ❏ 1. Things are getting worse and worse for me.
- ❏ 2. I worry all the time.
- ❏ 3. I think I'm worthless.
- ❏ 4. I never know what to say.
- ❏ 5. No one would miss me if I were dead.
- ❏ 6. I'm afraid that I'll get sick.
- ❏ 7. I think I'm a failure.
- ❏ 8. My thoughts race, and I obsess about things.
- ❏ 9. I don't look forward to much of anything.
- ❏ 10. I get really nervous around people I don't know.
- ❏ 11. The world would be better off without me.
- ❏ 12. Thoughts about past trauma keep rolling through my mind.
- ❏ 13. I find it impossible to make decisions.
- ❏ 14. I can't stand it when I'm the center of attention.
- ❏ 15. My life is full of regrets.
- ❏ 16. I can't stand making mistakes.
- ❏ 17. I don't see things getting any better in the future.
- ❏ 18. I worry about my health all the time.
- ❏ 19. I'm deeply ashamed of myself.
- ❏ 20. I over-prepare for everything.

Although these thoughts can occur to someone who's either depressed or anxious (or both), the odd-numbered items are most indicative of depression, and the even-numbered items reflect anxious thinking. There's no pass or fail mark on this quiz. However, the more items you endorse, the more you have cause for concern; specifically, if you check more than eight or ten items, you should think seriously about addressing your condition. At the same time, if you very strongly believe in any of these items, you just may have too much anxiety or depression.

If you have any thoughts of suicide or utter hopelessness, you should consult your primary care physician or a mental health professional immediately.

Walking in Quicksand: Apprehensive and Blue Behavior

If you were to follow a depressed or anxious person around, you might see some behavioral signs of their emotional turmoil. That's because depression and anxiety on the inside affect what people do on the outside. For example, a depressed person may look tired, move slowly, or withdraw from friends and family; an anxious person may avoid socializing or have a trembling voice.

Take the quiz in Worksheet 1-2 to see if your behavior indicates a problem with anxiety and/or depression. Check off each statement that applies to you.

Worksheet 1-2	The Distraught Behavior Quiz

❑ 1. I've been crying for no clear reason.

❑ 2. I pace around when I'm worried.

❑ 3. Sometimes I can't make myself get out of bed.

❑ 4. I avoid going into crowded areas.

❑ 5. I can't seem to make myself exercise.

❑ 6. I avoid risks because I'm afraid of failure.

❑ 7. I don't do things for fun lately.

❑ 8. I always play things on the safe side.

❑ 9. I've been missing work lately because I just don't have the motivation.

❑ 10. I'm really fidgety.

❑ 11. I've been doing everything at a much slower pace for no good reason.

❑ 12. I avoid people or places that remind me of a bad past experience.

❑ 13. I don't care what I look like anymore.

❑ 14. I spend too much time making sure I look okay.

❑ 15. I don't laugh anymore.

❑ 16. My hands shake when I'm nervous.

❑ 17. I've been letting things go that I need to attend to.

❑ 18. I feel compelled to repeat actions (such as hand washing, checking locks, arranging things in a certain way, and so on).

Again, there's no pass or fail on this quiz. The more items you check, the greater the problem. Even-numbered items are most consistent with anxiety, and odd-numbered items largely indicate depression. And, of course, like many people, you may have symptoms of both types of problems.

Feeling Funky

Depression and anxiety inevitably produce physical symptoms. In fact, some people primarily suffer from changes in appetite, sleep, energy, or pain while reporting few problematic thoughts or behaviors. These symptoms directly affect your body, but they're not as easily observed by other people as the behavioral signs covered in the preceding section.

Take The Sad, Stressed Sensations Quiz in Worksheet 1-3 to see if your body is trying to tell you something about your emotional state.

Worksheet 1-3	**The Sad, Stressed Sensations Quiz**

- ❏ 1. I have no appetite.
- ❏ 2. My palms sweat all the time.
- ❏ 3. I wake up too early each morning and can't go back to sleep.
- ❏ 4. I've been experiencing a lot of nausea and diarrhea.
- ❏ 5. I've been sleeping a lot more than usual.
- ❏ 6. I feel shaky all over.
- ❏ 7. I've been having lots of aches and pains for no good reason.
- ❏ 8. When I'm nervous, my chest feels tight.
- ❏ 9. I have no energy lately.
- ❏ 10. My heart races when I'm tense.
- ❏ 11. I've been constipated a lot more often than usual.
- ❏ 12. I feel like I can't catch my breath.
- ❏ 13. I'm eating all the time lately.
- ❏ 14. My hands are often cold and clammy.
- ❏ 15. I've lost my sex drive.
- ❏ 16. Sometimes I hyperventilate.
- ❏ 17. Every move I make takes more effort lately.
- ❏ 18. I get dizzy easily.

The symptoms in this quiz can also result from various physical illnesses, drugs in your medicine cabinet, or even your three-cup coffee fix in the morning. Be sure to consult your primary care physician if you're experiencing any of the symptoms in The Sad, Stressed Sensations Quiz. It's always a good idea to have a checkup once a year and more frequently if you experience noticeable changes in your body.

Although physical sensations overlap in anxiety and depression, even-numbered items in the quiz above are most consistent with anxiety, and the odd-numbered items usually plague those with depression. There's no cutoff point for indicating a problem. The more statements you check off, though, the worse your problem.

Reflecting upon Relationships

When you're feeling down or distressed for any length of time, odds are that your relationships with those around you will take a hit. Although you may think that your depression or anxiety affects only you, it impacts your friends, family, lovers, co-workers, and acquaintances.

Take the quiz in Worksheet 1-4 to see if your emotions are causing trouble with your relationships. Check off any statements that apply to you.

Worksheet 1-4	The Conflicted Connections Quiz

❏ 1. I don't feel like being with anybody.

❏ 2. I get very nervous when I meet new people.

❏ 3. I don't feel like talking to anyone.

❏ 4. I'm overly sensitive when anyone criticizes me in the slightest way.

❏ 5. I'm more irritable with others than usual.

❏ 6. I worry about saying the wrong thing.

❏ 7. I don't feel connected to anyone.

❏ 8. I worry about people leaving me.

❏ 9. I don't feel like going out with anyone anymore.

❏ 10. I'm plagued by visions of people I care about getting hurt.

❏ 11. I've withdrawn from everyone.

❏ 12. I feel uptight in crowds, so I stay at home.

❏ 13. I feel numb around people.

❏ 14. I always feel uncomfortable in the spotlight.

❏ 15. I feel unworthy of friendship and love.

❏ 16. Compliments make me feel uneasy.

You guessed it; there's no cutoff score here to tell you definitively whether or not you're anxious or depressed. But the more items you check off, the more your relationships are suffering from your anxiety, depression, or both. Odd-numbered items usually indicate problems with depression, and even-numbered items particularly accompany anxious feelings.

Many people are a little shy or introverted. You may feel somewhat anxious meeting new people and may be uncomfortable in the spotlight — these feelings aren't necessarily anything to be concerned about. However, such issues become problematic when you find yourself avoiding social activities or meeting new people because of your shyness.

Plotting Your Personal Problems Profile

The Personal Problems Profile provides you with an overview of your problematic symptoms. (If you skipped the quizzes in the previous sections of this chapter, go back and take some time to complete them; your answers to those quizzes come into play in this exercise.) The profile exercise in this section helps you identify the ways in which anxiety and depression affect you. One good thing about this profile is that you can track how these symptoms change as you progress through the rest of this book.

Tyler, a middle-aged engineer, doesn't consider himself depressed or plagued with any emotional problems. But when he sees his primary care doctor, Tyler complains of fatigue, recent weight gain, and a noticeable loss in his sex drive. After ruling out physical causes, the doctor suggests that he may be depressed. "Funny," Tyler says, "my girlfriend just bought me the *Anxiety & Depression Workbook For Dummies* and said she thought I was depressed too. Maybe I'll take a look at it."

When Tyler fills out his Personal Problems Profile (see Worksheet 1-5), he lists the following top ten symptoms and notes whether they indicate anxiety or depression (*A* or *D*).

Worksheet 1-5	Tyler's Personal Problems Profile

1. I have no energy lately. (D)

2. Every move I make takes more effort lately. (D)

3. I've lost my sex drive. (D)

4. I've been eating all the time lately. (D)

5. I don't feel like being with anyone. (D)

6. I don't look forward to much of anything. (D)

7. I find it impossible to make decisions. (D)

8. I worry about my health all the time. (A)

9. I feel shaky all over. (A)

10. Sometimes I can't make myself get out of bed. (D)

As you can see, Tyler suffers primarily from symptoms of depression. And most of these symptoms are physical in nature. Filling out his Personal Problems Profile helps Tyler see that he has a depression that he wasn't even consciously aware of. He reflects on his discovery (see Worksheet 1-6).

Worksheet 1-6	Tyler's Reflections

I can see that I do have signs of depression. I didn't realize that before. And I see that depression particularly shows up in my body. It's affecting my energy, sex drive, and appetite. It's also making me withdraw from my girlfriend, which I can see from my loss of sex drive and lack of desire to be with her. Apparently, I also have a few symptoms of anxiety, and I think I always have. It's time to do something about this.

This is the *Anxiety & Depression* **Workbook** *For Dummies.* You can't feel better without doing a little work. It isn't that difficult. Of course, you can skip a few exercises, but the more you do, the sooner you'll start feeling better. Odd as it may seem, writing things down does a world of good. Writing helps you remember, clarifies your thinking, and increases focus and reflection.

Now, complete your own Personal Problems Profile in Worksheet 1-7. Look back at the quizzes earlier in this chapter and underline the most problematic thoughts, feelings, behaviors, and relationship issues for you. Then choose up to ten of the most significant items that you've underlined and write them in the My Personal Problems Profile space that's provided.

In addition, put an *A* by the symptoms that are most indicative of anxiety (even-numbered items in the preceding quizzes) and a *D* by symptoms that are most consistent with depression (odd-numbered items).

Worksheet 1-7	**My Personal Problems Profile**
1.	
2.	
3.	
4.	
5.	
6.	
7.	
8.	
9.	
10.	

Do your symptoms mostly involve anxiety, depression, or a mix of the two? And do they seem to mostly affect your thoughts, feelings, behaviors, or relationships? Take some time to reflect on your profile. What conclusions can you draw? Record them in Worksheet 1-8.

Worksheet 1-8	**My Reflections**

Choosing Your Challenge

The next four parts of this workbook cover the areas of thoughts, feelings, behaviors, and relationships. One obvious way of deciding which area to begin in is to choose the one that causes you the most problems. Or, you can work through them in order. Wherever you choose to start, you should know that all these areas interact with each other. For example, if you have anxious *thoughts* about being judged, you're likely to avoid *(behavior)* the spotlight. And you could very well experience butterflies *(feelings)*. Furthermore, you may be overly sensitive to criticism from others *(relationships)*.

Nevertheless, we find that many people like to start out by tackling the problem area that best fits their personal styles. In other words, some folks are doers and others are thinkers; still others are feelers, and some are relaters. Use the Personal Style Questionnaire in Worksheet 1-9 to pinpoint and understand your preferred style.

Worksheet 1-9	Personal Style Questionnaire

Thinkers

❑ I like facts and numbers.

❑ I tend to be a very logical person.

❑ I'm a planner.

❑ I like to think through problems.

❑ I carefully weigh costs and benefits before I act.

Doers

❑ I can't stand sitting around and thinking.

❑ I like to take action on problems.

❑ I like accomplishing things each day.

❑ I like plowing through obstacles.

❑ I act first and think later.

Feelers

❑ I'm a very sensuous person.

❑ I pay a lot of attention to how I feel.

❑ I love massages and hot baths.

❑ Music and art are very important to me.

❑ I'm very in touch with my feelings.

Relaters

❑ I'm a people person.

❑ I'd rather be with people than anything else.

❑ I care deeply about other people's feelings.

❑ I'm very empathetic.

❑ Relationships are more important to me than accomplishments.

Are you predominately a thinker, doer, feeler, or relater? If you checked considerably more items in one area than the others, you may want to start your work in the part of this workbook that corresponds to that style:

✔ **Thinker:** Part II, Thought Therapy

✔ **Doer:** Part III, Behavior Therapy

✔ **Feeler:** Part IV, Physical Feelings

✔ **Relater:** Part V, Relationship Therapy

Knowing When to Get More Help

Self-help tools benefit almost everyone who puts in the effort. Many people find they can overcome minor to moderate emotional problems by working with books like this one. Nevertheless, some difficulties require professional help, perhaps because your anxiety or depression is especially serious or because your problems are simply too complex to be addressed by self-help methods.

Work through The Serious Symptom Checklist in Worksheet 1-10 to find out if you should seriously consider seeking treatment from a mental health professional.

Checking off any one item from the list means that you should strongly consider a professional consultation. Furthermore, please realize that no such list can be all-inclusive. If you're really not sure if you need help, see a mental health professional for an assessment.

Worksheet 1-10   The Serious Symptom Checklist

❏ I have thoughts about killing myself.

❏ I feel hopeless.

❏ My sleep has been seriously disturbed for more than two weeks (including sleeping too little or too much).

❏ I've gained or lost more than a few pounds without trying to do so.

❏ I'm ignoring major responsibilities in my life such as going to work or paying bills.

❏ I'm hearing voices.

❏ I'm seeing things that aren't there.

❏ My drug use and/or drinking are interfering with my life.

❏ My thoughts race, and I can't slow them down.

❏ Someone I trust and care about has said I need help.

❏ I've been getting into numerous fights or arguments.

❏ I've been making really poor decisions lately (such as making outlandish purchases or getting involved in questionable business schemes).

❏ Lately I've felt that people are out to get me.

❏ I haven't been able to get myself to leave the house except for absolute essentials.

❏ I'm taking risks that I never did before.

❏ Suddenly I feel like I'm a special person who's capable of extraordinary things.

❏ I'm spending considerably more time everyday than I should repeating actions such as hand washing, arranging things, and checking and rechecking things (appliances, locks, and so on).

❏ I have highly disturbing flashbacks or nightmares about past trauma that I can't seem to forget about.

If you checked one or more of the statements above and you're beginning to think that perhaps you need help, where should you go? Many people start with their family physicians, which is a pretty good idea because your doctor can also determine if your problems have a physical cause. If physical problems have been ruled out or treated and you still need help, you can:

> ✔ Check with your state's psychology, counseling, social work, or psychiatric association.
>
> ✔ Call your insurance company for recommendations.
>
> ✔ Ask trusted friends or family for recommendations.
>
> ✔ Contact your local university department of psychology, social work, counseling, or psychiatry for a referral.

Either before or during your first session, talk to the mental health professional and ask if you'll receive a scientifically validated treatment for anxiety or depression. Unfortunately, some practitioners lack necessary training in therapies that have shown effectiveness in scientific studies. And make sure whomever you see is a licensed mental health practitioner.

At this point, you should pat yourself on the back! Whether this is the first chapter you've read or not, you've made a good start. Every minute you spend with this workbook is likely to improve your moods.

Chapter 2

Discovering the Beginnings

*I*f you're reading this book, you probably feel a little anxious or depressed. But you may not know where those feelings come from. It's valuable to understand the origins of your feelings, whether its biology and genetics, personal history, or stress. This chapter helps you gain insight into the source of your problem and connect the dots, because knowing the origins of your emotions allows you to discard the baggage of guilt and self-blame.

In this chapter, we review the major causes of depression and anxiety: biology, personal history, and stress. Many of our clients come to us believing that they're to blame for having succumbed to emotional distress. When they discover the factors that contributed to the origins of their problems, they usually feel less guilty, and getting rid of that guilt frees up energy that can be used for making important changes.

Building the Body Connection

Feelings can have biological beginnings. Does your Uncle Paul seem down in the dumps? Was Cousin Jack a neat freak? Was your grandmother a recluse? What was your great-grandmother like? Why are these questions important? Because depression and anxiety tend to run in families. And genes could be responsible for a good portion of your emotional distress.

If you have access to family members, ask if they'd be willing to talk with you about your family's history. Ask them if any relatives, from either side of the family, suffered from any symptoms of anxiety or depression. You may want to review the symptoms covered in Chapter 1 first. There's no exact number of relatives required for determining if genetics are responsible for your symptoms. However, the more family members with similar problems, the more likely you've inherited a tendency for depression or anxiety. Fill in the blanks here with what you learn.

Members of my family with anxiety or depression (brothers, sisters, cousins, parents, uncles, aunts, and grandparents):

_____

_____

_____

_____

_____

In addition to genetics, depression and anxiety can have biological underpinnings in the drugs you take (legal or illegal) or as the result of physical illness. Drugs — whether over-the-counter, prescription, or illegal — have many side effects. Sometimes solving your problem is as simple as checking your medicine cabinet for possible culprits.

Almost any medication you're taking could influence your emotions negatively. Check with your pharmacist or primary care physician to see if your medication may be causing part of your problem. Don't stop taking the medication without medical consultation.

In addition, alcohol is widely known to contribute to depression or anxiety when it's abused. Some people find that even moderate amounts of alcohol exacerbate their problems with mood. Alcohol also interacts with a wide variety of prescribed and over-the-counter drugs to produce harmful and even deadly results.

Finally, illegal drugs such as marijuana, cocaine, heroin, methamphetamine, ecstasy, and so on are taken to alter moods. In the short run, they accomplish that goal; but in the long run, they almost inevitably worsen mood problems.

Physical illnesses can also produce symptoms of anxiety or depression. Not only can the illness itself cause mood problems, but worry and grief about illness can contribute to your distress. If you've been diagnosed with a medical condition, check with your doctor to see if your depression or anxiety is related to that condition.

Laying Out a Lifeline

The sadness and angst you feel today often sprout from seeds planted in your past. Therefore, exploring your personal history provides clues about the origins of your problems. The exercise in this section, called the Emotional Origins form, takes a little time.

The Emotional Origins exercise makes you revisit your childhood by asking questions about your parents and your childhood experiences. Some of the memories involved may evoke powerful emotions; if you become overwhelmed, you may wish to stop the exercise and consult a mental health professional for guidance and support.

Filling out this form is a lot easier after you look over an example. So, the following example shows you how Tyler filled out his Emotional Origins form.

Tyler suffers from many physical signs of depression such as lack of energy and increased appetite. He has little insight as to the origins of his depression. His physician refers him to a psychologist who suggests he fill out an Emotional Origins form (see Worksheet 2-1) to examine his childhood experiences.

Worksheet 2-1 **Tyler's Emotional Origins**

Questions About Mother (or other caregiver)

1. What was my mother's personality like?

She was self-centered and rarely thought much about what my sister and I needed. When things didn't go her way, she exploded. She was domineering and incredibly uptight. She was a perfectionist who talked about the "right way" or the "wrong way" to do things. I also remember that she always acted like a martyr.

2. How did my mother discipline me?

She mostly just yelled at us. Sometimes she'd ground us, but we'd talk our way out of it. I didn't get in a lot of trouble because she didn't catch me breaking the rules.

3. Was my mother warm or cold?

It's funny; she could be very warm sometimes. But in other ways, it felt like she couldn't care less about me.

4. Was she overly critical or supportive?

Again, she was inconsistent. She could be both. Sometimes, she'd encourage me to do things, and other times, she'd rip me to shreds. I never knew what to expect.

5. How did she spend time with me?

This seems odd, but I just don't remember doing much of anything with her. She was a den mother for my Cub Scout group, though. In retrospect, the things she did always seemed to be more about her than about me.

6. Were there special circumstances (for example, illness, death, divorce, military service, etc.)?

She had a miscarriage when I was about 6 years old. She was really depressed for several years after that.

7. Does anything else important about her come to mind, whether positive or negative?

She never seemed especially happy or satisfied with her life. I remember her getting furious with my father a number of times.

Questions About Father (or other important caregiver)

1. What was my father's personality like?

Everybody liked him. He could be very funny. But I can't say that I really knew him very well.

2. How did my father discipline me?

He mostly stayed out of the discipline area. But sometimes he'd explode over nothing.

3. Was my father warm or cold?

I guess he was warm, but looking back, it feels like it was pretty superficial. He never said, "I love you."

4. Was he overly critical or supportive?

Neither really. He didn't pay a lot of attention to me. He paid more attention to my sister than to me. I always felt I wasn't good enough to warrant his attention.

5. How did he spend time with me?

When I was little, he'd wrestle and roughhouse with me. He worked really long hours and just wasn't around that much.

6. Were there special circumstances (for example, illness, death, divorce, military service, etc.)?

Nothing really. To the outside world, we seemed like a pretty typical family with no particular problems.

7. Does anything else important about him come to mind, whether positive or negative?

When he tried to teach me to do things, he'd explode if I didn't get the hang of it right away.

Other Questions About Childhood

---

1. What are my earliest memories?

I don't remember much from when I was a little kid. My grandfather used to take us horseback riding. That was fun. I remember my father and my grandparents having a big fight over money. That was scary.

2. Did I have siblings or other people in the home who influenced me, and how?

I looked up to my older sister, but she didn't want anything to do with me after she went to junior high school. I think my parents favored her — at least my Dad did. I never felt like I measured up to her.

3. What do I remember about grade school? (Was I happy; what did I think about myself; how did I do in school; what were my friendships like; were there any important events?)

I remember being really shy. But I was a good student. I had a few good friends, but they were sort of nerds like me.

4. What do I remember about middle school or junior high school? (Was I happy; what did I think about myself; how did I do in school; what were my friendships like; were there any important events?)

> I was even shyer then. I felt clumsy and awkward all the time. I didn't get invited to parties much. I wasn't very happy. If I got upset, my mother sometimes would do some of my homework for me. Then she'd make me feel guilty about it.

5. What do I remember about high school? (Was I happy; what did I think about myself; how did I do in school; what were my friendships like; were there any important events?)

> I had a few more friends then and started dating some. I got pretty down when a girl jilted me. I remember staying in my room for hours at a time. I realize now that I didn't know how to handle my emotions very well — when I didn't know what else to do, I'd just withdraw. I worked just hard enough to get Bs, but I know I could have done much better in school.

6. What are the major events of my adulthood, such as trauma or winning the lottery?

> I graduated from college, got married, and had a couple of kids. My divorce after 14 years of marriage came as a shock, but I got through it okay.

7. What did this exercise teach me about the origins of my anxiety or depression?

> When I think back on my childhood, I realize it wasn't very happy. My dad didn't seem to care much about me. My mother cared more, but she was like an emotional roller coaster. I just shut down, and I think I've had that tendency my whole life. Maybe I'm shutting down now, too; it's what I do when I'm unhappy. I guess I realize that I'm not totally to blame for my problems. It sort of makes sense that I shut down whenever I face possible rejection, criticism, or when someone gets angry with me.

After completing the Emotional Origins form, Tyler has a better understanding of why he copes with stress the way he does. He sees that there's a reason he shuts down when facing certain types of situations. The exercise isn't about blame and faultfinding; rather, it helps Tyler forgive himself for being the way he is. These insights start him on the path toward a new beginning.

Now, complete your Emotional Origins form in Worksheet 2-2. This is an important exercise; take as much time as you need. If you happen to be receiving counseling or psychotherapy, your therapist will no doubt find this information useful and informative.

Start by reflecting on your childhood. You may jump-start your memory by talking with relatives or by looking through old photo albums. Then move on to answer the questions about your parents or caregivers as well as the questions about your childhood and adolescence. Don't worry about getting all the details right — just do the best you can. Memories aren't always completely accurate, but, in a powerful way, they impact the way you feel today.

Please realize that the intent of this exercise is not to place blame on your parents or other important people in your life. These people indeed may have made significant contributions to your problems, and that's useful to know. But they came by their own problems as honestly as you did. Understanding helps; blame and faultfinding do not.

Worksheet 2-2	My Emotional Origins

Questions About Mother (or other caregiver)

1. **What was my mother's personality like?**

_____

_____

_____

2. **How did my mother discipline me?**

_____

_____

_____

3. **Was my mother warm or cold?**

_____

_____

_____

4. **Was she overly critical or supportive?**

_____

_____

_____

5. **How did she spend time with me?**

_____

_____

_____

6. Were there special circumstances (for example, illness, death, divorce, military service, etc.)?

_____

_____

_____

_____

7. Does anything else important about her come to mind, whether positive or negative?

_____

_____

_____

_____

Questions About Father (or other important caregiver)

1. What was my father's personality like?

_____

_____

_____

_____

2. How did my father discipline me?

_____

_____

_____

_____

3. Was my father warm or cold?

_____

_____

_____

_____

4. Was he overly critical or supportive?

_____

_____

_____

_____

5. How did he spend time with me?

_____

_____

_____

_____

6. Were there special circumstances (for example, illness, death, divorce, military service, etc.)?

_____

_____

_____

_____

7. Does anything else important about him come to mind, whether positive or negative?

_____

_____

_____

_____

Other Questions About Childhood

1. What are my earliest memories?

_____

_____

_____

_____

2. **Did I have siblings or other people in the home who influenced me, and how?**

_____

_____

_____

_____

3. **What do I remember about grade school? (Was I happy; what did I think about myself; how did I do in school; what were my friendships like; were there any important events?)**

_____

_____

_____

_____

4. **What do I remember about middle school or junior high school? (Was I happy; what did I think about myself; how did I do in school; what were my friendships like; were there any important events?)**

_____

_____

_____

_____

5. **What do I remember about high school? (Was I happy; what did I think about myself; how did I do in school; what were my friendships like; were there any important events?)**

_____

_____

_____

_____

6. **What are the major events of my adulthood, such as trauma or winning the lottery?**

_____

_____

_____

_____

7. What did this exercise teach me about the origins of my anxiety or depression?

_____

_____

_____

_____

Surveying Stress

In the search for causes of your anxiety or depression, you need to include a review of your world. Open your eyes and observe. What's going on in your life that aggravates your distress? From daily traffic hassles to major losses, stressful events deplete your coping resources and even harm your health. Complete The Current Culprits Survey in Worksheet 2-3 to uncover the sources of your stress. You can't make your world less stressful unless you first identify the stress-causing culprits.

Worksheet 2-3   **The Current Culprits Survey**

---

1. In the past year or so, have I lost anyone I care about through death, divorce, or prolonged separation?

_____

_____

_____

_____

2. Have I suffered from any serious physical injury or illness?

_____

_____

_____

_____

3. Have finances caused me any difficulty recently? Or have I made any major purchases such as a new house or car?

_____

_____

_____

_____

4. Am I having arguments or conflicts with anyone?

_____

_____

_____

5. Are there problems at work such as new responsibilities, longer hours, or poor management?

_____

_____

_____

6. Have I made any major changes in my life such as retirement, a new job, or a new relationship?

_____

_____

_____

7. Do I have major responsibility for the care of a parent or child?

_____

_____

_____

8. Do I have daily hassles such as a long commute, disturbing noises, or poor living conditions?

_____

_____

_____

You may notice that a few of the items above have positive aspects to them. For example, retirement or the purchase of a new home may be exciting. However, all major changes, whether positive or negative, carry significant stress that tags along for the ride.

Drawing Conclusions

You didn't ask for depression or anxiety. Your distress is understandable if you examine the three major contributors: biology/genetics, your personal history, and the stressors in your world. Take a moment to summarize in Worksheet 2-4 what you believe are the most important origins and contributors to your depression or anxiety.

Worksheet 2-4   **My Most Important Contributors**

---

1. **Physical contributors (genetics, drugs, illness):**

_____

_____

_____

_____

2. **My personal history:**

_____

_____

_____

_____

3. **The stressors in my world:**

_____

_____

_____

_____

As you review your summary, we sincerely hope you conclude that you're truly not at fault for having depression or anxiety. At the same time, you're responsible for doing something about your distress — no one can do the work for you. Just remember that working on your emotional distress rewards you with lifelong benefits.

Chapter 3

Overcoming Obstacles to Change

● ●

In This Chapter
▶ Uncovering change-blocking beliefs
▶ Busting beliefs
▶ Sleuthing self-sabotage
▶ Slicing through self-sabotage

● ●

You don't *want* to feel depressed or anxious. And at times it probably seems as if you have no choice but to feel that way. You want to do something about your distress, but you may feel overwhelmed and incapable. Truth is, you *can* do something about your predicament. But first, you have to understand and overcome the obstacles in your mind that prevent you from taking action and moving forward.

In this chapter, we help you uncover assumptions or beliefs you may have that make it hard for you to tackle your problems. After you identify the beliefs that stand in your way, you can use a tool we provide to remove these obstacles from your path. We also help you discover whether you're unconsciously sabotaging your own progress. If you discover that you're getting in your own way, we show you how to rewrite your self-defeating script.

Discovering and Challenging Change-Blocking Beliefs

You may not be aware that people hold many beliefs about change. For example, some people believe that change is frightening. Others think they don't deserve to be happy and therefore don't change their lives to improve their situations. By stealing your motivation to change, assumptions such as these can keep you stuck in a depressed or anxious state. And, unfortunately, most people aren't aware of when and how these underlying assumptions can derail the most serious and sincere efforts for making changes.

The quizzes in this section are designed to help you discover whether any change-blocking beliefs create obstacles on your road to change. After the quizzes, you can find an exercise that assists you in ridding yourself of these beliefs through careful, honest analysis of whether each belief helps or hurts you.

Detecting beliefs standing in your way

People resist change because they are afraid, feel they don't deserve something better, and/or view themselves as helpless to do anything about their circumstances. Unknowingly holding any of these beliefs will inevitably impede your progress toward change. So take the following three quizzes to see which, if any, of these barriers exist in your mind. Put a check mark next to each statement in Worksheets 3-1, 3-2, and 3-3 that you feel applies to you.

Worksheet 3-1 **The Fear of Change Quiz**

❑ 1. If I take a risk, I'm likely to fail.

❑ 2. If I reach out to others, I'll get rejected.

❑ 3. Whenever I try something new, I manage to screw it up.

❑ 4. Every time I get my hopes up, I'm disappointed.

❑ 5. If I work on my problems, I'll fail.

❑ 6. I'd rather not try than fail.

❑ 7. I can't see myself as a success.

❑ 8. I'm too anxious and depressed to succeed.

Worksheet 3-2 **The Underlying Undeserving Belief Quiz**

❑ 1. I don't deserve to be happy.

❑ 2. I don't expect much out of my life.

❑ 3. I feel less worthy than other people.

❑ 4. I feel guilty asking anyone for help, so I'd rather not ask.

❑ 5. There's something fundamentally wrong with me; that's why I'm distressed.

❑ 6. I don't feel I'm as good as other people.

❑ 7. I'm uncomfortable when people are nice to me.

❑ 8. I feel like other people deserve a lot more than I do.

Worksheet 3-3 **The Unfair, Unjust Belief Quiz**

❑ 1. It's easy for me to dwell on how unfair life has been to me.

❑ 2. I feel helpless in dealing with my plight.

❑ 3. I can't stop thinking about how I've been mistreated.

❑ 4. I feel angry about all the bad things that have happened to me.

❑ 5. Other people don't understand how difficult my life has been.

❑ 6. Anyone with my life couldn't help but complain.

❑ 7. Hardly anyone could appreciate how much I've suffered.

❑ 8. Doing something about my problems would somehow discount the importance of the trauma that has happened in my life.

Now that you've taken the quizzes, you can probably see if any of these beliefs dwell in your mind.

✔ If you checked two or more items in The Fear of Change Quiz, you probably get scared at the thought of changing.

✔ If you checked two or more items from The Underlying Undeserving Belief Quiz, you may feel that you don't deserve the good things that could come to you if you were to change.

✔ If you checked two or more items from The Unfair, Unjust Belief Quiz, you may dwell so much on how you're suffering that you have trouble marshalling the resources for making changes.

✔ If, by chance, you checked two or more items in two or more quizzes, well, you have a little work cut out for you.

It's not your fault if you hold any of these change-blocking beliefs. People pick up on these ideas as children or through traumatic events at any time in their lives. And some change-blocking beliefs have a touch of truth to them; for instance,

✔ Life is often unfair.

✔ It's reasonable sometimes to feel a little angry.

✔ You can't always succeed.

However, people deserve to feel happy, including you. You can succeed in the things you do, and you can move past the bad things that have happened to you. Even if you've experienced horrific trauma, moving on doesn't diminish the significance of what you experienced. Getting better simply makes you more powerful and allows you to live again.

Jasmine, a mother of three, worries all the time. As a child, she was sexually abused by a babysitter. Now, she tends to be overly protective of her own children. Lately, she's been sleeping poorly; her youngest child has asthma, and Jasmine finds herself listening to the child's breathing throughout the night. She panics when her middle child is late from school. Her oldest son is an exchange student in another country and rarely calls home, so images of him being hurt or kidnapped float through Jasmine's mind throughout the day. Her doctor is concerned about her rising blood pressure, so Jasmine decides to work on her anxiety and stress. She takes the three change-blocking beliefs quizzes (presented earlier in this section) and discovers a variety of change-blocking beliefs, although the fear and undeserving beliefs predominate. She then fills in her Top Three Change-Blocking Beliefs Summary, which you can see in Worksheet 3-4.

Worksheet 3-4   Jasmine's Top Three Change-Blocking Beliefs Summary

---

1. Whenever I try something new, I manage to screw it up.

2. Every time I get my hopes up, I'm disappointed.

3. I feel guilty asking anyone for help, so I'd rather not.

Next, Jasmine jots down her reflections on both this exercise and the change-blocking beliefs she's identified in the summary (see Worksheet 3-5).

Worksheet 3-5   Jasmine's Reflections

I can see that I do have some of these change-blocking beliefs. I guess I've always thought that this is just the way my life is. But now that I reflect on it, I guess I can see how these beliefs could get in the way of doing something about my problems. Nothing is going to change if I hold on tightly to these assumptions. But what can I do about them?

In the next section, Jasmine sees what she can do about her problematic beliefs. But before jumping to her resolution, try filling out your own Top Three Change-Blocking Beliefs Summary in Worksheet 3-6. Go back to the three change-blocking belief quizzes and look at the items you checked. Then write down the three beliefs that seem to be the most troubling and the most likely to get in the way of your ability to make changes.

Worksheet 3-6	My Top Three Change-Blocking Beliefs Summary
1.	
2.	
3.	

In Worksheet 3-7, jot down your reflections about these beliefs. What have you learned? Do you think these beliefs are helping you or getting in your way? Write down anything that comes to mind.

Worksheet 3-7	My Reflections

Blasting through beliefs blocking your path

After completing the exercises in the last section, you should have an idea of which change-blocking beliefs may be holding up your progress. If you've tried to make changes in the past and failed, it's very likely that one or more of these beliefs are responsible. *Unfortunately,* ridding yourself of such problematic beliefs isn't as easy as sweeping them out the door; it's more than a matter of knowing what they are and declaring that you no longer believe in them. *Fortunately,* we have some tools to help you revise your way of thinking.

Changing beliefs requires that you appreciate and understand the extent to which your assumptions cause trouble for you. If you've only just now discovered what your beliefs are, you can't be expected to fully understand the pros and cons associated with them. We find that analyzing advantages and disadvantages helps achieve this insight.

Jasmine fills out an Analyzing Advantages and Disadvantages Form (see Worksheet 3-8) in order to more fully comprehend how her change-blocking beliefs affect her. She starts by writing down the reasons her change-blocking beliefs feel good and advantageous to her. Next, she writes about how each belief gives her problems — in other words, how it stands in her way. Finally, she reviews both lists very carefully and writes down her conclusions. She fills out this form for each belief in her Top Three Change-Blocking Beliefs Summary. (This example only includes analysis of two of Jasmine's beliefs.)

Worksheet 3-8   Jasmine's Analyzing Advantages and Disadvantages Form

Change-Blocking Belief #1: Whenever I try something new, I manage to screw it up.

Advantages of This Belief	Disadvantages of This Belief
If I don't try, I don't have to risk failing.	Of course, this means I can never succeed either.
I don't have to go through the effort. Change is a lot of work.	This belief keeps me feeling miserable.
I don't know why, but change is scary, and this belief keeps me from dealing with that fear.	I miss out on opportunities by clinging to this belief. It's just possible that even if I do fail, I could end up learning something useful for my life. This view simply keeps me stuck.

Change-Blocking Belief #2: I feel guilty asking anyone for help, so I'd rather not.

Advantages of This Belief	Disadvantages of This Belief
I don't expect anyone to help me, so I don't end up disappointed.	I don't get the chance to share my worries with anyone.
People don't have to worry about me leaning on them.	I don't get as close to people as I could.
I don't worry anyone because they never know when I'm upset.	When I'm really upset I get quiet, and people sometimes think I'm angry when I'm not. Sometimes, everyone needs a little help from others, and I'm at a disadvantage when I don't seek it.

After completing her Analyzing Advantages and Disadvantages Form, Jasmine takes some time to reflect. She considers whether the advantages she listed are truly advantages and concludes that her original change-blocking beliefs are causing her more harm than good. She then writes down her reflections in Worksheet 3-9.

| **Worksheet 3-9** | **Jasmine's Reflections** |

I realize that when I don't try, I still end up failing, so not trying isn't really an advantage. And yes, change may be a lot of work and seem overwhelming, but I'm utterly miserable. When I think about it, I get satisfaction from helping others. So logically, they wouldn't mind helping me from time to time. I could use some help, and it might feel really nice to get close to people. On balance, these change-blocking beliefs are keeping me stuck.

Clearly, Jasmine can see that her assumptions about change are causing her to remain in limbo. Now that she's completed the exercises and disputed those assumptions, she can start moving forward. Because she's aware of these beliefs, she can be on the lookout for them to pop up again and remind herself of their considerable disadvantages.

Now it's your turn.

1. **In Worksheet 3-10, write down each of your change-blocking beliefs (see Worksheet 3-6).**

2. **Jot down all the reasons that each belief feels right, true, and useful to you.**

3. **For each belief, write down the other side of the argument; in other words, make a list of all the ways in which your belief may actually be causing you harm.**

| **Worksheet 3-10** | **My Analyzing Advantages and Disadvantages Form** |

Change-Blocking Belief #1: _____

Advantages of This Belief	*Disadvantages of This Belief*

Change-Blocking Belief #2: _____

Advantages of This Belief	Disadvantages of This Belief

Change-Blocking Belief #3: _____

Advantages of This Belief	Disadvantages of This Belief

(continued)

Worksheet 3-10 *(continued)*

Advantages of This Belief	Disadvantages of This Belief

Now, read over the advantages and disadvantages you've listed for each change-blocking belief. Reflect on the advantages, and you're likely to see that they actually aren't all that advantageous. Weigh the pros and the cons of holding onto your beliefs, and write all your reflections in Worksheet 3-11.

Worksheet 3-11 **My Reflections**

_____

_____

_____

_____

_____

If you get stuck on any of these exercises, or if you see more advantages than disadvantages to your change-blocking beliefs, consider talking with your therapist or possibly a close friend for further help and advice.

Looking Out for Self-Sabotage

Overcoming anxiety or depression is tough and sometimes even frightening work. (Even positive change evokes fear in most people!) As a result, people tend to resist, avoid, or procrastinate working on their problems. This means you have to be on the lookout for *self-sabotage.* Self-sabotage describes the things you do to keep from addressing and correcting your problems, and it appears in various forms and disguises.

Some people self-sabotage by telling themselves that change is impossible. Others defeat themselves by finding reasons to put off working on their issues. What are your reasons for avoiding making changes?

Complete the checklist in Worksheet 3-12 to see if you're falling into the self-sabotage trap. Check off any statements you hear running through your mind.

Worksheet 3-12	The Hindering Change Checklist

❑ 1. I feel my situation is hopeless.

❑ 2. I'll never be okay because of my past.

❑ 3. I want to wait to make changes until just the right time, but that time never comes.

❑ 4. I want a guarantee that I'll get better before I'm willing to risk change.

❑ 5. I use a lot of excuses for not dealing with my problems.

❑ 6. It's hard for me to stick with something if it doesn't help right away.

❑ 7. Sometimes I get confused or out of it when I try to tackle my issues.

❑ 8. If I don't succeed 100%, I get very critical of myself.

❑ 9. If I do something well, it's hard for me to give myself credit for it.

❑ 10. I want fast results, or else I just can't get motivated to try.

❑ 11. I dwell so much on my past failures that it's hard to try something new.

❑ 12. My depression or anxiety is biological, so I can't do anything about it.

It isn't hard to see how thoughts like these could bog you down and prevent active efforts to change. Yet almost everyone engages in at least a little self-sabotage, whether consciously or not.

Don't make your problems worse by pummeling yourself when you see that you're self-sabotaging. Self-criticism merely piles on more self-sabotage. Instead, monitor your self-sabotaging thoughts. When you feel them getting in your way, fight back and argue against them using the Self-Sabotage Diary presented in the next section.

Stopping self-sabotage

Throughout this book, we ask you to write out your thoughts, feelings, beliefs, and life events. That's because writing is an invaluable tool for battling problematic emotions, sorting out issues, achieving important insight, and solving problems. In this section, we invite you to track and record your inevitable acts and thoughts of self-sabotage in a diary. But first, see how Molly fills out her Self-Sabotage Diary.

Molly is a busy, highly successful professional at the top of her career. None of her colleagues are aware that she suffers from considerable anxiety and depression. She worries that others will discover that she doesn't deserve her professional success. She realizes that, for the last decade, she has neglected friends and family in pursuit of success. Now, she feels lonely and despondent; success hasn't brought her the happiness she expected, and her anxiety and depression have only increased. Molly sees a psychologist, and together they identify her self-sabotaging tendencies. She keeps a diary in which she records her acts of self-sabotage and responses to them. Worksheet 3-13 contains five days' worth of Molly's diary.

Worksheet 3-13		**Molly's Self-Sabotage Diary**
Day	*Self-Sabotage*	*Response to Self-Sabotage*
Sunday	It was raining today, so I didn't feel like going to the gym like my psychologist suggested.	Obviously, not a helpful thing to do. I'm using an excuse. Everyone does that sometimes, but I want to try and push through excuses next time.
Monday	I scraped my car on a pole in the parking lot. I was so upset — it ruined my day. I hate myself when I mess up.	I guess dumping on myself isn't particularly useful. I need to accept my flaws and imperfections if I'm going to get somewhere.
Tuesday	I was supposed to complete an exercise for my therapist, but I got too busy.	Wow, I guess that's just another excuse. The exercise only takes ten minutes. I'll be on the lookout for that one.
Wednesday	One of my clients complimented me on my work, and I couldn't accept the compliment. I gave credit to someone else.	That didn't help me. I tend to discount positive things that happen to me. No wonder my self-esteem suffers sometimes.
Thursday	My assignment today was to ask a friend out for coffee. When I started thinking about calling, I felt confused and disoriented. So I didn't do it.	When I try to do something difficult, I become so anxious I can't think clearly. I need to slow down, give it some time, and relax — then go back at it.

Now, it's time for you to make a Self-Sabotage Diary. Remember to take your time.

1. **In the middle column of Worksheet 3-14, write down any thought or action from that day that you feel limits your efforts at overcoming your anxiety or depression.** If you get stuck, review The Hindering Change Checklist for examples.

2. **In the right-hand column, write down how helpful (if at all) you think the self-sabotage may have been as well as any arguments you can find against it.**

3. **Maintain this diary for at least one week; keep it up much longer if you continue to see lots of self-sabotage.**

Criticizing yourself for the sabotage you notice yourself committing only leads to more sabotage. Stop the cycle!

Worksheet 3-14		My Self-Sabotage Diary
Day	*Self-Sabotage*	*Response to Self-Sabotage*
Sunday		
Monday		
Tuesday		
Wednesday		
Thursday		
Friday		
Saturday		

You can download extra copies of this form at www.dummies.com/go/adwbfd.

Rewriting your self-sabotaging scripts

Our minds create stories — about ourselves, our lives, and our worlds. If you feel stuck, your stories are probably cloaked in themes of failure. For example, you may have a long-running play in your mind that has you as its central character. That character has a series of mishaps, failures, and missed opportunities. If this sounds familiar, it's time to rewrite the script. Try creating a new story about you and your life that allows you to ultimately succeed. But remember, in addition to success, the new story needs to contain realistic struggle and difficulty. After all, life isn't a fairy tale.

To the outside world, **Molly** is successful. On the inside, she feels like a fraud. Worksheet 3-15 illustrates her personal story.

Worksheet 3-15	Molly's Current Life-Script

I might have money and a little prestige, but I deserve none of it. I don't believe I'm as talented as I should be for the position I have. No one likes me because I'm irritable. I have no friends or close family. I'm different than other people. I'll never really fit in. I'm going to die lonely and forgotten. My life means nothing.

Molly struggles to rewrite her script. When she finishes, she reads her new story every day for a month. Although it takes her a while to start believing it, gradually she begins to see her life in a new light. Worksheet 3-16 contains her revised story.

Worksheet 3-16	Molly's New Life-Script

I have a good job, and I worked very hard to get it. I don't need to discount my accomplishments. Yes, I do get irritable sometimes, and who doesn't? Besides, I'm capable of learning new behaviors, and I'm working on my irritability. I don't have many friends because I'm a workaholic. This will be a struggle for me, but I see myself cutting back a little on my work and making new friends. I'm going to put more meaning in my life. For starters, I plan to do some volunteer work.

Now it's your turn. Follow these instructions:

1. **In Worksheet 3-17, write your current life-script, including how you see yourself today and in the future. How do you view your accomplishments, relationships, and failures?**

2. **In Worksheet 3-18, write a new life-script. Be sure to include your thoughts on hope, change, possibilities, as well as struggle.**

3. **Read your new life-script daily for a month. Feel free to make changes to it as you see fit.**

Worksheet 3-17	My Current Life-Script

_____

_____

_____

_____

_____

Worksheet 3-18	My New Life-Script

_____

_____

_____

_____

Chapter 4

Minding Your Moods

● ●

In This Chapter

▶ Listening to your body

▶ Figuring out your feelings

▶ Connecting events and feelings

▶ Tracking thoughts, events, and feelings

● ●

You can't overcome anxiety and depression by running on autopilot. Learning how to feel better starts with self-observation. In this chapter, we provide instructions for observing the relationships among your feelings, your thoughts, and the happenings in your life.

First, you monitor your body's response to events. This information helps you become more aware of the physical components of depression and anxiety. Next, you keep track of your feelings. Some people aren't very good at identifying their feelings, so we help you by providing a list of feeling words. Then you observe how events, feelings, and bodily sensations go hand in hand. Finally, we show you how to become aware of how thoughts link up with feelings, events, and bodily sensations. The path to feeling better starts with understanding these connections.

Deciphering Body Signals

Your heart may race or your hands may sweat when you feel anxious. Changes in appetite and sleep may accompany feelings of sadness and depression. These physical reactions signal that something important is going on internally. Monitoring your bodily sensations gives you an early warning that a storm of emotional distress is brewing.

Tyler is surprised when his doctor diagnoses him with depression. His friends say he's out of touch with his feelings. Tyler begins to understand his body's signals by monitoring physical sensations on a daily basis. He fills out the Body Responses Tracking Sheet shown in Worksheet 4-1. He jots down any time that he feels something uncomfortable in his body and includes information about what was going on at the time.

Worksheet 4-1	Tyler's Body Responses Tracking Sheet	
Body Response	*How did my body feel?*	*When did this happen? What was I doing?*
Muscle tightness	I felt pain in my shoulders and back.	Monday morning. I was going over the new project with my boss.

(continued)

Worksheet 4-1 *(continued)*

Body Response	How did my body feel?	When did this happen? What was I doing?
Breathing/Increased heart rate	I could tell my breathing was rapid and shallow.	Tuesday evening while talking with my ex-wife.
Stomach symptoms	None	
Fatigue	My body feels heavy. It feels like I'm walking through mud.	Lately, I've felt this way every day.
Headaches	None this week	
Posture	I noticed I'm walking around stooped over. And I've been slumped at my desk.	I notice this mostly after lunch on Thursday and Friday.
Other: Dizziness, sweating, lightness, tingling, constriction in throat or chest, or feeling spacey and disoriented	Spacey and light-headed	Saturday morning before paying bills.

After filling out his Body Responses Tracking Sheet, Tyler takes some time to reflect on the exercise (see Worksheet 4-2).

Worksheet 4-2 **Tyler's Reflections**

I noticed that my body seems to react to what's going on in my life. I really wasn't aware of that before. These sensations aren't very pleasant, and maybe the doc is right that I'm depressed. I realize that talking with my ex-wife and my boss both make me feel pretty weird and stressed. I also think I'm worried about finances although I haven't wanted to admit it. Now that I know all this, I really want to do something to get myself to a better place.

Now fill out your own Body Responses Tracking Sheet (see Worksheet 4-3) and record your reflections on the exercise (see Worksheet 4-4).

1. **Once or twice a day, review each of the body responses in the left-hand column.**

2. **If you experienced a reaction in a given category, elaborate and specify how your body reacted (in the middle column).**

3. **Record when the body response happened and what was going on at the time. This information should help you connect the dots between events and responses.**

4. **After completing the tracking sheet, take some time to think about what you see. Write a few reflections.**

Worksheet 4-3	My Body Responses Tracking Sheet	
Body Response	*How did my body feel?*	*When did this happen? What was I doing?*
Muscle tightness		
Breathing		
Stomach symptoms		
Fatigue		
Headaches		
Posture		
Other: Dizziness, lightness, tingling, constriction in throat or chest, or feeling spacey and disoriented		

Visit `www.dummies.com/go/adwbfd` to obtain extra copies of this form. We recommend stashing a couple of them in your purse or briefcase so they're handy whenever you experience unpleasant physical sensations.

Worksheet 4-4	My Reflections

_____

_____

_____

_____

_____

Connecting the Mind and Body

After you become more observant of your body's signals, it's time to connect your mental and physical states. *Feeling words* connect and label these combined states. If you're unaccustomed to describing your feelings, spend some time looking over the list of words in the following chart and ponder whether they apply to you. Take your time, and don't rush the process.

Track your feelings every day for a week using the Daily Unpleasant Emotions Checklist in Worksheet 4-5. See Chapter 17 for exercises relevant to positive emotions.

1. **Each day, circle all the feeling words that describe your emotions.**

2. **At the end of the week, look back over your checklist and tally the most prevalent feelings. Use Worksheet 4-6 to reflect on the exercise.**

Worksheet 4-5		Daily Unpleasant Emotions Checklist		
Day	**Sadness**	**Fear**	**Shame**	**Anger**
Sunday	Despondent, miserable, hopeless, gloomy, grief, joyless, dispirited, dejected, sad	Panicked, nervous, tense, afraid, timid, terrified, apprehensive, worried	Guilty, regretful, remorseful, embarrassed, disgraced, dishonored	Outraged, bitter, furious, resentful, mad, annoyed, irritable, indignant
Monday	Despondent, miserable, hopeless, gloomy, grief, joyless, dispirited, dejected, sad	Panicked, nervous, tense, afraid, timid, terrified, apprehensive, worried	Guilty, regretful, remorseful, embarrassed, disgraced, dishonored	Outraged, bitter, furious, resentful, mad, annoyed, irritable, indignant
Tuesday	Despondent, miserable, hopeless, gloomy, grief, joyless, dispirited, dejected, sad	Panicked, nervous, tense, afraid, timid, terrified, apprehensive, worried	Guilty, regretful, remorseful, embarrassed, disgraced, dishonored	Outraged, bitter, furious, resentful, mad, annoyed, irritable, indignant

Day	Sadness	Fear	Shame	Anger
Wednesday	Despondent, miserable, hopeless, gloomy, grief, joyless, dispirited, dejected, sad	Panicked, nervous, tense, afraid, timid, terrified, apprehensive, worried	Guilty, regretful, remorseful, embarrassed, disgraced, dishonored	Outraged, bitter, furious, resentful, mad, annoyed, irritable, indignant
Thursday	Despondent, miserable, hopeless, gloomy, grief, joyless, dispirited, dejected, sad	Panicked, nervous, tense, afraid, timid, terrified, apprehensive, worried	Guilty, regretful, remorseful, embarrassed, disgraced, dishonored	Outraged, bitter, furious, resentful, mad, annoyed, irritable, indignant
Friday	Despondent, miserable, hopeless, gloomy, grief, joyless, dispirited, dejected, sad	Panicked, nervous, tense, afraid, timid, terrified, apprehensive, worried	Guilty, regretful, remorseful, embarrassed, disgraced, dishonored	Outraged, bitter, furious, resentful, mad, annoyed, irritable, indignant
Saturday	Despondent, miserable, hopeless, gloomy, grief, joyless, dispirited, dejected, sad	Panicked, nervous, tense, afraid, timid, terrified, apprehensive, worried	Guilty, regretful, remorseful, embarrassed, disgraced, dishonored	Outraged, bitter, furious, resentful, mad, annoyed, irritable, indignant

Worksheet 4-6	**My Reflections**

_____

_____

_____

_____

_____

Putting Events, Feelings, and Sensations Together

As you work through this chapter, you should become more aware of how your body reacts to events in your life. And thanks to the Daily Unpleasant Emotions Checklist in the previous section, you have feeling words to label your mental and physical states. It's time to connect these body sensations and feeling words to the events that trigger them.

Jasmine suffers from constant worry and anxiety. She thinks that her worries mainly center on her children, but at times she has no idea where her anxiety comes from. So, she fills out a Mood Diary. She pays special attention to her body's signals and writes them down whenever she feels something unpleasant. She then searches for a feeling word that captures her emotion. She rates the emotions and sensations on a scale of 1 (almost undetectable) to 100 (maximal). She then asks herself what was going on when she detected her distress. Worksheet 4-7 is a sample of Jasmine's Mood Diary; specifically, it's a record of four days on which Jasmine noticed undesirable moods.

Worksheet 4-7	Jasmine's Mood Diary	
Day	*Feelings and Sensations (Rated 1–100)*	*Corresponding Events*
Sunday	Apprehension, tightness in my chest (70)	I was thinking about going to work tomorrow morning.
Tuesday	Anger, trembling (85)	My secretary messed up my schedule.
Thursday	Worry, tightness in my chest (60)	My middle child has a cold, and I'm worried she'll have an asthma attack.
Saturday	Nervous, tension in my shoulders (55)	I have a party to go to, and I won't know many people there.

Jasmine keeps track of her moods over the course of a couple of weeks. After studying her complete Mood Diary, she comes to a few conclusions (see Worksheet 4-8).

Worksheet 4-8	Jasmine's Reflections

Well, I'm surprised. I thought that all I worried about was the kids. Truth is, my job really gets me stirred up. Conflict isn't easy for me either. I'd better do something about that. My shyness gets in my way, too. I didn't realize how often I have these feelings.

Now it's your turn to fill out a Mood Diary (see Worksheet 4-9). This exercise can provide you with invaluable information about patterns and issues that consistently cause you distress. This knowledge helps you see what needs to change in your life. The exercise also lays a foundation for changing your thinking, which we get into in Part II of this book.

1. **For at least one week, pay attention to your body's signals and write them down whenever you feel something unpleasant.**

2. **Search for a feeling word that captures your emotion and jot it down.** Refer to the Daily Unpleasant Emotions Checklist earlier in this chapter for help finding the right feeling words.

3. **Rate your feeling on a scale of intensity from 1 (almost undetectable) to 100 (maximal).**

4. **Ask yourself what was going on when you started noticing your emotions and body's signals.** The corresponding event can be something happening in your world, but an event can also be in the form of a thought or image that runs through your mind. Be concrete and specific; don't write something overly general such as "I hate my work." Instead, ask yourself what happened at work that you didn't like.

5. **Look over your Mood Diary to see if you can draw any conclusions or come up with any new insights into where your body signals come from. Write a few sentences of reflection in Worksheet 4-10.**

Worksheet 4-9	My Mood Diary	
Day	*Feelings and Sensations (Rated 1–100)*	*Corresponding Events*
Sunday		
Monday		
Tuesday		
Wednesday		
Thursday		
Friday		
Saturday		

Visit www.dummies.com/go/adwbfd for extra copies of this form. Continue filling them out for several weeks for maximum benefit.

Worksheet 4-10	My Reflections

Becoming a Thought Detective

Imagine yourself in a parking lot at night. You're tired and back your car into a cement pole. Crunch. What's your reaction? Do you have angry thoughts like "Who the bleep put that post there!?" Do you feel anxious and worried about the costs of repair? Or do you feel distraught and upset with yourself because you believe you were careless?

Anyone is likely to feel upset for a little while after banging up a car. However, if your thoughts are intense or persistent, they provide clues about your *negative thinking habits*. These habits dictate how you interpret the accident and thus the way you feel about it. If you feel terribly worried, it's probably because you tend to have lots of anxious thoughts. If the accident leaves you overly down on yourself, you may be prone to depressive thoughts.

Thought Trackers show you how feelings, events, and thoughts connect — they lay it all out for you. What are you saying to yourself when you feel upset? See how Molly, Tyler, and Jasmine complete their Thought Trackers before you try a few for yourself.

Molly runs her car into a pole one night. Her psychologist has been having her fill out Thought Trackers for the past week whenever she notices upsetting feelings. So later that night she completes a Thought Tracker on the incident (see Worksheet 4-11).

Worksheet 4-11	Molly's Thought Tracker	
Feelings and Sensations (Rated 1–100)	*Corresponding Events*	*Thoughts/Interpretations*
Despair (70); nauseous	Crunched my car fender.	I can't believe I did that. I'm such an idiot. Everyone at work will notice.
Tense (90); tightness through my back and shoulders		I don't have time to deal with this. I'll have to call the insurance company, get estimates on the repair, and arrange alternative transportation. I'm already feeling way behind on the Bradley contract. I'll never get it done on time now.

Strange as it may seem, **Tyler** slams his car into that same pole, although not until the next night. He also fills out a Thought Tracker on the incident (see Worksheet 4-12), having read about them in the *Anxiety & Depression Workbook For Dummies*.

Worksheet 4-12	Tyler's Thought Tracker	
Feelings and Sensations (Rated 1–100)	*Corresponding Events*	*Thoughts/Interpretations*
Rage (80); flushed face and rapid breathing	I hit that stupid pole with my new sports car.	There's not a single good reason that anyone would have a pole there! I should sue whoever owns this parking lot.
Sad (65); tired		This is terrible. I've only had that car for three months. Cars are never the same after you wreck them. Bad things are always happening to me.

Now, you're going to find this *really* hard to believe, but **Jasmine** happens to be in that same parking lot a week later. Cars seem drawn to that pole. Like Molly and Tyler, Jasmine completes a Thought Tracker (see Worksheet 4-13) following her run-in with that pesky pole.

Worksheet 4-13	Jasmine's Thought Tracker	
Feelings and Sensations (Rated 1–100)	*Corresponding Events*	*Thoughts/Interpretations*
Panic (95); terrified, sweaty, rapid shallow breathing, dizzy	I slammed my car into a pole.	At first I thought I might have run into someone's car and could have hurt somebody. I never know how to handle things like this. I'll probably lose my driver's license or my insurance will drop me. My husband will be furious with me. I can't stand it when he's mad at me.

Three people, same event. You can see how their thoughts contribute to the way they feel. All three of them look at this event in unique ways, and they feel differently as a result. Molly worries about the consequences of the accident and puts herself down. Because of the way she interprets the event, Molly's at risk for anxiety and depression. Tyler gets mad and catastrophizes the fender-bender. He tends to have problems with anger and depression. On the other hand, Jasmine panics about the bash into the pole; her reaction is the product of her frequent struggles with anxiety and panic.

Sometimes people say they really don't know what's going on in their heads when they feel distressed. They know how they feel and they know what happened, but they simply have no idea what they're thinking. You may experience this problem. If so, ask yourself the questions in Worksheet 4-14 about an event that accompanied your difficult feelings.

Worksheet 4-14	The Thought Query Quiz

1. What meaning does the event have for me in my life?

_____

_____

_____

_____

2. Will this event affect my future in any way?

_____

_____

_____

_____

3. What bothers me about the event?

_____

_____

_____

_____

4. Does the event say something about me as a person?

_____

_____

_____

_____

5. What passed through my mind as I noticed the event?

_____

_____

_____

_____

Thought Trackers give you important information about the way your mind interprets events and your related feelings. That's why we recommend that you do them often. See Part II for ways of changing your thinking habits and improving your moods.

The Thought Tracker demonstrates how the way you think about occurrences influences the way you feel. Sad feelings inevitably accompany thoughts about loss, low self-worth, or rejection. Anxious or worried feelings go along with thoughts about danger, vulnerability, or horrible outcomes. To complete your Thought Tracker in Worksheet 4-15, follow these instructions:

1. **Pay attention to your body's signals and write them down whenever you feel something unpleasant.**

2. **Search for a feeling word that captures your emotion and jot that down, too.** Refer to the Daily Unpleasant Emotions Checklist earlier in this chapter for help.

3. **Rate your feeling on a scale of intensity from 1 (almost undetectable) to 100 (maximal).**

4. **Ask yourself what was going on when you started noticing your emotions and body's signals.** The corresponding event can be something happening in your world, but an event can also come in the form of a thought or image that runs through your mind. Be concrete and specific; don't write something overly general such as "I hate my job." Instead, ask yourself what happened at work that you didn't like.

5. **Record your thoughts in the thoughts and interpretation column.** Describe how you perceive, interpret, or think about the event. Refer to the preceding Thought Query Quiz if you experience any difficulty figuring out your thoughts about the event.

Worksheet 4-15	My Thought Tracker	
Feelings and Sensations (Rated 1–100)	*Corresponding Events*	*Thoughts/Interpretations*

(continued)

Worksheet 4-15 *(continued)*

Feelings and Sensations (Rated 1–100)	Corresponding Events	Thoughts/Interpretations

Visit www.dummies.com/go/adwbfd to download extra copies of this form.

Do you notice any patterns to the types of thoughts you have? Are these thoughts associated with certain types of feelings? Take the time to reflect on this exercise using Worksheet 4-16.

Worksheet 4-16 **My Reflections**

_____

_____

_____

_____

_____

Part II
Thinking About Thinking: Thought Therapy

The 5th Wave   By Rich Tennant

@RICHTENNANT

"Okay, you were depressed because you didn't win, but couldn't you have been happy enough about finishing second to pick up the $100,000 check?"

In this part . . .

*W*e help you understand the connection between your thoughts and feelings by way of cognitive therapy, a well established, research-based approach for the treatment of depression and anxiety. We reveal how distortions in your thinking can make you more upset than you need to be, and we show you how to prosecute your distorted thoughts for the trouble they cause and rehabilitate those thoughts into clear, beneficial thinking.

Finally, we help you uncover the deep, core beliefs and assumptions that may be responsible for many of your distorted thoughts. These beliefs may act like cracked or dirty lenses that you see yourself and your world through, so we help you regrind those lenses for clear vision.

Chapter 5

Untangling Twisted Thinking

- -

In This Chapter

▶ Discovering distortions in your thinking

▶ Prejudging yourself

▶ Assigning blame

- -

*I*n this chapter, we cut to the chase and help you apply the principles of *cognitive therapy*, which is based on the premise that the way you interpret or think about events largely determines the way you feel. The great thing about cognitive therapy is that changing the way you think changes the way you feel.

With the possible exception of our book editors, all human beings have some distorted thinking. Distorted means that your thinking doesn't accurately reflect, predict, or describe what's going on. Have you ever heard a noise in the night that woke you up and scared you? Perhaps your mind filled with thoughts of dread and images of someone breaking into your house. Only rarely are such thoughts accurate. More often than not, the noise results from wind or creaking floorboards. But when you hear a bump in the night, your fear is very real. Your thoughts, while understandable, are distorted.

Distorted thinking can be overly positive as well as negative. For example, we have a dog we think is truly beautiful, but most of our friends and neighbors think he's a peculiar-looking mutt. No doubt our perception is slightly flawed; it's understandable because we love our dog, but it's distorted nevertheless.

Distorted thinking is a problem when it leads to depression and anxiety. We call these kinds of distortions *reality scramblers*. The three types of reality scramblers are:

✔ The Information Reality Scramblers

✔ The Self-Judging Reality Scramblers

✔ The Self-Blame Reality Scramblers

Although this chapter makes distinctions among various types of reality scramblers, in *reality,* scramblers often overlap or exist in groups. To put it another way, a single thought can involve several Information Reality Scramblers as well as scramblers involving self-judging and self-blame. The examples used throughout this chapter show you how scramblers combine.

The Information Reality Scramblers

Information Reality Scramblers warp your perceptions of your world and events occurring around you; they distort how you think about what's really happening. You may not know that Information Reality Scramblers affect your thinking, but if you give it a little thought, you're likely to see that they do.

Information Reality Scramblers consist of the various ways in which the mind distorts the information coming into it. For example, suppose a depressed man receives a mediocre performance review at work. He's likely to enlarge this event and turn it into a complete catastrophe by assuming that he's totally worthless as a person. That Information Reality Scrambler is called *enlarging*. Without the scrambler, the reality is simply that his performance was considered average even though he would have preferred a better rating.

This exercise shows you all the various ways that Information Reality Scramblers can affect your thinking and ultimately the way you feel.

1. **Read the description of each type of Information Reality Scrambler and the accompanying examples in Worksheet 5-1.**

2. **Think about when your thoughts might have been influenced by the Information Reality Scrambler.**

3. **Reflect and write down any examples of specific thoughts that you've had which might be distorted by an Information Reality Scrambler.** If you can't think of an example for each type of Information Reality Scrambler, that's okay. We give you more exercises for seeing how they do their work later in this chapter.

Worksheet 5-1   **Information Reality Scramblers Exercise**

---

1. **Enlarging and shrinking:** Your mind magnifies the awfulness of unpleasant events and minimizes the value and importance of anything positive about yourself, your world, or your future. For example, we may think, "It's *horrible* that we have to write six pages today. We *can't stand it!*" Truth is, we may not feel like writing six pages, but the task hardly compares with more trying events such as losing someone close or being diagnosed with a serious health problem.

   _____

   _____

   _____

   _____

2. **Filtering:** Your mind searches for dismal, dark, or frightening data while screening out more positive information. The not-too-surprising result? The world (or yourself) looks bleak or more frightening than it is. For example, suppose you receive a job evaluation that rates you highly on most areas but contains one average rating. You proceed to focus exclusively on the average rating and conclude that the evaluation was mediocre.

   _____

   _____

   _____

   _____

3. **Seeing in black-or-white, all-or-none terms:** Your mind views events and your character as either black or white, with no shades of gray. Thus, a single bad grade or performance, for example, indicates complete failure. Or when teenagers notice blemishes on their faces, they often conclude that they look totally horrible. The problem with such polarized thinking is that it sets you up for inevitable failure, disappointment, and self-abuse.

_____

_____

_____

_____

4. **Dismissing evidence:** Your mind discards evidence that may contradict its negative thoughts. For example, suppose you're preparing a speech and have the thought that when it comes time to give the speech, you'll be so scared that you won't be able to talk. Your mind automatically dismisses the fact that you've given numerous speeches before and have never been so afraid you couldn't talk.

_____

_____

_____

_____

5. **Overgeneralizing:** You look at a single, unpleasant occurrence and decide that this event represents a general, unrelenting trend. For example, a wife tells her husband that she's furious because he's *always* late, but in reality he's late only about 10 percent of the time. Words like *always* and *never* are clues to overgeneralization.

_____

_____

_____

_____

6. **Mind reading:** You assume that you know what others are thinking without checking it out. Thus, when your boss walks by you without saying hello, you automatically think, "She's really angry with me; I must have messed something up." In reality, she's merely distracted.

_____

_____

_____

_____

7. **Emotional reasoning:** You treat feelings as facts. For example, if you feel guilty, you conclude that you must have done something wrong. Or if you don't feel like working on your depression, you assume that means you're unable to. And if you're afraid of something, it must be dangerous merely because you fear it.

_____

_____

_____

_____

8. **Unreliable forecasting:** You presume a negative outcome without any real evidence. For example, you have an argument with your partner and believe that he or she will certainly leave you. Or, you avoid driving on the freeway because you're convinced that you'll get in an accident.

_____

_____

_____

_____

Recording Information Reality Scramblers on Thought Trackers

Tracking your thoughts and looking for distortions in them helps clear your thinking, which in turn starts improving your mood. Before you get to work on your own Thought Tracker, see what **Bradford** (see Worksheet 5-2) and **Sheila** (see Worksheet 5-3) discover when they track their thoughts and analyze them for reality scramblers.

Worksheet 5-2		Bradford's Thought Tracker	
Feelings and Sensations (Rated 1–100)	**Corresponding Events**	**Thoughts/ Interpretations**	**Information Reality Scramblers**
Despondent (70), anxious (65); tightness in my chest	My boss said we had to increase our productivity.	I hate this job. The boss must hate me. It will never get better. I can't possibly meet this standard; what then?	Enlarging, mind reading, seeing in black-and-white terms, overgeneralizing, unreliable forecasting
Sad (75); overwhelming heaviness and fatigue	My bid on that house fell through. The real estate agent said we could get just as good a deal on another house.	I'll never find a deal that good. Things like this never work out for me.	Overgeneralizing, seeing in black-and-white terms, dismissing evidence

Worksheet 5-3		Sheila's Thought Tracker	
Feelings and Sensations (Rated 1–100)	*Corresponding Events*	*Thoughts/ Interpretations*	*Information Reality Scramblers*
Panic (90); racing pulse, shaky, nausea	Jason's 20 minutes late coming home from school.	He's never this late; something horrible must have happened. I just feel it in my gut.	Emotional reasoning, unreliable forecasting
Nervous (70); queasy stomach	Getting the house ready for a party.	No one is going to show up. I know people came to the last party, but they felt they had to come. Even though they said they had a good time, I know they were just being polite.	Unreliable forecasting, mind reading, dismissing evidence

Now that you've seen a couple examples of Information Reality Scramblers at work, it's time to take a challenge and see if you can pick out Information Reality Scramblers in different situations. Worksheet 5-4 presents an incomplete Thought Tracker with samples from an assortment of people and events. Review the feelings and sensations, events, and thoughts and interpretations of those events provided, and then fill in the Information Reality Scramblers that you believe apply. We give you our answers later in this section, but don't peek!

Worksheet 5-4		Thought Tracker Information Reality Scrambler Practice		
Scenario	*Feelings and Sensations (Rated 1–100)*	*Corresponding Events*	*Thoughts/ Interpretations*	*Information Reality Scramblers*
1	Miserable (65), embarrassed (75); tired	My wife said I've gained a little weight.	It's true. I've let myself go completely. I'll probably die of a heart attack. I feel out of control, so I must have no willpower at all.	

(continued)

Worksheet 5-4 (continued)

Scenario	Feelings and Sensations (Rated 1–100)	Corresponding Events	Thoughts/ Interpretations	Information Reality Scramblers
2	Apprehensive (70); spacey, tense	I was appointed Department Chair.	The Dean is setting me up for failure; he wants to get rid of me. I'll get more money, but the only reason I got the job is because no one else wanted it.	
3	Bitter (80), gloomy (65); muscle tightness, back pain	Some jerk keyed my car.	This kind of thing always happens to me. This is going to cost a fortune to fix.	

Here are the answers to the Thought Tracker Information Reality Scrambler Practice exercise. Don't worry if your answers don't perfectly match ours — the point is simply learning to observe distortions at work. And sometimes the precise distortions involved are debatable.

✔ **Scenario 1:** Enlarging, unreliable forecasting, seeing in black-and-white terms, emotional reasoning

✔ **Scenario 2:** Dismissing the evidence, mind reading, filtering

✔ **Scenario 3:** Enlarging, overgeneralizing, unreliable forecasting

It's time to start tracking your own thoughts and looking for possible Information Reality Scramblers. This process helps you to see that some of your unpleasant feelings actually come from the way your mind misinterprets events in your world. The following instructions guide you in building your own Thought Tracker in Worksheet 5-5, but for more complete information about Thought Trackers, see Chapter 4.

1. **Pay attention to your body's signals and write them down whenever you feel something unpleasant.**

2. **Search for a feeling word that captures your emotion and jot it down.** Refer to the Daily Unpleasant Emotions Checklist in Chapter 4 for an extensive list of feeling words to get you started.

3. **Rate your feeling on a scale of intensity from 1 (almost undetectable) to 100 (maximal).**

4. **Ask yourself what was going on when you started noticing your emotions and your body's signals, and record that event.** The event can be something happening in your world or it can come in the form of a thought or image that runs through your mind. Be concrete and specific when recording events. Don't write something overly general such as "I hate my work;" instead, ask yourself what happened at work that you didn't like.

5. **Record your thoughts in the appropriate column by describing how you perceive, interpret, or think about the event.** Refer to The Thought Query Quiz in Chapter 4 if you experience any difficulty figuring out your thoughts about the event.

6. **Using the Information Reality Scramblers information from Worksheet 5-1, record the distortions you believe are at work.**

Worksheet 5-5	Thought Tracker Information Reality Scrambler Practice		
Feelings and Sensations (Rated 1–100)	**Corresponding Events**	**Thoughts/ Interpretations**	**Information Reality Scrambler**

For extra copies of this form, visit www.dummies.com/go/adwbfd.

In working through the exercise in Worksheet 5-5, were you able to find the Information Reality Scramblers in your thinking? If so, we expect you'll begin questioning whether or not your thoughts about events are always accurate. With that doubt comes the possibility of seeing things a little differently — more realistically, actually. Record your reflections in Worksheet 5-6. We hope we're beginning to shake up your thinking (see Chapter 6 for a variety of strategies for replacing distorted thinking with more accurate perceptions).

Worksheet 5-6	My Reflections

The Self-Judging Reality Scramblers

The Self-Judging Reality Scramblers twist the way you view yourself and your behavior. Depressed and anxious minds tend to be harshly critical, judgmental, and self-abusive. Why is that a problem? Because self-judging is another form of self-sabotage. Although you may think otherwise, self-criticism doesn't motivate you to do anything positive or productive; rather, it only makes you feel worse and leaves you with less energy for changing.

Self-Judging Reality Scramblers come in three different forms:

✔ Shoulds

✔ Critical comparisons

✔ Loathsome labels

Shoulding on yourself

One of our favorite quotes comes from psychologist Dr. Albert Ellis, who said, "Stop shoulding on yourself." That phrase rings true for the vast majority of clients we see in our practices as psychologists. And we must admit, we occasionally fall victim to the tyranny of the should as well. *Shoulding* involves putting yourself down by telling yourself that you *should* be or act different in some way. It can refer to past, present, or future actions. Shoulding scrambles accurate self-views and turns them into self-criticisms.

To identify your own shoulds, take the quiz in Worksheet 5-7, putting a check mark next to each thought that has run through your mind.

Worksheet 5-7	The Shoulding-on-Yourself Quiz

❏ I should have known better.

❏ I shouldn't eat that much.

❏ I should be a better person.

❏ I should have been more careful.

❏ I shouldn't have distorted thoughts!

❏ I shouldn't be so crabby.

❑ I shouldn't make so many mistakes.

❑ I should exercise more.

❑ I should be nicer to people.

❑ I shouldn't get so upset about things.

So what's wrong with these thoughts? (We can almost hear you thinking, "But I *SHOULD* eat less, be a better person, or not get so upset about things!") Well, there's no rule chiseled in granite stating that you should or must act or think in certain ways. Shoulding is a form of criticism that makes you feel bad because guilt and shame don't motivate positive behavior. The bottom line is that shoulding doesn't help. You *shouldn't* should on yourself — just kidding, sort of.

The alternative to shoulding on yourself is recognizing that it may be a good idea to do things differently but refusing to engage in harsh self-judgment. Before you get to your own should alternatives, in Worksheet 5-8, you can read **Murphy**'s should statements and see how she develops alternatives to shoulding on herself.

Worksheet 5-8	Murphy's Should Alternative Exercise
Should Statement	*Should Alternative Statement*
I shouldn't get upset so often.	I wish I didn't get upset so often, but I do. And I'm trying to master relaxation as an alternative.
I shouldn't get in bad moods so often.	I don't like bad moods, but they're tough to change. I do want to work on them, but I don't need to pummel myself when they happen.
I shouldn't let myself get out of shape.	I would prefer to get into better shape. It's difficult to find the time to exercise. I'll try to make more time for taking care of myself.
I should spend more time on the exercises in this workbook.	I do want to spend more time on these exercises, but every bit that I do is worth something.
I shouldn't make mistakes.	I prefer not to make mistakes, but I'm human, after all.

Review any items you endorsed from The Shoulding-on-Yourself Quiz (see Worksheet 5-7) and also listen to your self-dialogue. Then fill out the Should Alternative Exercise in Worksheet 5-9 by following these instructions:

1. **Tune into what you're telling yourself when you feel upset.**

2. **Listen for any time that you tell yourself, "I should" or "I shouldn't."**

3. **Record those statements in the left-hand column.**

4. **Come up with alternative perspectives for each should statement and write them in the right-hand column.** Words like "prefer," "would like to," "wish," and "would be better if," make good alternatives to "should."

Worksheet 5-9	My Should Alternative Exercise
Should Statement	*Should Alternative Statement*

Making critical comparisons

Are you the richest, best-looking, or smartest person in the world? Neither are we. There's always someone who has more of something than you do. Even if you're the best at something, that doesn't mean you're the best at everything. People have strengths and weaknesses, and if you do think you're the best at everything, you have a problem that's quite different from anxiety or depression.

Everyone engages in comparing themselves to others sometimes. But anxious and depressed folks tend to rate themselves more negatively and place more value on those comparisons.

To identify your negative personal comparisons, put a check mark next to each item in Worksheet 5-10 that you sometimes examine in yourself and then compare to others.

Worksheet 5-10 **The Critical Comparison Quiz**

❏ Finances or wealth

❏ Looks and appearance

❏ Intelligence

❏ Popularity

❏ Fame

❏ Gadgets (a guy thing)

❏ House

❏ Car

❏ Clothes

❏ Status

❏ Age

❏ Knowledge

Essentially, the less comparing you do, the better off you are. However, the seduction of comparisons lies in the fact that they contain a kernel of truth. The reality is that there's always someone richer, younger, or higher on the ladder than you. Comparisons may be unavoidable, but they become problematic when you conclude that you're not good enough because you're not the top or the best.

What's the alternative to making critical comparisons that scramble the way you see yourself? Like should alternative statements (see "Shoulding on yourself"), comparison alternatives are all about looking at an issue from a different, less harsh perspective. Before creating your own alternative statements, take a look at Worksheet 5-11 for an example.

Worksheet 5-11 **Scott's Comparison Alternative Exercise**

Critical Comparison	*Comparison Alternative*
My friend Joe has done a lot better than I have in his career.	Well, he has. But I've done fine. I spend a lot of time with my family, and that's my real priority.
When we went to that Super Bowl party, I was really jealous of that 60" plasma TV. Our TV is pitiful in comparison.	There was nothing wrong with my TV before that party. I don't even watch that much TV.
I went to the gym and noticed that everyone was more fit than I am.	Of course, most of the really unfit people don't even go to the gym. I'm in better shape than I was a month ago; that's progress, and that's what matters.
I read an article on retirement and got anxious when I realized that I don't have as much put away as a lot of people do.	Having kids was more expensive than I thought it would be, but I wouldn't trade it for the world. Once Trevor's college is paid for, we'll prioritize saving.

Review the items you checked on your Critical Comparison Quiz (see Worksheet 5-10) and listen to your self-dialogue. Then fill out the Comparison Alternative Exercise in Worksheet 5-12 by following these instructions:

1. **Tune into what you're telling yourself when you feel upset, and listen for any time that you critically compare yourself to others.**

2. **List those statements in the left-hand column.**

3. **Come up with alternative perspectives and record them in the right-hand column.**
   Because only one person in the world is at the top on any given issue or activity, try to accept that you'll be average, normal, or even occasionally less than average at many things. Comparing yourself to the very top only leaves you disappointed, so appreciate your own strengths, weaknesses, and chosen priorities.

Worksheet 5-12	My Comparison Alternative Exercise
Critical Comparison	*Comparison Alternative*

Tagging yourself with loathsome labels

Sticks and stones can break your bones, and words *can* really hurt you. The final Self-Judging Reality Scrambler amounts to calling yourself bad names. It's so easy to tag yourself with demeaning labels, and when you do, you inevitably feel worse.

To pinpoint the loathsome labels you give yourself, take the quiz in Worksheet 5-13. Check off the words that you use to describe yourself when things go wrong.

Worksheet 5-13	The Loathsome Label Quiz

❏ Loser

❏ Pathetic

❏ Misfit

❏ Freak

❏ Clod

❏ Klutz

❏ Fat pig

❏ Failure

❏ Nerd

❏ Pitiful

❏ Stupid

❏ Monster

❏ Disturbed

❏ Crazy

❏ Idiot

❏ Jerk

❏ Imbecile

❏ Fool

❏ Moron

❏ Dummy (well . . . not really!)

Labels erode your self-worth. They always involve overgeneralization and black-and-white thinking (see the section "The Information Reality Scramblers" earlier in this chapter). Labels represent concepts that hold no redeeming value; they don't help you, and they often lead to increased emotional distress. So what should you do when you hear these labels floating through your mind? See Worksheet 5-14 for examples of self-labels and new ways of looking at them.

Worksheet 5-14	Label Replacement Exercise	
Event	*Corresponding Label*	*Label Replacement Thought*
I spilled a drink at a restaurant.	I'm a total klutz!	I've seen other people spill drinks. Good grief, it's not a big deal.
I started to tear up when I was talking about my mother's illness.	I'm pathetic and pitiful.	There's nothing wrong with showing some emotion.

(continued)

EXAMPLE

Worksheet 5-14 *(continued)*

Event	Corresponding Label	Label Replacement Thought
My voice started to shake during a meeting at work.	I'm a loser.	I was talking about something very important to me. At times like that I do get a little tense. I wish I didn't, but that doesn't make me a loser.
I didn't get into the graduate school I wanted.	I'm a failure.	It was very competitive. I did get my third choice. Sure, I wish I'd gotten my preference, but I can still succeed in my chosen career.
I can't seem to lose weight.	I'm a fat pig!	The doc said that after 50, metabolic changes make it harder to lose weight. I do have extra weight, and I don't like it, but it doesn't help to call myself a pig.

PRACTICE

If you stop calling yourself useless, hurtful names, and replace the labels with more reasonable perspectives, you'll feel better. Therefore, we recommend that you complete the Label Replacement Exercise in Worksheet 5-15 each time you hear those destructive labels in your mind:

1. **Tune into what you're telling yourself when you feel upset, and listen for any time that you tag yourself with a hurtful label.**

2. **Write the triggering event in the left-hand column.**

3. **Write the label you're putting on yourself in the middle column.**

4. **Come up with alternative perspectives to the labels and record them in the right-hand column.** In creating label replacements, try to accept any portion of the event that has truth in it, such as having gained some weight, but look at the issue more realistically. Try to be self-forgiving. Because labels tend to be overarching ratings (that is, they imply a bigger problem than the event that triggered them), your replacement thoughts should be specific and look for positive possibilities.

TIP

If you have trouble coming up with label replacement thoughts, don't worry. Jump to Chapter 6 for lots of ideas for challenging negative self-talk.

Worksheet 5-15	My Label Replacement Exercise	
Event	*Corresponding Label*	*Label Replacement Thought*

Now that you've completed the Label Replacement Exercise, take a few minutes to reflect on what self-labels have been doing to you and how it feels to change them (see Worksheet 5-16).

Worksheet 5-16	My Reflections

The Self-Blame Reality Scrambler

When sadness or anxiety clouds your thinking, you're likely to add to your distress by assuming full responsibility for your misery. You may accuse yourself of being inept, incapable, or inadequate and therefore fully culpable for all your suffering. When the Self-Blame Reality Scrambler is at work, you attribute all fault and blame to yourself. Doing so leads you to wallow in shame and self-loathing.

In this section, we give you a tool for figuring out if you use the Self-Blame Reality Scrambler. After you begin to understand that your problem isn't completely your fault, you can take action on the portion for which you own responsibility. The Rating Responsibility Exercise helps you see that most problems have many causes and that you only own a portion of the responsibility. Accepting these facts can help you lessen the guilt and shame you feel. After you understand the causes of the problem, you'll be more ready to do something productive about it.

Robin blames herself for her recent divorce and believes that she is almost entirely responsible for her husband leaving the marriage for another woman. Robin considers herself boring and unattractive, and she berates herself for not seeing the signs early enough to prevent what happened. Robin decides to take the Rating Responsibility Exercise (see Worksheet 5-17), focusing on the blame she places on herself for her divorce.

Worksheet 5-17	Robin's Rating Responsibility Exercise

I blame myself for: My recent divorce

I rate the blame at: 95%

All Possible Causes of Your Problem	Percentage of Responsibility
My husband's roving eye.	10%: He does have a roving eye!
My husband's hostility.	15%: He's a difficult man.
Diana's conniving, manipulative plan to steal him.	20%: She was after him for months, no doubt about it.
The strain of our financial problems.	10%: This didn't help.
My husband's grief over losing his mother, father, and brother over the last year and a half.	10%: He could never talk about these losses, and I know they got to him.
The stress of our daughter's bout with cancer. She's recovered now, but my husband still worries.	10%: Again, he couldn't talk about it.
I gained ten pounds during our marriage.	5%: I know I'm not that overweight.
My husband can easily find women more attractive than me.	5%: Yeah, but I do look better than many women my age.

All Possible Causes of Your Problem	Percentage of Responsibility
We had stopped talking about our days.	10%: I probably should have paid more attention to that issue.
Random events.	5%: I'm sure there are things I'm not factoring into this equation.

As you can see, Robin initially assigns 95 percent of the blame for the divorce on herself. At the end of the quiz, Robin reassesses her level of responsibility because she's able to see things a bit more objectively. She re-rates the level of blame she puts on herself and identifies that 20 percent seems more appropriate — she's only partly responsible. This knowledge helps her to feel less guilty and self-disparaging.

Now that you've seen the Rating Responsibility Exercise in action, it's time to evaluate the level of responsibility you feel you carry. In other words, you're figuring out how much of the problem is you. Complete your Rating Responsibility Exercise in Worksheet 5-18 by following these steps:

1. **Name the problem you're blaming yourself for. Write this at the top of the worksheet.**

2. **Using a percentage from 1 to 100, rate how much blame you put on yourself for this problem. At the top of the worksheet, write this percentage under the problem you've identified.**

3. **In the left-hand column, list all imaginable causes of your problem.**

4. **In the right-hand column, using a number from 1 to 100, estimate the percentage of actual responsibility for this problem that each cause in the left-hand column owns. Also record your contributions to the problem.**

5. **Re-rate the percentage of responsibility you have for the problem you identified.**

Worksheet 5-18   **My Rating Responsibility Exercise**

I blame myself for: _____

I rate the blame at: _____

All Possible Causes of Your Problem	Percentage of Responsibility

(continued)

Worksheet 5-18 *(continued)*

All Possible Causes of Your Problem	Percentage of Responsibility

My re-rated level of responsibility is: _____

Some people deny any and all responsibility for problems they encounter. These folks usually find a convenient scapegoat such as a mother, father, significant other, society, or event to blame for all their woes. Failing to accept any responsibility for your troubles makes you see yourself as helpless and the world as unfair and unjust (check out Chapter 3 for more information about such self-sabotaging beliefs). Realize that you don't want to fall into that trap — read the next section to see how to avoid it.

Doing What You Can to Solve the Problem

In this section, you face your problem and take action to change it. By assessing your responsibility and determining what you can do about your problem, you avoid immersing yourself in self-loathing and harsh self-blame. This approach allows you to take responsibility for an appropriate portion of the problem and do what you can with it. If your responsibility involves something that's over and done with, no action is possible. But you can still try to let go of the shame that leads nowhere and does nothing to help you. And you may be able to do some things to prevent a similar problem in the future.

Robin reviews her Rating Responsibility Exercise (see Worksheet 5-17) and notices that she owns partial responsibility for some of the problems that led to her divorce. She lists those contributions and then plans steps for productive action on the Action Strategy Worksheet shown in Worksheet 5-19.

Worksheet 5-19	Robin's Action Strategy Worksheet

The problem: My divorce.

My Specific Contributions to the Problem	Specific Actions I Can Take
I am ten pounds overweight.	I can lose ten pounds by increasing my exercise and watching my diet. It won't help this divorce, but my counselor said exercise will lift my spirits, and I'll be healthier.
I'm not the most attractive woman in the world.	I can't do a lot about my appearance other than realize it's not that important. I don't want a man who wants me just for the way I look anyway.
I ignored our lack of communication in the marriage.	When I find another relationship, I need to pay attention to how we talk and any other problems that crop up. I don't want to bury my head in the sand.

After completing your Rating Responsibility Exercise in Worksheet 5-18, the next step is to create an action strategy to determine how you can begin solving your problem. By identifying productive actions to address the problem, you're able to move forward and stop berating yourself. Follow these steps to create an action strategy in Worksheet 5-20:

1. **Name the problem you're blaming yourself for and write it at the top of the worksheet.**

2. **In the left-hand column, list the specific contributions you've identified that you have some control over.** In other words, record anything you did that may have led to the problem or made it worse.

3. **In the right-hand column, list any steps you can take now or in the future that may be useful in solving this problem.**

Worksheet 5-20	My Action Strategy Worksheet

The problem: _____

My Specific Contributions to the Problem	Specific Actions I Can Take

(continued)

Worksheet 5-20 *(continued)*

My Specific Contributions to the Problem	Specific Actions I Can Take

As you finish this chapter, take the time to reflect on what you've discovered about your patterns of thinking and how they affect your view of yourself. Write down your feelings, thoughts, and insights in Worksheet 5-21.

Worksheet 5-21 **My Reflections**

_____

_____

_____

_____

Chapter 6

Indicting and Rehabilitating Thoughts

Most people simply assume that thoughts they have about themselves and the world are true. But thoughts don't always reflect reality, just as funhouse mirrors don't reflect the way you really look. In Chapter 5, we help you uncover the distortions (also known as *reality scramblers*) in your thoughts.

In this chapter, you become a thought detective. No, you don't need a magnifying glass or sharp-looking hat and trenchcoat. All you need are the tools and instructions we provide in this chapter . . . and an open mind. We show you how to take your distorted thoughts to court and charge them with the crime of inflicting misery on yourself. If you find them guilty (and we think you will), you see how to rehabilitate those criminal thoughts so that they can contribute to your well-being.

From Arraignment to Conviction: Thought Court

We base our technique called Thought Court on the principles of *cognitive therapy*. Cognitive therapy was founded in the late 1950s by Dr. Aaron T. Beck, who discovered that changing the way people think changes the way they feel. Many studies attest to the fact that cognitive therapy works very well to alleviate anxiety and depression. Therefore, we recommend that you regularly work on the exercises in this section. Do this work until you find yourself starting to think and feel differently . . . then do it for a little while longer.

Thought Court begins with a Thought Tracker. Thought Trackers show you how feelings, events, and thoughts connect. We give you examples of Thought Trackers in this section, but for more information, flip to Chapter 4.

Thought Court is a process of indicting the accused thought (the one you pinpoint in your Thought Tracker) and then bringing it to trial. You play the roles of defense attorney, prosecutor, and judge. As the defense attorney, you present the evidence that supports the validity or accuracy of the thought. In other words, the defense claims that your thought is true and isn't culpable for your anguish. On the other side, you, as the prosecutor, lay out a case demonstrating that the thought is actually guilty of distortion and therefore has caused you unnecessary emotional distress. In Thought Court, you're also the judge. If you find the thought guilty, we give you ways to replace or rehabilitate your thought.

Frankly, you're very unlikely to find the thought innocent, but if you manage to consistently find your thought justified or innocent of causing you unnecessary harm, you should seek consultation with a mental health professional. You may need a fresh perspective to help sort out your troubles.

Most people learn better through stories and examples than through laborious explanations. With that in mind, we help you master the process of Thought Court by presenting a case example in the next section. Then we give you the chance to put *your* thoughts on trial, and in case you need more help, we follow up your practice with more case examples.

Examining a sample case in Thought Court

Jeremy is a good looking 23-year-old personal trainer who takes pride in his healthy lifestyle. People admire his strength and athleticism. He's known at the gym for the colorful, long-sleeved T-shirts that he always wears. Jeremy gets more than his share of attention from women, but he never gets involved because he has a secret: He was seriously burned as a child, and his chest and arms are deeply scarred. Jeremy has never had a serious relationship; he believes any woman seeing his body would recoil in disgust. Rather than face rejection and ridicule, he locks himself away in solitary confinement.

Jeremy finds himself very attracted to a young woman he meets at the gym. She's obviously drawn to him as well. When she asks him out for coffee, he panics and puts her off. His combination of fear and yearning motivates him to see a therapist, and he manages to tell his therapist about his lifelong secret. Jeremy's therapist suggests that he start examining his thoughts with a Thought Tracker (see Worksheet 6-1) and then take his thoughts to Thought Court.

Worksheet 6-1	Jeremy's Thought Tracker	
Feelings & Sensations (Rated 1–100)	**Corresponding Events**	**Thoughts/Interpretations**
Anxiety (85), fear (95); shaking hands, flushed face	Chelsea asks me out for a cappuccino.	I can't possibly go out with her. If she ever saw my scars, she'd freak out. I couldn't stand to see the look of repulsion on her face.
Anxiety (75), shame (85), bitter (85); sweaty, sinking feeling in the pit of my stomach	The guys asked me to go into the hot tub with them after work.	The shame would overwhelm me. I look like a monster. It's not fair that I was burned and have to go through life this way. This will never end.

After he completes his Thought Tracker, Jeremy and his therapist pull out his most troubling thoughts, what we call the *most malicious thoughts*.

Jeremy's most malicious thoughts:

1. I couldn't stand to see the look of repulsion on her face.

2. It's not fair that I was burned and have to go through life this way.

Jeremy finds the Thought Tracker exercise interesting. He realizes that two thoughts create the most emotional pain for him. Next, his therapist suggests that Jeremy put the first of these thoughts on trial using a worksheet (later on, they address his other malicious thought). As you can see in Worksheet 6-2, Jeremy writes down the malicious thought first and then in one column defends the thought by listing all the reasons, logic, and evidence he can muster to support the case that the thought is true. In the other column, Jeremy attempts to prosecute the thought by demonstrating that it's false.

Worksheet 6-2   Jeremy's Thought on Trial Worksheet

Accused thought: I couldn't stand to see the look of repulsion on her face.

Defending the Thought	*Prosecuting the Thought*
People are repulsed by burn scars.	The medical team doesn't seem shocked.
I've seen the look of shock on people's faces before.	My family seems to have gotten used to my scars.
I can remember my mother crying when she saw how badly I was burned.	
After one surgery, a physical therapist made a comment that my burns were permanently deforming and I'd just have to learn to live with them.	
Sometimes when I go for a checkup, I hear people talking about me.	

So far, this case is going very well for the defense and very poorly for the prosecution. Thus, Jeremy remains quite convinced that his thought is a true reflection of reality; it's just the way things are. He can't imagine being persuaded to change his thought. The therapist tells him he's made a good start but asks him to consider the Prosecutor's Investigative Questions in Worksheet 6-3 and write down his reflections on those questions (see Worksheet 6-4).

Worksheet 6-3   Prosecutor's Investigative Questions

1. Is this thought illogical or distorted in any way? (See Chapter 5 for a list of reality scramblers that indicate distortions in thoughts.)

2. Is this event as horrible as I'm letting myself believe it is?

3. Were there any times in my life when this thought wouldn't have held true?

(continued)

Worksheet 6-3 *(continued)*

---

4. Do I know of friends or acquaintances who have experienced similar events but for whom this thought wouldn't apply?

---

5. Am I ignoring any evidence that may dispute this thought?

---

6. Is this thought really helping me?

---

7. Have I ever coped with something like this before and gotten through it okay?

---

8. What would happen if I just started acting as though the thought weren't true?

Worksheet 6-4   **Jeremy's Reflections**

These questions are a little difficult to contemplate. But let's see. Are there any distortions in my accused thought? Well, I guess I would really dislike seeing repulsion on her face, but I could probably "stand it." So I might be enlarging somewhat. And I suppose I've seen attractive women who are with guys who have substantial disabilities like morbid obesity, missing limbs, and so on. I was in that burn support group, and I admit there were some people who had nice relationships after they'd been burned. So I guess it's possible she may not be repulsed. And I guess the thought is doing me more harm than good because it keeps me from ever considering a relationship. Maybe it's worth testing out if it's true or not.

After Jeremy reflects on the list of Prosecutor Investigative Questions, his therapist advises him to take another look at his Thoughts on Trial Worksheet and try to add more evidence and logic to his case (see Worksheet 6-5).

Worksheet 6-5   **Jeremy's Revised Thought on Trial Worksheet**

Accused thought: I couldn't stand to see the look of repulsion on her face.

Defending the Thought	*Prosecuting the Thought*
People are repulsed by burn scars.	Actually, there are a few people I know who haven't been shocked or repulsed by my scars. That thought is overgeneralizing.
I've seen the look of shock on people's faces before.	My family seems to have gotten used to my scars. If they can, it's certainly possible that others could do the same — especially if they cared about me.
I can remember my mother crying when she saw how badly I was burned.	Just because my mother cried doesn't mean that she can't stand looking at me.

Defending the Thought	Prosecuting the Thought
After one surgery, a physical therapist made a comment that my burns were permanently deforming and I'd just have to learn to live with them.	The physical therapist was right in that I do have to live with this. But that doesn't mean I can't have a relationship. This thought involves enlarging and overgeneralizing.
Sometimes when I go for a checkup, I hear people talking about me.	My burns are noticeable; it doesn't mean people don't like me when they talk about me. Here, I'm mind reading.
	Lots of people with disfiguring disabilities have partners. In many cases, they found those partners after the disfigurement occurred.
	If someone really likes and cares about me, she ought to be able to look past my scars.
	If I don't try, I'll never have a relationship. This thought isn't helping me.
	If she does reject me, it doesn't mean that everyone will. I've handled the pain of burns; rejection can't be that much worse.

At this point, Jeremy carefully reviews the case presented in his Revised Thought on Trial Worksheet. He finds his accused thought guilty of inflicting unnecessary misery. He and his therapist agree to work on a replacement thought for his most malicious thought (see the section "After the Verdict: Replacing and Rehabilitating Your Thoughts" later in this chapter). After he creates the first replacement though, he continues putting his other malicious thoughts on trial and replacing them, one at a time.

Putting your thoughts on trial

You guessed it; it's your turn to visit Thought Court. Don't be concerned if you struggle in your initial attempts; this important exercise takes practice. (And if you're still confused after examining your own thoughts, you can find several more examples to illustrate further how this process works.) The first step is to complete a Thought Tracker (see Worksheet 6-6) by following these instructions:

1. **Pay attention to your body's signals and write them down whenever you feel something unpleasant.**

2. **Search for a feeling word that captures your emotion and jot it down.** Refer to the Daily Unpleasant Emotions Checklist in Chapter 4 for help finding the right feeling words.

3. **Rate your feeling on a scale of intensity from 1 (almost undetectable) to 100 (maximal).**

4. **Ask yourself what was going on when you started noticing your emotions and your body's signals.** The corresponding event can be something happening in your world, but an event can also be in the form of a thought or image that runs through your mind. Be concrete and specific; don't write something overly general such as "I hate my work." Instead, ask yourself what happened at work that you didn't like.

5. **Record your thoughts in the Thoughts/Interpretations column of the worksheet. Describe how you perceive, interpret, or think about the event.** Refer to The Thought Query Quiz in Chapter 4 if you experience any difficulty figuring out your thoughts about the event.

6. **Review your thoughts and write down the thought or thoughts that evoke the greatest amount of emotion — your *most malicious thoughts*.**

Worksheet 6-6	My Thought Tracker	
Feelings & Sensations (Rated 1–100)	*Corresponding Events*	*Thoughts/Interpretations*

My most malicious thoughts:

1. _____

2. _____

You can find this worksheet on the Web at: www.dummies.com/go/adwbfd. Download as many copies as you need and be sure to practice this technique often. In time, you're likely to start changing the way you think and, therefore, the way you feel. Just give it some time.

The Thought Tracker prepares you for the next step: Thought Court. Thought Court takes some planning and preparation. Take a malicious thought and consider the Prosecutor's Investigative Questions in Worksheet 6-3. Reflect on your answers in Worksheet 6-7.

Worksheet 6-7	**My Reflections**

_____

_____

_____

_____

_____

Now you're ready to put a malicious thought on trial. After you put one thought on trial using the instructions that follow, proceed to put other malicious thoughts through the same process.

1. **In Worksheet 6-8, designate one of your most malicious thoughts as the accused thought and write it down.**

2. **In the left-hand column, write all the reasons, evidence, and logic that support the truth of your accused thought.** In other words, defend your thought as best you can.

3. **In the right-hand column, write refutations of all the reasons, evidence, and logic presented by the defense. Then write down any additional points that help prosecute the thought.**

Worksheet 6-8	**My Thought on Trial Worksheet**

Accused thought: _____

Defending the Thought	*Prosecuting the Thought*

(continued)

Worksheet 6-8 *(continued)*

Defending the Thought	Prosecuting the Thought

You can download extra copies of this form at www.dummies.com/go/adwbfd. After all, you need to use the Thought Court method numerous times to feel the full benefit.

After you complete the Thought Court process, decide for yourself whether or not your thought is guilty of causing you unneeded emotional distress such as anxiety, depression, or other difficult feelings. Even if you conclude that your thought has some grain of truth, you're likely to discover that it's highly suspect of causing you more harm than good. In Thought Court, you don't judge your thought guilty only on the basis of "beyond a reasonable doubt." Rather, we suggest you judge your thoughts on the "preponderance of evidence"; in plain English, convict your thought if the evidence weighs heaviest on the guilty side.

Reviewing more Thought Court cases

To help you understand Thought Court better, this section contains a few more examples. Because the Thought Tracker also appears in Chapters 4 and 5, we start with the accused thought here, which comes from the most malicious thoughts at the end of a Thought Tracker (see "Putting your thoughts on trial").

Connor: Doomed to unhappiness

Over the years, **Connor,** a 58-year-old high school teacher, became an avid outdoorsman, spending his summer vacations camping, fishing, and hiking. Although his arthritis has been getting progressively worse, Connor has tried to ignore the pain. In fact, he only consults his doctor when the pain becomes overwhelming. His doctor refers him to an orthopedic specialist who tells Connor he needs a hip replacement. Connor slips into depression at the news. He fills out some Thought Trackers and zeroes in on a malicious thought: "I'll never be happy again. Life will just be a downhill slide from here." He accuses this thought of increasing his misery and puts it on trial (see Worksheet 6-9).

Worksheet 6-9	Connor's Thought on Trial Worksheet

Accused thought: I'll never be happy again — life will just be a downhill slide from here.

Defending the Thought	Prosecuting the Thought
This hip replacement is just the beginning of the end.	Many people get hip replacements without experiencing a series of health problems. This thought is enlarging reality and using unreliable forecasting.
I get my greatest pleasure from the outdoors. If I can't do that anymore, I can't imagine being happy.	That's hogwash — I do get pleasure from other things such as going to movies, reading novels, and going out to dinner. I'm filtering out these other pleasures.
I'll be suffering from chronic pain the rest of my life. Pain will rob me of all joy.	That's unreliable forecasting and magnification. I need to check with the doctor before I come to this conclusion. And there are many ways to manage pain. There are other people with arthritis who manage to have a good quality of life.
No one wants to be around someone who's sick and feeble.	That's probably true if I act like a whining victim. But I don't have to do that. I'm mind reading.
I won't even be able to climb the stairs to my classroom.	Here I go again with unreliable forecasting. I just read that most people with hip replacements return to active lives.
I should have exercised more and kept my weight down; if I had, I would never have needed this hip replacement.	Now I'm shoulding on myself. That doesn't help me at all.
I'm sure I'll be confined to a wheelchair soon.	That's distorted logic; it's using unreliable forecasting. I realize I do that a lot! And even if it turned out to be the case, people in wheelchairs also can lead productive lives.
	Most likely, I'll have some discomfort after the surgery, and it will take some time to get better. But, odds are, I'll be almost back to normal if I go to physical therapy.
	Good grief; one of the other teachers at school had a hip replacement last summer and he looks good as new.

Connor carefully considers the evidence. His verdict: Guilty as charged. He now realizes the thought, "I'll never be happy again — life will just be a downhill slide from here," is far from the truth and certainly doesn't help him cope with his reality.

Emma: Filled with anxiety

Emma, a 37-year-old loan officer, regularly puts in a 50-hour workweek. A divorced mom, she juggles the responsibilities of work and parenting. She's also a perfectionist and expects to be able to handle everything. Understandably, Emma is often plagued with anxiety. She worries about keeping up with her job and being a good mother to her two children. So when Emma's son brings home a mediocre report card, she crashes into a terrible depression. She loses her temper and screams at her son, and then she berates herself for being a terrible mother. Emma completes a Thought Tracker and then puts her most malicious thought on trial (see Worksheet 6-10).

Worksheet 6-10	Emma's Thought on Trial Worksheet

Accused thought: I'm a complete failure as a mother; my son is falling apart.

Defending the Thought	*Prosecuting the Thought*
My son is doing horrible in school.	He had one bad report card. It wasn't even all that bad, just worse than his usual. Overall, he has done okay. I'm enlarging here.
I screamed at him. I shouldn't have done that.	I'm not the only mother to lose it. Usually, I'm pretty calm. I'm shoulding on myself; I don't need to do that.
If I were a good mother, I would have known that he needed more help in school.	I wonder why the teacher didn't contact me before report card time.
My son started to cry when I yelled at him.	That's pretty normal; after all he is a child. It doesn't mean he's falling apart. I'm mind reading here.
I haven't gone on a field trip with my son's class because of work.	Out of 30 kids, only a few parents were able to drive on field trips.
Other mothers even volunteer in the classroom. That's what good moms do.	I wish I could spend more time with my son, but I also need to support the family. I'm engaging in critical comparisons of myself to others.
I have been putting my job ahead of my children.	That's not really true; when my kids really need me, I take the time off. I'm overgeneralizing.

Defending the Thought	Prosecuting the Thought
I don't know what to do to help him.	I guess I'll do what the teacher suggests and put him on a weekly grade check.
	If my son were falling apart, he certainly wouldn't have so many friends.
	Up until this last report, he's carried a B+/A- grade average. I just need to see what's going on lately.
	Clearly I do a lot of things with my son. I can't be Supermom.

Thought Court is one of the most effective tools for combating anxiety, depression, and other unpleasant emotions. If you have trouble with the exercise, spend more time going over the Prosecutor's Investigative Questions in Worksheet 6-3. It also doesn't hurt to review Chapter 5 and re-read the examples in this chapter. If you still struggle, we recommend you consult a mental health professional who's proficient in cognitive therapy.

After the Verdict: Replacing and Rehabilitating Your Thoughts

Hopefully, the prosecution presents a convincing case against a variety of your malicious thoughts, and you begin to see that many of your thoughts are guilty of scrambling reality and causing excessive emotional distress. When criminals are convicted, society usually tries to rehabilitate them and give them a second chance. The same thing goes for guilty thoughts.

In this section, we show you how to rehabilitate your guilty thoughts, one at a time. Rehabilitating your thoughts decreases feelings of depression and anxiety because rehabilitated thoughts are less distorted, judgmental, and critical. We call rehabilitated thoughts *replacement thoughts* because they replace your old malicious thoughts.

A replacement thought is a balanced, realistic appraisal of your problem. The reason for forming a *single* replacement thought is that you can use that new thought repeatedly whenever the old, malicious thoughts start rumbling through your mind. The new thought is a quick and easy comeback to negative, distorted, reality-scrambled thinking.

You can use a number of different techniques to develop effective replacement thoughts. The strategies outlined in the following sections help you discard distortions and straighten out your thinking. With these strategies, you discover how to replace your twisted thoughts with more helpful, realistic replacement thoughts. We provide four separate strategies for developing replacement thoughts. If one doesn't work for you, be sure to try the others.

Getting a little help from a friend

This rehabilitation strategy is pretty simple. You start by imagining that a good friend of yours is going through the same kind of problem as you are. Your friend has the same kind of thoughts as you do about the problem. Now imagine your friend sitting across from you. You feel empathy for your friend, and you want to help.

What do you say? How do you suggest your friend think about this situation? It's important that you look at your friend's problem from an honest viewpoint. We don't want you to simply try to make your friend feel better by sugarcoating the issue; rather, tell your friend about a reasonable way to think about the problem.

The essence of this powerful, yet surprisingly simple, technique is that the advice you would give a friend is advice you can give to yourself. The strategy works by helping you get a little distance from your problem. Viewing thoughts and feelings from a distance helps you be more objective. The following example shows you how to use Getting Help from a Friend to your advantage.

Emma (see "Emma: Filled with anxiety" earlier in this chapter) has taken her most malicious thought to Thought Court and found it guilty. Now she turns to Getting Help from a Friend to rehabilitate that thought. She thinks about her best friend, Louise. She imagines Louise coming to her with the same problem and concerns about her son. In other words, Louise is thinking Emma's most malicious thought and seeking advice (see Worksheet 6-11).

Emma's/Louise's most malicious thought:

I'm a complete failure as a mother; my son is falling apart.

Worksheet 6-11	Emma's Getting Help from a Friend (Louise)

Well, Louise, I know you feel like a failure, but your son only came home with two C's and three B's. That's not exactly catastrophic. Sure, you haven't spent as much time with him lately, but you've been pretty tied up at work. That happens. You don't need to beat up on yourself. Talk with his teacher and see what you can do to help. Quit sounding like a helpless victim. Besides, your son is 16 now; don't you think he has something to do with his own success and failure? It isn't all about you.

Emma reviews her imaginary discussion with Louise. She sees that her perspective changes when she gives Louise advice rather than listen to the negative automatic dialogue in her own head. Next, she distills this perspective into a single replacement thought (see Worksheet 6-12).

Worksheet 6-12	Emma's Replacement Thought

My son isn't falling apart and I'm not a failure. All I can do is see what I can do to help — the rest is up to him.

Take one of your most malicious thoughts and use the Getting Help from a Friend strategy to devise an effective response to that thought. Of course, it helps to take the malicious thought to Thought Court first, which you've done — right? We did mention this is a workbook? That means you need to do the work for this book to help you. So if you haven't worked on these exercises yet, no problem. Start now!

1. Write down one of your most malicious thoughts from your Thought Tracker (see Worksheet 6-6).

2. Think of someone you know and respect.

3. Imagine that the friend has a problem very similar to your own and has similar thoughts about the problem.

4. Imagine you're talking with your friend about a better way to think about and deal with the problem.

5. Write down the advice you would give your friend in Worksheet 6-13.

6. Look over that advice and try to rehabilitate your most malicious thought into a more balanced, summary replacement thought in Worksheet 6-14.

My most malicious thought:

_____

_____

Worksheet 6-13	**My Getting Help from a Friend**

_____

_____

_____

_____

_____

Worksheet 6-14	**My Replacement Thought**

_____

_____

_____

_____

_____

Traveling to the future

The events that disrupt your life today rarely have the same meaning after a few days, weeks, or months. For example, have you ever felt distraught about any of the following?

- Someone cutting you off in traffic
- Being embarrassed
- Locking yourself out of your car
- Forgetting someone's name
- A minor illness or injury
- Spilling something
- For women (well, mostly women anyway): A run in your nylon hose
- For men (again, for the most part): Cutting your face shaving
- A bad hair day
- A fender bender
- A traffic ticket
- Running late

Events like these so often lead to very malicious thoughts and highly distressing feelings. If you think back on these events after some time has passed, however, rarely can you muster up the same intensity of emotion. That's because most upsetting events truly aren't all that important if you look at them in the context of your entire life. Check out the following example of the Traveling to the Future technique in action.

Joel owns a piece of land on a busy corner. He'd like to sell the property, but he knows it's worth far more if it can be zoned for commercial purposes first. In order to do that, Joel must present his case in front of the Zoning Commission. He expects some opposition and criticism from homeowners in the area, and he's been putting this task off for months because of the intense anxiety it arouses in him.

He fills out a Thought Tracker (see "From Arraignment to Conviction: Thought Court" earlier in this chapter) and identifies his most malicious thought: "I'll make a fool out of myself. I'll probably stumble all over my words and sound like an idiot." He travels to the future with this thought to help him gain a better perspective; Joel asks himself how he'll look at this issue at various times in the future (see Worksheet 6-15). He rates the emotional upset and effect on his life that he feels right now, and then he re-rates the impact on his life at the conclusion of the exercise.

Worksheet 6-15   Joel's Traveling to the Future

If I do indeed make a fool out of myself, I'll probably feel pretty bad and the impact on my life will feel like 30 or even 40 on a 100-point scale. I'll still feel embarrassed a week later. I suspect that images of the incident will go through my mind fairly often, but six months from now, I doubt I'll think about the incident much at all. I'm sure that a year later I will have almost completely forgotten about it. So I guess the overall effect on my life will likely be about a 1 on a 100-point scale.

After pondering what his malicious thought will seem like in the future, Joel feels ready to develop a more realistic replacement thought (see Worksheet 6-16).

Worksheet 6-16	**Joel's Replacement Thought**

Even if I should happen to make a fool out of myself, it's hardly going to be a life-changing event. I may as well just go ahead and present the case.

The Traveling to the Future technique won't apply to all your thoughts and problems, but it works wonders with quite a few. In Joel's case, he could have analyzed his malicious thought for obvious distortions such as labeling and enlarging. He also could have taken the malicious thought to Thought Court. In other words, be sure to try out a variety of strategies for rehabilitating your thoughts in order to find the one that works best for you and for a particular thought or thoughts.

Take one of your most malicious thoughts and use the Traveling to the Future strategy to devise an effective response to that thought.

1. **Write down one of your most malicious thoughts from your Thought Tracker (see Worksheet 6-6).**

2. **In Worksheet 6-17, rate the overall amount of upset and impact you feel at the moment (on a scale of 1 to 100, with 100 representing the highest imaginable impact).**

3. **Think about how your thoughts are likely to change in a week.**

4. **Think about how your thoughts are likely to change in six months.**

5. **Think about how your thoughts are likely to change in a year.**

6. **Re-rate how much impact you'll feel as a whole.**

7. **In Worksheet 6-18, write down a balanced, summary replacement thought based on any new perspective you obtain with this strategy.**

My most malicious thought:

_____

Worksheet 6-17	**My Traveling to the Future**

_____

_____

_____

_____

_____

Worksheet 6-18	**My Replacement Thought**

_____

_____

_____

_____

Recalculating risks

When you're anxious, worried, or depressed, your mind frequently focuses on the future and makes dire predictions. People worry about things yet to happen to them, such as facing a plane crash, catching germs, encountering heights, and experiencing embarrassment. They predict that whatever they undertake will result in horror, misery, or unhappiness. Yet, such worries typically far exceed the actual odds of unwanted outcomes. In other words, people tend to overestimate the risks of negative outcomes, and they do so more often when they're in emotional distress.

When you predict negative outcomes, you have malicious thoughts that paralyze you from taking action. In order to develop replacement thoughts for your malicious ones, you first need to rethink your negative predictions. Then we suggest that you recalculate your actual risks. After you analyze your predictions, you'll be able to rehabilitate your malicious thoughts. The following example illustrates this technique.

Melinda's boss, Allison, takes a month off work after the birth of her baby. Melinda takes on Allison's responsibilities in her absence and assumes the extra work without thinking about it. She performs flawlessly. After a month, Allison announces that she isn't returning to work. Melinda is offered Allison's job. Oddly, Melinda now finds herself racked with fear and anxiety. She predicts that she won't be able to handle the job, and she can't see herself as a boss. Her most malicious thoughts are, "I'm not cut out to handle supervising others — I'm a follower, not a leader. I can't do this."

Melinda takes the Rethinking Negative Predictions Quiz shown in Worksheet 6-19 to prepare her to test out her negative predictions.

Worksheet 6-19   Melinda's Rethinking Negative Predictions Quiz

1. **How many times have I predicted this outcome and how many times has it actually happened to me?**

   There are other challenges in my life that I thought I couldn't do. I didn't think I'd make it through college and I did. I actually can't think of any times that I failed at something important to me.

2. **How often does this happen to people I know?**

   I can't recall a single instance in this company when someone has been promoted and then fired.

3. **If someone else made this prediction, would I agree?**

   Not necessarily. I would base my prediction on past performance. I guess mine has been pretty good.

4. **Am I assuming this will happen just because I fear that it will, or is there a reasonable chance that it will truly happen?**

   Of course, there's a small chance I won't be able to handle the job. But clearly, I'm making some unwarranted assumptions here. After all, I've done the job successfully for a month.

5. **Do I have any experiences from my past that suggest my dire prediction is unlikely to occur?**

Again, for the past month, I have done fine. I've never really failed at anything, come to think of it.

After filling out her answers to this quiz, Melinda decides to act on her recalculated risk by taking the job. She finds she actually enjoys the new challenges. She looks back over her most malicious thought and develops a replacement thought (see Worksheet 6-20).

Worksheet 6-20   **Melinda's Replacement Thought**

While I don't "feel" like a leader, the evidence says otherwise. I'm capable, and I'm doing it!

Take one of your most malicious thoughts and use the Testing Thoughts strategy to devise an effective response to that thought.

1. **When you find yourself making a negative prediction about some upcoming event or situation, write down your most malicious thought.**

2. **Take the Rethinking Negative Predictions Quiz in Worksheet 6-21.**

3. **Act on your recalculated risk by doing the thing you fear.**

4. **In Worksheet 6-22, write out a replacement thought for your original prediction and use it in similar future situations.**

Worksheet 6-21   **My Rethinking Negative Predictions Quiz**

---

1. **How many times have I predicted this outcome and how many times has it actually happened to me?**

_____

_____

_____

_____

2. **How often does this happen to people I know?**

_____

_____

_____

_____

3. **If someone else made this prediction, would I agree?**

_____

_____

_____

_____

4. **Am I assuming this will happen just because I fear that it will, or is there a reasonable chance that it will truly happen?**

_____

_____

_____

_____

5. **Do I have any experiences from my past that suggest my dire prediction is unlikely to occur?**

_____

_____

_____

_____

Assuming your answers tell you that the odds are in your favor, go ahead and test out your negative predictions. Jump right in and do what you fear. Then jot down a replacement thought (in Worksheet 6-22) for your original malicious thought.

If the odds of a bad outcome are high, go to the Worst-Case Scenario strategy in the next section of this chapter, where you can find techniques for coping with bad outcomes.

Worksheet 6-22	**My Replacement Thought**

_____

_____

_____

_____

Imagining the worst

The preceding section shows you how to rethink risks because, in general, when people are depressed or anxious, they greatly overestimate the odds of bad things happening. _And_ they grossly underestimate their abilities to cope.

But just in case you're starting to think otherwise, we're not trying to convince you that bad things never happen. They do. People get sick, accidents happen, and relationships end. Stuff happens. Sometimes really bad stuff. What then? Imagining yourself dealing with worst-case scenarios is a useful exercise because it helps you understand that you can get through whatever it is that you fear. The following example shows you how the Worst-Case Scenario Quiz helps Martha make a decision and develop a replacement thought for her malicious thought.

Martha has been single for the past 20 years. Since her painful divorce, she's had a number of casual dates, but work and raising her child have kept her attention away from developing a serious relationship. Now at age 50, Martha has fallen in love with someone special, and he feels the same way. However, she finds herself withdrawing out of fear that things won't work out. She predicts that if she commits to the relationship, her companion will ultimately reject her, and she couldn't stand that. Martha identifies her most malicious thought as, "I'd rather be alone forever than risk the pain of rejection again; I don't think I could deal with that."

Martha takes the Worst-Case Scenario Quiz shown in Worksheet 6-23 to identify and work through her greatest fear.

Worksheet 6-23   **Martha's Worst-Case Scenario Quiz**

---

1. Have I ever dealt with anything like this in the past?

I was rejected by my ex-husband. It took me quite a while, but I got through it. Today, I'm actually fairly happy.

2. How much will this affect my life a year from now?

If he rejects me, I'll be hurt and alone. I've been okay alone for a while now. A year from now, I suspect I'll be sad, but I think I'll be getting over the worst of the rejection.

3. Do I know people who have coped with something like this, and how did they do it?

I have lots of friends who've lost relationships. They got through it by staying active and seeking support from others. A couple of my friends went to therapy, which they said helped.

4. Do I know anyone I could turn to for help or support?

Over the years, I've developed a pretty good network of friends. I know I could get support from them. My family has always been there for me, too.

5. Can I think of a creative, new possibility that could result from this challenge?

If this relationship doesn't work, I think I'll volunteer to work with Habitat for Humanity in another country. I've always wanted to do something like that. I love travel and meeting new people. I think that experience would be very meaningful to me.

Now, Martha's ready to devise a more realistic replacement thought (see Worksheet 6-24).

Worksheet 6-24 **Martha's Replacement Thought**

If I do get rejected, I can handle it. I love this guy. Now I feel more like taking the risk, committing myself to this relationship, and seeing what happens.

Take one of your most malicious thoughts and use the Worst-Case Scenario strategy to devise an effective response to that thought.

1. **When you find yourself thinking of a worst-case scenario that you think you can't cope with, write down your most malicious thought.**

2. **Take the Worst-Case Scenario Quiz in Worksheet 6-25.**

3. **Rehabilitate your malicious thought with a replacement thought written in Worksheet 6-26.**

Worksheet 6-25 **My Worst-Case Scenario Quiz**

---

1. **Have I ever dealt with anything like this in the past?**

_____

_____

_____

_____

2. **How much will this affect my life a year from now?**

_____

_____

_____

_____

3. **Do I know people who have coped with something like this, and how did they do it?**

_____

_____

_____

_____

4. **Do I know anyone I could turn to for help or support?**

_____

_____

_____

_____

5. Can I think of a creative, new possibility that could result from this challenge?

_____

_____

_____

_____

Worksheet 6-26	My Replacement Thought

_____

_____

_____

_____

Use the techniques in this chapter to combat malicious thoughts. Take each of your malicious thoughts and develop a replacement, one at a time. The more thoughts you rehabilitate, the more you'll benefit.

Reflections on Chapter 6

This chapter is full of exercises and ideas for overcoming anxious and depressed thinking. Work through it carefully — this isn't a timed test. Be sure to download any extra forms you need from www.dummies.com/go/adwbfd. After completing the exercises and looking at your thoughts in new and different ways, take time to reflect on your new insights using the space in Worksheet 6-27.

Worksheet 6-27	My Reflections

_____

_____

_____

_____

_____

Chapter 7

Correcting Your Life-Lenses: A New Vision

When people get out of bed every morning, they open their eyes and look at their world. Some folks grab glasses off the nightstand, others need to get up and put in their contacts to see better. Some lucky people have 20/20 vision.

What most people don't know is that everyone's vision of reality is altered by special *life-lenses*. Life-lenses are strongly held beliefs or assumptions that you have about yourself, your relationships with others, and your world. Life-lenses powerfully influence how you respond to, interpret, and feel about events, but you may not be aware that you look through them.

Perhaps you know of people who view the world through rose-colored glasses. As perpetual optimists, they see the best in everything and everyone. On the other hand, you probably know a few folks who view the world through dark, gloomy shades. They expect the worst and rarely see the positive side of things.

In this chapter, we help you understand the nature of life-lenses. Your views of people, events, and even your self-image depend upon which lenses you look through. This chapter helps you realize whether your lenses are dirty, cracked, smoky, colored, or clear. A quiz shows you which lenses you look through and how they may cause you emotional trouble, and the exercises demonstrate how to change problematic life-lenses.

Examining Life-Lenses

Everyone has certain unquestioned assumptions about life. Many assumptions are rather useful. For example, it's not a bad idea to assume that day follows night, taxes must be paid, food is located at grocery stores, most drivers stop at red lights, and hard work usually pays off. Not questioning these assumptions makes life more efficient. Think about how snarled traffic would be if no one assumed that red means stop and green means go. Or just consider how much time you'd waste if you searched for food in department stores, schools, and libraries rather than assuming that you'd find it in grocery stores.

Life-lenses are special types of unquestioned assumptions. These assumptions or beliefs color the way you feel about yourself and the things that happen to you. For example, you may look through a *perfectionistic* life-lens and therefore believe that you must be perfect all the time. Or perhaps you have a *vulnerable* life-lens and thus assume that the world is a dangerous place. As we explore assumptions (that is, life-lenses) such as these, you can see that they form the foundation of your most distressing emotions, such as depression, anxiety, worry, irritability, apprehension, and even anger.

Life-lenses are the broad themes or assumptions you live by. These themes directly influence the kinds of thoughts you have and, in turn, how you feel about what happens to you. Each life-lens can be activated by many types of events.

Susan and **Diane** work as nurses at a local hospital. They both apply for one open management position. Although Susan and Diane are both well qualified, a nurse from another hospital gets the job. Susan reacts with anger and comments, "I deserved that job; the administration had no right to give that job away. I'll never cooperate with the creep that stole my job."

Diane reacts quite differently. She feels gloomy and says, "I'm sure they made the right decision picking someone else. I shouldn't have let my supervisor talk me into applying. I'm not management material."

Susan and Diane have different life-lenses. Susan has the life-lens of *entitled*. She believes that she always deserves the best; Susan feels that the world owes her and that if she wants something, it should be hers. On the other hand, Diane has the life-lens of *inadequacy*. She thinks that she's not good enough and that others have more skill and talent than she does. Diane assumes that she couldn't do the job even though her supervisor told her she has the appropriate ability and background.

Same event. Different thoughts and different feelings. Susan's *entitled* life-lens makes her prone to tension and anger when her needs aren't met. Diane's *inadequacy* life-lens steers her in the direction of depression when her adequacy is called into question.

Susan and Diane apply their respective life-lenses to many different events in their lives. For example, when they're both caught in an unexpected traffic jam, they view the event through their own life-lenses and thus experience different thoughts and feelings. Susan's *entitled* life-lens leads her to feel rage and have thoughts like, "No one in this town knows how to drive. What idiots!" Diane, who looks through an *inadequacy* life-lens, scolds herself, "I should have left earlier. Why didn't I listen to the traffic report this morning? I'm an idiot!"

With some understanding of life-lenses, it's time to take a look at which lenses may be affecting you and your life. After all, changing the way you feel starts with identifying your problematic life-lenses. If you aren't aware of your own life-lenses, you're powerless to do anything about them.

The questionnaire in Worksheet 7-1 is designed to clarify which life-lenses may be causing you trouble. After you identify them, we tell you a little more about how they work, where they come from, and most importantly, what you can do about them. Before you start marking the life-lenses in the worksheet that apply to you, consider the following tips:

- ✔ **Answer as honestly as possible.** Sometimes, people respond how they think they "should" answer rather than responding with honest self-appraisals. Self-deception isn't useful.

- ✔ **Take your time to reflect on various events and situations that have happened to you that are relevant to each lens.** For example, in answering questions about abandonment-fearful versus intimacy-avoidant, ponder the relationships you've had and how you feel and react to those close to you. You shouldn't rush this task.

✔ **Base your answer on how you feel and react in situations that relate to each lens.** For example, if you frequently feel inadequate but know in your head that you're actually not inadequate, answer on the basis of how you feel when your adequacy comes into question, such as when you're asked to make a speech.

✔ **Don't worry about inconsistencies.** As you see in Worksheet 7-1, life-lenses come in opposite pairs. And you very well may find yourself using both lenses from time to time. For example, if you're a perfectionist, you may also quite often feel inadequate when you make a mistake. Or if you normally feel unworthy and undeserving, you may find yourself feeling quite angry and entitled on occasions when your needs unexpectedly go unmet. People often flip between opposite lenses, so don't worry if you seem a little inconsistent.

✔ **Answer on the basis of how often each lens describes you.** If you see parts of the description that apply and others that don't, underline the parts that fit and rate yourself on those parts in terms of how often they apply to you.

Use a scale of 1 to 5 for your frequency rating.

✔ **1** if the lens almost never describes you

✔ **2** if it occasionally describes you

✔ **3** if it sometimes describes you

✔ **4** if it usually describes you

✔ **5** if it almost always describes you

Worksheet 7-1	Problematic Life-Lenses Questionnaire
Lens	*Opposite Lens*
____ *Unworthy* I don't feel like I deserve to have good things happen to me. I feel uncomfortable whenever someone does something nice for me.	____ *Entitled* I deserve the best of everything. I should have almost anything I want. If my needs unexpectedly go unmet, I feel threatened, sad, or angry.
____ *Abandonment-fearful* I need lots of reassurance to feel loved. I feel lost without someone in my life, and I worry about losing those I care about. I feel jealous and cling to my loved ones because of my fear.	____ *Intimacy-avoidant* I don't like to get close to anyone. I'd just as soon stay away from any emotional involvement; I don't really want anybody in my life.
____ *Inadequate* I feel like I'm not as talented or skillful as most other people. I just don't measure up. I don't like taking on things I've never done before if they look difficult.	____ *Perfectionistic* I feel like I must do everything perfectly. I feel like there's a right way and a wrong way to do things, and I want to do things the right way.
____ *Guilty and blameworthy* I feel like everything that goes wrong is my fault. I worry about whether I've done the wrong thing. I can't stand hurting anyone else.	____ *Guiltless* I don't let stupid things like morality and conscience stand in my way if I want something bad enough. I never care about what other people think.
____ *Vulnerable* Bad things happen all the time. I worry a lot about the future. I'm scared; the world feels very dangerous.	____ *Invulnerable* I'm invincible — nothing can ever hurt me. The world treats me extremely well. I always have great luck, and I never worry about taking precautions.

(continued)

Worksheet 7-1 *(continued)*

Lens	Opposite Lens
____ *Help-seeking* I depend on others a lot, and I feel better when other people take care of me. I can't handle life by myself.	____ *Help-avoidant* I hate asking for favors, and I don't like it when other people try to help me.
____ *Under-control* If I want to do something, I follow my impulses. It's hard for me to set limits with people, so I tend to get walked on. I'd rather express my emotions than control them.	____ *Over-control* Nothing is worse than losing control. I never let anyone see how I feel. I like to keep my hand in everything. I don't like working for someone else, and I can't stand leaving my fate in the control of others.

Any life-lens that you rate as *3* or above probably gives you trouble now and then. If you discover that you have many life-lenses that you rate as *3* or above, don't worry. Many people have a range of these problematic assumptions. Change takes time, but you can do it — one lens at a time.

Take a few minutes now to reflect on the results of your Problematic Life-Lenses Questionnaire. In Worksheet 7-2, jot down thoughts about how these life-lenses may be causing you to have troubling emotions. Don't worry if you're not quite sure of the connections; we give you more ways of seeing the lenses' influence on your life in the next few sections of this chapter.

Worksheet 7-2　　　　　　　　　**My Reflections**

_____

_____

_____

_____

_____

How life-lenses work

You may wonder just how much trouble life-lenses create and why we say they're the root cause of most emotional turmoil. The examples in this section give you an idea about how they work their mischief. The exercise in this section is likely to convince you of just how much life-lenses affect your vision and your emotional life.

After you identify your life-lenses, it's a good idea to consider more examples of how the lenses lead to problematic thoughts and feelings. Notice how the life-lenses are a broad theme and the thoughts are specific to a given event.

Jim, Paul, and **Wayne** are friends and neighbors. All three have teenage daughters who are the same age and also best friends. One evening, the girls are late coming home. Jim, Paul, and Wayne have very different reactions. See how life-lenses influence how the fathers interpret this identical event and respond to their daughters.

Jim has a *guilty and blameworthy* life-lens. He feels like he's done something wrong, even when it's not his fault (see Worksheet 7-3).

Worksheet 7-3	Jim's Influence of Life-Lenses

Event: My daughter is 30 minutes late getting home.

Life-Lens & Definition	Thoughts	Feelings
Guilty and blameworthy: I worry about whether I've done the wrong thing.	I must be a terrible father; otherwise, my daughter would be home on time.	Sad and depressed

Paul has an *over-control* life-lens. He likes to be in charge and feels uncomfortable when others challenge his authority (see Worksheet 7-4).

Worksheet 7-4	Paul's Influence of Life-Lenses

Event: My daughter is 30 minutes late getting home.

Life-Lens & Definition	Thoughts	Feelings
Over-control: I like to be in charge of everyone and everything.	How dare she be late? I'm her father; she had better respect me and do what I say.	Anger

Wayne's major life-lens is *abandonment-fearful.* He worries that the people he cares about will leave him and needs frequent reassurance that he's loved (see Worksheet 7-5).

Worksheet 7-5	Wayne's Influence of Life-Lenses

Event: My daughter is 30 minutes late getting home.

Life-Lens & Definition	Thoughts	Feelings
Abandonment-fearful: I worry about losing people I care about; I don't think I could stand it if I lost someone close to me.	Oh no, she's probability had an accident. She might be hurt. I couldn't go on if I lost her.	Fear and anxiety

These three examples show you how life-lenses affect people's thoughts and feelings. Guess what? It's your turn to complete an Influence of Life-Lenses worksheet (see Worksheet 7-6). Filling out these exercises works a whole lot better than just reading about them, so don't forget to do the work.

1. **When events happen and you notice distressing feelings, write the event down.** The event can be something happening in your world or something that runs through your mind. Whatever it is, be specific.

2. **In the middle column, write down the thoughts or interpretations you have about the event.** In other words, describe how you perceive or think about the event. If you have difficulty with this step, flip to Chapter 6 for more information about events and thoughts.

3. **In the right-hand column, write down any feelings you have about the event.** Check out the Daily Unpleasant Emotions Checklist in Chapter 4 for a list of feelings.

4. **Review the Problematic Life-Lenses Questionnaire in Worksheet 7-1 (you did do it, didn't you?). Think about which life-lens fits your thoughts and feelings best and write that in the left-hand column.** You may discover that more than one lens applies. Also, include a brief definition of the life-lens based on the reflections you recorded in Worksheet 7-2. Feel free to shorten and/or tailor the definition so that it fits you better.

5. **In Worksheet 7-7, reflect on what this exercise tells you about your problematic emotions and where they come from.**

Worksheet 7-6	The Influence of My Life-Lenses	

Event: _____

Life-Lens & Definition	Thoughts	Feelings

Event: _____

Life-Lens & Definition	Thoughts	Feelings

Event: _____

Life-Lens & Definition	Thoughts	Feelings

For more copies of this form, visit www.dummies.com/go/adwbfd. The more forms you fill out, the more you'll understand how life-lenses impact your life.

Worksheet 7-7	My Reflections

The origins of life-lenses

Usually, the prescription for your life-lenses is established in your childhood. People don't come into the world seeing themselves as *inadequate, undeserving, entitled,* or *perfectionistic.* Rather, they learn these patterns through repeated experiences. Life-lenses emerge from abuse, abandonment, betrayal, criticism, natural disasters, loss, rejection, and other emotionally powerful events.

Some life-lenses even develop from well-meaning parents who unwittingly go overboard (probably because of their own life-lenses). For example, some parents worry so much that they overprotect their children, who subsequently feel vulnerable. Other parents overindulge their children in the name of love and caring, and their kids may end up feeling entitled.

On the road to understanding and changing your life-lenses, it helps to reflect on what caused you to acquire the lenses you look through in the first place. When you understand these origins, you can release the notion that you're crazy, weird, or messed up. Self-forgiveness releases energy that you can use for grinding new lenses for better vision.

Hannah struggles with depression and anxiety. She takes the Problematic Life-Lenses Questionnaire shown in Worksheet 7-1 and identifies the life-lenses of *intimacy-avoidant* and *entitled.* She also realizes that she's *perfectionistic* but flips to feeling *inadequate* when she makes a mistake. Hannah reflects on her childhood for possible causes of her life-lenses. She then completes the Childhood Origins of Life-Lenses exercise shown in Worksheet 7-8 and reflects on her findings in Worksheet 7-9.

Worksheet 7-8	Hannah's Childhood Origins of Life-Lenses
Lens	*Opposite Lens*
Unworthy: This life-lens doesn't apply to me.	Entitled: My mother always made me feel like our family was better than others. I have to admit she spoiled me, too.
Abandonment-fearful: This life-lens doesn't really fit.	Intimacy-avoidant: Although I was told I was special, I never felt anyone listened to me. Whenever I was sad or lonely, my parents told me how lucky I was to have all the toys, clothes, and luxuries I did. I decided it was better to never need anyone.

(continued)

Worksheet 7-8 *(continued)*	
Lens	*Opposite Lens*
Inadequate: Whenever I made a mistake, my father made me feel stupid.	Perfectionistic: My family was incredibly concerned about how we looked to other people. My parents were so critical that I tried to be perfect.

Worksheet 7-9	Hannah's Reflections

When I look back on my childhood, I realize that my family was pretty cold. They expected me to be perfect, and when I wasn't, I was treated with scorn. It's no wonder I feel anxious about being perfect and feel depressed when I'm not. There wasn't a lot of love in my family, so I've learned to keep my distance from others. I was taught that possessions and status are more important than people, so I've invested too much time and effort on getting the things I want. But I feel empty and lonely.

To uncover the origins of your life-lenses in the same way that Hannah did, follow these instructions and complete Worksheets 7-10 and 7-11.

1. **Review each life-lens that you rated as 3 or above on your Problematic Life-lens Questionnaire (see Worksheet 7-1).**

2. **For each of those lenses, reflect on your childhood.** Feel free to look back at Chapter 2 for help with ways of recalling past feelings and events.

3. **Jot down anything from your childhood that you believe may have contributed to each of your problematic life-lenses.**

4. **After you complete this exercise, take some time to reflect on any new insights you've discovered and record them in Worksheet 7-11.**

Worksheet 7-10	Childhood Origins of Life-Lenses
Lens	*Opposite Lens*
Unworthy:	Entitled:
Abandonment-fearful:	Intimacy-avoidant:
Inadequate:	Perfectionistic:
Guilty and blameworthy:	Guiltless:

Lens	Opposite Lens
Vulnerable:	Invulnerable:
Help-seeking:	Help-avoidant:
Under-control:	Over-control:

Worksheet 7-11 **My Reflections**

_____

_____

_____

_____

_____

Changing the Prescription of Your Life-Lenses

After you complete the exercises in the preceding sections, you should know which life-lenses cause you problems. In this section, we give you three techniques for regrinding your life-lenses. It would be nice if you could toss the old lenses in the trash or throw them on the ground and stomp on them. But these lenses consist of almost shatterproof material — after all, they're cast from the emotional turmoil of childhood (see "The origins of life-lenses"). Thus, you need to proceed slowly and cautiously.

You may find the task of changing your life-lenses more challenging than you expected. Even if you put a lot of time and work into it, when you're tired or stressed, you may find yourself looking through your outdated prescription. That's okay. Your new prescription takes a while to break in. You're bound to use the old one out of habit. Your goal is simply to use the new lenses more often than the old ones (until you can't even find the old ones). If you find the task too difficult, please consult a mental health professional.

Distinguishing the past from the present

Life-lenses develop from emotionally significant events in childhood, and they make sense when viewed in conjunction with those events. Your world has no doubt changed a great deal over the years, but you probably still look through many of the same old lenses. And those lenses don't give you a clear vision of present-day reality.

As you can see in Worksheet 7-8, **Hannah** developed the life-lens of *perfectionistic*. As a kid, she was harshly criticized when she wasn't perfect, so the lens helped her avoid some of that criticism. The lens was a healthy adaptation to her life at the time. But today, as an adult, her *perfectionistic* life-lens causes her anxiety, stress, and even depression when she fails. Furthermore, no one in her life is nearly as critical as her father was. So she doesn't need to be perfect to avoid harsh criticism today. Her *perfectionistic* lens distorts her vision. Hannah completes the Then and Now Exercise in Worksheet 7-12 in order to help her understand how her past experiences cause her to overreact to current triggers. Seeing this connection will help her change her life-lens.

Worksheet 7-12	Hannah's Then and Now Exercise	
Problematic Life-Lens	*Childhood Image(s)*	*Current Triggers*
Perfectionistic: I feel like I must do everything perfectly. And if I don't, it's awful.	My mother would scream at me if I got my clothes dirty.	If I get a snag or a run in my hose, I freak. And a stain on my blouse drives me insane.
	My father was never satisfied with anything but straight A's. Even when I got them, he was never impressed.	I can't stand being evaluated at work. I lose sleep for days. Even a single rating just one notch below "Outstanding" sends me into a depression.
	Both of my parents always talked about other people critically. They put people down for just about anything.	I judge everything I do — my hair, my housecleaning, my job, everything. And sometimes I judge other people too harshly over trivial things.

Eleven-year-old **Adam** had a warm and caring family. He lived in a nice neighborhood and attended a reputable public middle school. He was bright but not brilliant. He played sports well enough and had many friends. In short, he was an unlikely candidate for developing problematic life-lenses.

Tragically, one beautiful fall day a highly disturbed classmate brought a gun to school and shot three students. Adam witnessed the event and was slightly injured. Subsequently, Adam suffered from nightmares, experienced intrusive images of the event, and was easily startled. Understandably, Adam developed a *vulnerable* life-lens.

As an adult, anxiety often overwhelms Adam. His *vulnerable* life-lens is activated by events only superficially similar to the original trauma. Adam completes the Then and Now Exercise in Worksheet 7-13 in order to help him understand how his past experiences contribute to his current responses. This connection helps him begin to change his life-lens.

Worksheet 7-13	Adam's Then and Now Exercise	
Problematic Life-Lens	*Childhood Image(s)*	*Current Triggers*
Vulnerable: I'm scared. The world feels very dangerous.	The image of a gun pointing at me is burned deeply into my brain. I hear the screams of the kids. I see blood and feel searing pain. I thought I was going to die.	When someone suddenly cuts me off in traffic, I feel the same surge of adrenaline and fear. Crowds make me feel nervous. I find myself watching my back. Whenever I meet someone new, I get anxious and have trouble trusting them. I wonder about the motives of even the nicest people.

You know the routine. Take some time to fill out the Then and Now Exercise (see Worksheet 7-14) for each problematic life-lens that you identified in Worksheet 7-1 earlier in this chapter. Whenever one of your problematic life-lenses is activated, refer back to this form in order to remind yourself that your feelings and reactions today have more to do with yesteryear than with your current reality.

1. **In the left-hand column, write down one of the problematic life-lenses that you rated as 3 or above on your Problematic Life-Lens Questionnaire (see Worksheet 7-1).** Also include a brief definition of the life-lens based on your reflections from Worksheet 7-2. Feel free to shorten and/or tailor the definition so that it fits you better.

2. **Reflect on your childhood and, in the middle column, record any memories or images that probably had something to do with the development of your life-lens.** Review Worksheet 7-10 for ideas.

3. **Be on the lookout for events that trigger your life-lens, and write those events down in the right-hand column as they occur.**

Because each lens often has multiple images and a variety of triggers, you should fill out a separate form for each problematic life-lens. And whenever your problematic life-lens is triggered, review this Then and Now Exercise as a reminder of what your reaction is actually all about.

Worksheet 7-14	My Then and Now Exercise	
Problematic Life-Lens	*Childhood Image(s)*	*Current Triggers*

Check out www.dummies.com/go/adwbfd to download extra copies of this form for your use.

For almost any problematic life-lens, you need to employ an array of strategies in order to feel significant benefit. Don't expect a single exercise to "cure" you, and always consider professional help if your own efforts don't take you far enough.

After you complete the exercise, take some time to reflect on what you've learned about yourself and your feelings, and record your reflections in Worksheet 7-15.

Worksheet 7-15	My Reflections

Tallying up costs and benefits of current life-lenses

The process of changing life-lenses stirs up some anxiety in most people. That's because people believe (whether consciously or unconsciously) that life-lenses either protect or benefit them in some important ways. For example, if you have a *vulnerable* life-lens, you probably think that seeing the world as dangerous helps you avoid harm. Or if you possess a *dependency* life-lens, you likely think that it guides you to find the help from others that you truly need.

But you may not have as much awareness of the *costs* of your life-lenses. This section helps reveal the hidden costs of problematic life-lenses. Only when you fully believe that your life-lenses cause you more harm than good do you have the motivation to change them.

Cameron, a 22-year-old college student, loves to have a good time. He looks at his world through the *under-control* life-lens. Cameron rarely sets limits on himself or others and doesn't think he should have to. He says what he thinks and does what he wants. His high intelligence and easy-going personality have enabled him to get by — until recently.

Lately, Cameron's drinking, which has never been under great control, escalates. He hangs out at bars until they close. Hangovers often cause him to miss classes, and his grades, previously hovering just above passing, sink into the failure zone. Cameron gets picked up for a DWI and is put on academic probation in the same week. He reels from the impact of these events and becomes depressed. Alarmed, his parents encourage him to see someone at the Student Mental Health Center.

After discovering that Cameron looks through an *under-control* life-lens, his therapist suggests that he fill out a Cost/Benefit Analysis of his life-lens. Because patients often downplay the benefits of their life-lenses when they're in therapy, his therapist suggests that he first ponder the advantages of his life-lens (see Worksheet 7-16).

Worksheet 7-16	Cameron's Cost/Benefit Analysis (Part I)

Life-Lens: Under-control. I believe it's best to let it all hang loose. I should be able to do what I feel like. It's good to express feelings and do what feels good.

Benefits	Costs
It feels good to do what I want.	
I know how to have a good time.	
I don't have to be a slave to rules and to what people tell me to do.	
My friends know that I say what I think and that I'm honest.	
I like showing how I feel no matter what.	
I don't have to deny my needs.	

Cameron doesn't have much trouble figuring out benefits for his problematic life-lens. In fact, at this point, he's not even sure the lens is problematic at all. However, his therapist urges him to carefully consider any negative consequences, or *costs,* of his *under-control* life-lens. Worksheet 7-17 shows Cameron's completed Cost/Benefit Analysis.

Worksheet 7-17	Cameron's Cost/Benefit Analysis (Part II)

Life-Lens: Under-control. I believe it's best to let it all hang loose. I should be able to do what I feel like. It's good to express feelings and do what feels good.

Benefits	Costs
It feels good to do what I want.	It feels good at the moment, but later I get hangovers.
I know how to have a good time.	I have a good time for a while, but my grades have suffered.
I don't have to be a slave to rules and to what people tell me to do.	When I didn't follow the rules about drinking and driving, I got a DWI and spent a night in jail. I never want that to happen again.
My friends know that I say what I think and that I'm honest.	I know I've hurt some good friends by what I've said. I don't like doing that.
I like showing how I feel no matter what.	It's not always smart to express everything I feel. I'm a lousy poker player. And my anger gets me in trouble sometimes.

(continued)

Worksheet 7-17 *(continued)*

Benefits	Costs
I don't have to deny my needs.	Eventually, this is all going to catch up with me.
	My life is spinning out of control this way.
	I want to succeed in life, and that's not where I'm headed at all.
	A lot of my friends seem more mature than I am. I used to think they were just boring, but I see that, in some ways, they seem happier than I am.

As Cameron wraps up his Cost/Benefit Analysis, he comes to a realization: "My *under-control* life-lens is ruining my life!" He feels an increased desire to do something about what he now sees as a real problem.

A Cost/Benefit Analysis helps you boost your motivation to regrind problematic life-lenses. Take the time to carefully complete this exercise in Worksheet 7-18.

1. **Write down one of the problematic life-lenses that you identified in Worksheet 7-1.** Also, include a brief definition of the life-lens based on your reflections in Worksheet 7-2. Feel free to shorten and/or tailor the definition so that it fits you better.

2. **Think about any and all of the conceivable benefits for your problematic life-lens and record them in the left-hand column.** Sometimes these may come readily; other times, you may need to reflect a while. Write down everything you come up with.

3. **In the right-hand column, record any and all conceivable costs of your problematic life-lens.** It's a good idea to start by looking at the presumed benefits and responding with a counterargument. Then, add any additional costs that you come up with.

4. **Review your Cost/Benefit Analysis carefully. Make a decision about whether the disadvantages or costs outweigh the advantages or benefits. Write down your conclusions in Worksheet 7-19.**

Worksheet 7-18   My Cost/Benefit Analysis

Life-Lens:

Benefits	Costs

Benefits	Costs

Go to www.dummies.com/go/adwbfd to print out extra copies of this form. You need to fill one out for each problematic life-lens you identify.

Worksheet 7-19	My Reflections

_____

_____

_____

_____

_____

Taking direct action against problematic life-lenses

The exercises in the previous two sections were designed to increase your motivation and set the stage for altering your life-lenses. In this section, our guidelines for developing an action plan show you how to prepare for an all-out assault on your life-lenses. Ready . . . set . . . go!

To tackle the action steps, you start by figuring out the effect your life-lens has had on you, your emotions, and your life. For example, if you have the *perfectionistic* life-lens, you may realize that this lens causes inordinate tension and worry; basically, you obsess over every little error.

The next step in taking action is to devise a plan that tests the assumptions behind your life-lens. For example, an action step for the *perfectionistic* life-lens tests out the assumption that you must never make mistakes. The test is an experiment in which you intentionally make small mistakes and see what happens.

To help you devise your own action steps, Worksheet 7-20 contains some examples for each problematic life-lens. But don't let our list stifle your own creativity. Be adventurous and take risks.

Worksheet 7-20	Sample Life-Lens Action Steps
Lens	*Opposite Lens*
Unworthy: I will ask someone for what I want. I will repeatedly tell myself that I deserve good things.	Entitled: I will refrain from demanding that others meet my needs. I will donate to charity.
Abandonment-fearful: I will resist checking on my loved ones so often. I will quit asking for reassurance that my husband loves me.	Intimacy-avoidant: I will reveal more about myself and express my feelings to people. I will join a social organization and work hard to get to know the people there.
Inadequate: I will join Toastmasters and learn to give public speeches. I will volunteer to lead a project at work.	Perfectionistic: I will wear two different-colored socks and see what happens. I will try to make as many trivial mistakes as I can in one day (go in an exit door, park over a line, and so on).
Guilty and blameworthy: When I feel guilty about something, I'll ask a trusted friend if I'm being too hard on myself. When I feel at fault, I will make a list of all the possible causes for the problem.	Guiltless: I will work hard to find something to apologize for at least once a week. I will admit to making mistakes.
Vulnerable: I will do something I'm afraid of, such as fly in an airplane. I will stop overprotecting my kids so much.	Invulnerable: I will volunteer at a hospital to see what can happen to people who ignore risks. I will start wearing my seat belt.
Help-seeking: I will do a project on my own without asking for help. I will help someone else without them asking me to.	Help-avoidant: I will ask someone for help on something once a week. I will start asking for directions when I'm lost.

Lens	Opposite Lens
Under-control: I will join AA. I will join a gym and develop some self-discipline.	Over-control: I will allow my partner to make more decisions. I will keep my mouth shut instead of giving advice to my adult son.

These sample action steps are just ideas, but if one or more of them fit your situation, great! However, your action steps need to specifically address the ways in which your life-lenses are affecting your life. Make your steps small, doable, and personalized. After you develop your action steps, don't forget to actually do them! And if you have trouble carrying out some action steps, try breaking them into smaller steps.

Fill out Worksheet 7-21 with your Life-Lens Action Steps.

Worksheet 7-21	My Life-Lens Action Steps
Lens	**Opposite Lens**
Unworthy:	Entitled:
Abandonment-fearful:	Intimacy-avoidant:
Inadequate:	Perfectionistic:
Guilty and blameworthy:	Guiltless:
Vulnerable:	Invulnerable:
Help-seeking:	Help-avoidant:
Under-control:	Over-control:

The life-lenses you see through were largely ground by circumstances and events rooted in your childhood, events over which you had little control. Thus, you don't deserve blame for carrying your lenses around. However, you do own the responsibility for doing something about regrinding your lenses. Regrinding life-lenses is slow, arduous work that takes patience, but the new, clear vision that results from your efforts is worth the wait.

Squeeze your eyes shut. Now open them up. How is your vision? Any clearer? Jot down a few of your thoughts and feelings in Worksheet 7-22.

Worksheet 7-22	My Reflections

Chapter 8

Managing Mindfulness and Achieving Acceptance

. . . .

In This Chapter

▶ Taking your thoughts less seriously

▶ Embracing your feelings

▶ Staying connected to the present

. . . .

Sit quietly for a few moments and pay attention to your breathing. Feel the air as it passes through your nostrils and slowly fills your lungs. Experience the sensation of your lungs deflating as you exhale. If thoughts come into your mind, notice them as an observer and allow them to pass through. Go back to focusing on your breathing.

This breathing exercise is designed to introduce you to *mindfulness.* Mindfulness is a state of awareness of the present in the absence of judgment, analysis, and reasoning. In other words, it's awareness without dwelling on your *thinking.* (That's why we think the term mindfulness really ought to be "mindlessness," but alas, the world has adopted the term "mindfulness," so we'll go along with that.) You can't achieve mindfulness without *acceptance,* which involves patience and tolerance as well as willingness to feel and experience "what is" without resistance. In this chapter, we guide you through the acceptance of your thoughts and feelings so that you can achieve mindfulness.

Start by Losing Your Mind!

You aren't the same as your mind. What's that? Confused? You may be thinking, "These authors sound like the ones who are losing their minds. This sounds like flakey hogwash!" It's perfectly okay with us if you wish to think that, but how about you play along with us for a few moments more and work through the next few sections?

Distinguishing between observing and evaluating

Sit back and wait for a thought to enter your mind. Don't rush it; we're sure one will come along pretty soon. When it does, ask yourself this question: Who noticed that thought? The obvious answer is *you.* The you that observes, breathes, and experiences isn't the same thing as your thoughts or your mind.

The following exercise helps you connect with the mindful, observant you by first demonstrating the ease with which you can slip into thoughts that come from an overly evaluative, judgmental state of mind.

As we sit in our office working on this chapter, we're connecting with our evaluative, judgmental minds. In this exercise, our job is to criticize everything we see. Therefore, we make the following critical thoughts and judgments about our surroundings:

- Papers are piled and stacked everywhere. What a disastrous mess!
- Who could ever work around this place?
- How could anyone type endlessly on a keyboard like this one that's tethered in one spot?
- How many glasses and cups are we going to accumulate before one of us finally breaks down and takes them to the kitchen?
- That picture on the wall of the memorial at the University of Kansas is wrinkled and warped.
- Look at this mess of computer wires under the desk. It looks like a snake pit.
- There are way too many books on the shelves — and just look at all that dust on them!
- See that basket full of last year's tax records? When are we ever going to file them away?
- With all this chaos, we'll never be able to finish this ^*!&*%#^@! book!

We found this exercise quite simple to do because we, like everyone else, easily slip into judgmental, critical states of mind. The more difficult task is to access the observing, nonevaluative you — in other words, to merely look at and experience what's around you. Here's what we experience when we're being mindful:

Right now, we can hear birds chirping outside, a fly let in through an open door buzzing around the room, and in the background, the sound of the dryer warning us that the laundry is ready. We see papers piled in stacks of varying heights, the flat computer screen, smooth-finished wood desks and shelves, a telephone, and the dogs napping on the floor. We see black and white wires entangled underneath the desk in patterns. We feel the plastic keys of the keyboard, the textured fabric of our chairs, slick paper lying on the desk, and a cold glass of iced tea. We also feel our breath as it gently goes in and out.

After the first, judgmental look at our present moment, we felt a little irritable, overwhelmed, and discouraged. When we simply allowed ourselves to experience what was in front of us without evaluation, we felt relaxed. The tasks at hand seemed less daunting. We pulled back from self-disparagement and soon found ourselves absorbed by our writing.

Do this three-part exercise right now. Don't let thoughts like "This is stupid," "What can this do for me?," or "I'll do this when I have more time" get in your way. Follow these instructions to complete Worksheet 8-1. Then move on to Worksheets 8-2 and 8-3.

1. **Sit and look at everything around you.**

2. **Find something negative in everything you see.**

3. **Write down each and every critical thought that comes to mind.**

4. **Notice how you feel when you're finished, and write those feelings down.**

Worksheet 8-1	**Your Critical State of Mind**

Critical thoughts:

1. _____
2. _____
3. _____
4. _____
5. _____
6. _____
7. _____
8. _____
9. _____
10. _____

Feelings after writing critical thoughts:

_____
_____
_____

1. **Take a new look around you, but this time don't judge or evaluate. Connect with your senses. Describe what you experience as objectively as you can, and write these experiences as they come to you in Worksheet 8-2.** Don't worry about sentence structure, punctuation, or grammar.

2. **Notice how you feel now. Jot these feelings down in Worksheet 8-2.**

3. **Reflect on this exercise, and write your conclusions under My Reflections in Worksheet 8-3.**

Worksheet 8-2	**Observing Your State of Mind**

Observations, sensations, and experiences:

_____
_____
_____
_____

Feelings after writing observations and experiences:

_____
_____
_____

Worksheet 8-3	My Reflections

Tuning in and tuning out mind chatter

Depressed and anxious minds chatter constantly. And usually the chatter predicts, judges, and evaluates in harsh or frightening ways. Think of part of your mind as a chatter machine that produces a stream of toxic verbiage, including:

- ✔ I'm not good enough.
- ✔ I'm a terrible person.
- ✔ I'll never make it.
- ✔ I don't deserve good things.
- ✔ I'm a screw-up.
- ✔ I'll fail if I try.
- ✔ I can't do this.
- ✔ No one will like me.
- ✔ If I ask her out, she'll reject me.
- ✔ Pretty soon, people will know I'm a phony.
- ✔ I'm going to fall apart.
- ✔ What if I get cancer?
- ✔ I might throw up.
- ✔ What if I cry?

Do you have thoughts like these? Tune into them using this exercise.

1. **Listen to your mind chatter as it rumbles through your mind.**

2. **In the left-hand column of Worksheet 8-4, write down the comments that you hear over and over.**

3. **Think of a good friend of yours. Change your mind chatter to a statement about your friend, and write that statement in the right-hand column.** For example, change "Pretty soon, people will know I'm a phony" to "Pretty soon, people will know you're a phony, Richard." Or change "I'm a terrible person" to "You're a terrible person, Richard."

4. **Imagine what it would feel like to express this mind chatter to your friend, and record your reflections in Worksheet 8-5.** You'd *never* say such things to a good friend, would you?

Worksheet 8-4	Mind Chatter Turned on Its Head
Mind Chatter	*Mind Chatter Said to a Friend*

Worksheet 8-5	My Reflections

Consider treating yourself as well as your friend better, and stop being so mean to yourself. When your mind chatters, remind yourself that you want to be a friend to yourself.

Playing with your mind chatter

In Chapters 5, 6, and 7, we show you how thoughts and beliefs that run through your mind contribute to emotional distress. These thoughts are almost always distorted and built on a foundation of sand (that is, they are based on flimsy evidence or outright distortions). Flip back to those chapters for a review of how you can wage war against unhelpful thoughts and beliefs.

You can certainly wage war on your unhelpful thoughts, but sometimes a warrior needs a break or a change in tactics. In this section, we ask you to change tactics and put down your weapons. Instead of going to war, we show you how to disarm damaging thoughts with humor. After all, it's hard to be upset when you're laughing. When you hear negative chatter, thank your mind for having those thoughts. Tell your mind how creative it's being (yes, this involves more than a hint of sarcasm). Take a look at an example, and then have some fun taking on your own thoughts.

Joseph works as a correction officer during the day and attends college at night. He hates his job and hopes that getting a counseling degree will allow him to change careers. His schedule is grueling, and at times he gets discouraged. He tracks his mind chatter and notices three recurring thoughts. After reading about thanking his mind, he comes up with the responses shown in Worksheet 8-6.

Worksheet 8-6	Joseph's Thank You Mind Exercise
Mind Chatter	*Playful Response*
I'll never be able to finish the degree.	Thanks, mind. That's such a useful way to look at things!
Even if I finish the degree, I'll make a lousy counselor.	Wow, mind. That's sooo helpful! Thanks!
I'm going to be stuck with this job for the rest of my life.	Good thinking! I really like it when you come up with such creative ways of helping me!

Try thanking your mind when you hear unhelpful mind chatter. If you take such chatter seriously, it's sure to drag you under. But if you play with the thoughts, you can take away their power. Follow these instructions to complete the exercise in Worksheet 8-7, and then record your overall reflections in Worksheet 8-8.

1. **Pay attention to your negative mind chatter.**

2. **In the left-hand column, write down upsetting thoughts that you hear repeatedly.**

3. **In the right-hand column, write a playful response to your mind chatter machine. Consider complimenting or thanking your mind.**

Keep this exercise in mind when your mind starts to chatter. Thank your mind for those thoughts, and smile!

Worksheet 8-7	My Thank You Mind Exercise
Mind Chatter	*Playful Response*

Just for fun, consider trying out some other ways of playing with your mind's chatter. Try singing the negative thoughts to the tune of "Happy Birthday to You" or "Row, Row, Row Your Boat." You can also speak the thoughts out loud in a different voice — how's your Homer Simpson impression? Or how about Donald Duck? When you sing or say your self-downing thoughts in a humorous manner, it's much harder to take them seriously.

Worksheet 8-8	My Reflections

Arriving at Acceptance

Once or twice each winter, we take a drive up to the crest of New Mexico's Sandia Mountains, elevation 10,000 feet. We like to tromp around in the snow and sometimes go cross-country skiing. We bring our dogs, and they appear to love the snow more than we do.

The parking lot at the crest is usually plowed, but the last time we went, we managed to get stuck in a snowbank. I mean *really* stuck. As the wheels began spinning uselessly, I (Charles) uttered a few choice words of frustration. Laura reminded me that we had written about this very subject (getting stuck in the snow) in our last book, *Depression For Dummies*. She said, "Remember, you have to accept where you're at to get where you want to go."

So, I took my foot off the accelerator and allowed the car to rock back. I gently applied the gas again until the tires started to spin, and once again, I took my foot off the accelerator. I continued rocking the car until we finally escaped from the snow.

No, this isn't a lesson in how to extract your car from a snowbank. Rather, the message here is that in order to move forward, it's important to ease up and accept where you're at for a moment. When the time is right, you can gently push ahead.

Are you wondering what acceptance has to do with anxiety and depression? Well, everyone feels anxious or sad now and then. Recognizing and accepting those feelings is important because if you absolutely can't stand to be worried or down, then you'll inevitably feel more upset when you experience these normal feelings. In other words, you get more upset and distressed about getting distressed. That's clearly not very helpful.

Don't get us wrong; we want you to feel good most of the time. But as far as we know, the only humans who don't feel some anxiety or sadness are, well . . . dead. Besides, if you don't know sadness, it's difficult to know what happiness is. Without worry, you wouldn't appreciate calm. Accept a certain degree of difficult emotions as part of your life.

One way to accept a few negative feelings is to view them objectively. Imagine that you're writing a report on the experience of anxiety or depression. To accurately express the experience, you need to acquire a dispassionate understanding of the essence of your emotions. In other words, observe and accept your feelings without judgment. As you do, you'll likely see that your distress lessens. Whether you're depressed or anxious, accepting the emotional angst dispassionately will help you handle your bad feelings without becoming more upset. Read through the following example, and try out the exercise when you're feeling troubled.

Kelsey needs to renew her driver's license, so she runs over to the Motor Vehicles Department on her lunch hour. Although there's only one clerk on duty, she's pleased to see only four people ahead of her. Then, the man at the front of the line starts arguing with the clerk. The argument continues, and the supervisor is summoned. As the discussion at the front of the line drags on, Kelsey looks at her watch and starts to worry about getting back to work on time. She recalls the Accepting Angst Dispassionately exercise (see Worksheet 8-9) and runs through it in her mind.

Worksheet 8-9	Accepting Angst Dispassionately

---

1. **Write about your current physical feelings. Is your stomach upset? Are you sweating? Is your heart pounding? Do your shoulders feel tight? Describe everything going on in your body in objective terms.**

   Huh, I'm jiggling and rocking back and forth. I can feel the tension in my shoulders. My breathing is becoming fast and shallow. My heart is even starting to race. How interesting.

2. **Notice fluctuations in these physical feelings. Over time, feelings vary in intensity. Are the waves long or short? How high do they go at their peaks and how low at their ebbs?**

   Now that I'm paying attention, I can see that these feelings go up and down every few minutes; they aren't constant. As I'm observing them, they actually seem to be lessening.

3. **Predict how long you will have these physical feelings. An hour, a minute, a day, a year?**

   They probably won't last more than however long I'm here.

4. **Notice with dispassion the thoughts that go through your mind. Imagine those thoughts floating away on clouds. Write them down and say goodbye as they float away.**

   It's interesting to notice my thoughts. I'm thinking things like, "I'm going to be late and that's horrible," and "That stupid man; who does he think he is anyway?" It's funny, but as I listen to these thoughts objectively, they don't seem so important.

5. **Predict how long you will have these thoughts. An hour, a minute, a day, a year?**

   They're already floating away as I zero in on them.

The next time you notice unpleasant feelings, work through the exercise in Worksheet 8-10. If you happen to have this book in front of you at the time, write your reactions down immediately. If you don't have your workbook on hand, recall as many of these questions as you can and answer them in your mind. The main goal is simply to adopt an objective perspective that describes your feeling without judging it.

Worksheet 8-10	**Accepting Angst Dispassionately**

1. Write about your current physical feelings. Is your stomach upset? Are you sweating? Is your heart pounding? Do your shoulders feel tight? Describe everything going on in your body in objective terms.

   _____

   _____

   _____

   _____

2. Notice fluctuations in these physical feelings. Over time, feelings vary in intensity. Are the waves long or short? How high do they go at their peaks and how low at their ebbs?

   _____

   _____

   _____

   _____

3. Predict how long you will have these physical feelings. An hour, a minute, a day, a year?

   _____

4. Notice with dispassion the thoughts that go through your mind. Imagine those thoughts floating away on clouds. Write them down and say goodbye as they float away.

   _____

   _____

   _____

   _____

5. Predict how long you will have these thoughts. An hour, a minute, a day, a year?

   _____

REMEMBER

The point of this exercise is to accept the way you feel in the moment without jumping to evaluation or judgment. Think of yourself as a scientist interested in objective observation and description. This exercise is particularly useful when you find yourself in frustrating, unavoidable predicaments, such as

✔ Being stuck in a traffic jam.

✔ Waiting in long lines.

✔ Sitting through boring meetings.

✔ Moving through crowds.

✔ Suffering through travel delays.

✔ Waiting for someone who's late.

✔ Meeting a deadline.

✔ Getting rejected.

✔ Receiving criticism.

✔ Feeling afraid.

✔ Taking a risk such as giving a speech.

✔ Getting sick.

Connecting with Now

People have the rather curious habit of allowing their thoughts to dwell on the past or the future. In the process, they make themselves miserable. If you really think about it, most of what you get unhappy or worried about has to do with events that happened in the past or are yet to occur. You feel guilty about past transgressions and worry about future calamities.

When you spend too much time in the past or future, you're bound to ruin your present. You lose the enjoyment and pleasure you may otherwise feel about the present. Rarely is the present as miserable as your memories or predictions.

For example, we have a great dog named Murphy. She's a Wheaton Terrier (looks like a little sheep dog). Murphy loves to ride in the car. What's odd is that most of the time she's in the car, we're taking her to the groomer. Murphy hates the groomer — as in *really* hates the groomer. Nevertheless, every time we open the car door, she eagerly bounds in and enthusiastically sticks her head out the window to enjoy the wind. When we arrive at the groomer's shop, she gleefully jumps out of the car, hoping to go for a walk. About 20 feet from the door, however, she sees where she's going and promptly plops down on the parking lot pavement. She refuses to move, so we end up carrying her in.

If Murphy were a person, she'd mark her calendar with her grooming dates and then worry and obsess about the appointment for days, if not weeks, ahead of time. She certainly would *not* enjoy the car ride — like how *you* miss your present because you're focusing on the past or future — and all those enjoyable moments would be lost.

The exercise laid out in Worksheet 8-11 facilitates becoming more now- or present-focused. Practice it for four or five minutes during your day; you can do it almost anywhere. This exercise will refresh you. (Some people need to use a stopwatch or timer because the five-minute rule is hard to follow at first, but it'll become easier as your practice becomes routine.)

Worksheet 8-11 **Embracing Present Moments**

---

1. **Sit comfortably in a chair or on the floor.** (Location doesn't matter as long as you're comfortable.)

2. **Extend your legs and place your feet about shoulder width apart.**

3. **Put your hand on your abdomen and feel your breath go in and out.** Take your time breathing, keep it low and slow.

4. **When you feel comfortable, close your eyes. Continue to think about your breathing.**

5. **When thoughts intrude, let them be.** Notice them and watch them float away. Just keep breathing — low and slow.

6. **Sit quietly.** When you first start this practice, you may feel an urge to scratch some part of your body. When that sensation occurs, concentrate mentally on the area and the desire is likely to pass.

7. **Remain for just five minutes of stillness.** If you feel a muscle tensing, send your mental effort to that area. Study the feeling, and it will pass.

Five quiet minutes is all it takes to become mindful of the present. Follow the steps above, and then take a few moments to reflect in Worksheet 8-12 on how you felt.

Worksheet 8-12   **My Reflections**

_____

_____

_____

_____

Almost any activity can be carried out mindfully, connecting only with the activity itself without judgment, evaluation, or analysis. For example, eating is an activity that occurs often and thus gives you numerous opportunities for practicing mindfulness. Relatively few present moments elicit high distress, and mindfulness connects you with the present. Mindful connection with the present takes some practice, so don't rush the process or judge your success or failure. Instead, simply practice, practice, practice.

Try this mindfulness exercise at any meal (see Worksheet 8-13). You'll find yourself slowing down and enjoying your food more than before. In fact, people who eat mindfully typically lose weight more easily (if that's what they're trying to do) because they're no longer eating to rid themselves of unpleasant feelings. After you work through the steps, record your reflections in Worksheet 8-14.

Worksheet 8-13   **Eating Mindfully**

---

1. **Look at what you're about to eat.** What colors are in front of you? Are they shiny or dull? What does the texture look like? Is it smooth, rough, or varied?

2. **Smell the food.** Does it smell sweet, garlicky, fishy, pungent, or something else?

3. **Take a small piece of food and place it on your tongue.** What does it feel like?

4. **Gently, slowly, move the piece around your mouth.** Are you salivating? Does this food need to be chewed?

5. **As you chew, note the different tastes and textures that are released.**

6. **As the food begins to break down, feel it as it gets close to the back of your throat. Swallow.**

7. **Start again with the next piece of food.**

Worksheet 8-14	My Reflections

Part III
Actions Against Angst: Behavior Therapy

The 5th Wave   By Rich Tennant

"It's just a little device I use to help relieve the anxiety from meeting new people."

In this part . . .

One approach to fighting depression and anxiety is by
changing your behavior. By changing what you do,
you can change the way you feel. We guide you step by
step through methods for overcoming fear and anxiety.
Furthermore, we provide encouragement for engaging in
healthy and pleasurable activities.

People who are emotionally upset usually find themselves unable to solve many of their everyday problems.
Therefore, we conclude this part by offering a structured
problem-solving skill we call S.O.C.C.E.R.

Chapter 9

Facing Feelings: Avoiding Avoidance

This chapter is all about fear and anxiety. We know what you're thinking — this book is supposed to be about both anxiety and depression; so what does fear have to do with depression? Well, quite a lot actually. Fear is connected to anxiety, and anxiety, especially chronic anxiety, frequently leads to depression. And if you're already depressed, anxiety is likely to deepen your depression.

If you experience fear and anxiety, you probably avoid the things that make you feel uneasy. For example, if you're dreadfully afraid of snakes, you probably don't hang out in swamps. Or if crowds make you nervous — really nervous, that is — you likely avoid the shopping mall during the holidays. So what's wrong with that?

The problem is that avoidance increases or intensifies anxiety. When you make the decision to avoid something you fear, you instantly feel relief, and relief feels pretty good. In a sense, you've rewarded yourself for avoidance. People tend to do things more often when they're rewarded; therefore, you're more likely to avoid again. In fact, you'll probably find yourself avoiding more frequently and in response to other, somewhat similar events.

If crowds make you really nervous, you may start out avoiding only huge crowds. That avoidance feels pretty good until smaller crowds start making you nervous, too. So you avoid smaller and smaller crowds, and your avoidance continues to grow until you're barely able to get yourself out of your house, lest you run into even a few people.

In this chapter, we give you a list of common anxieties and fears that people commonly experience so that you can identify the ones that cause you the most distress and choose one to battle. We show you how to break your fear into manageable pieces, guiding you up the Staircase of Fear, one step at a time. Don't worry; you can do it! Finally, we review a special type of anxiety known as *obsessive-compulsive disorder* (OCD) and explain its treatment, which is similar to the treatment of other anxieties and fears but with a few special modifications.

What, Me Worry?

Most people have at least a few minor worries or anxieties, and that's no big deal. A little anxiety prepares you for action. When the guy in the car in front of you slams on his brakes, the sudden anxiety you feel helps your body to respond quickly — and that's a good thing.

But when fears and worries start dominating your life, you probably want to take action. The first step in doing so involves figuring out exactly what makes you anxious. Go through our 50 Fears Checklist in Worksheet 9-1 and check off each item that causes you significant concern.

Worksheet 9-1	50 Fears Checklist

❑ 1. Germs

❑ 2. Crowds

❑ 3. Airplanes

❑ 4. Snakes

❑ 5. Feeling panicky or out of control

❑ 6. Leaving the house

❑ 7. Heights

❑ 8. Giving a speech

❑ 9. Rodents

❑ 10. Being trapped in a small place

❑ 11. Bugs

❑ 12. Leaving appliances turned on

❑ 13. Leaving doors unlocked

❑ 14. Getting a disease

❑ 15. Being alone

❑ 16. Thunderstorms

❑ 17. Drowning

❑ 18. Being buried alive

❑ 19. Dogs

❑ 20. Getting contaminated by chemicals, radiation, and so on

❑ 21. Getting sick in public

❑ 22. Driving on the highway or busy roads

❑ 23. Sexual performance

❑ 24. Meeting new people

❑ 25. Talking on the telephone

❑ 26. Rejection

❑ 27. Running out of money

❑ 28. Blurting out something inappropriate

❑ 29. Making mistakes

❑ 30. Needles and injections

❑ 31. Having blood pressure taken

❑ 32. Going to the doctor

❑ 33. Going to the dentist

❑ 34. Going shopping

❑ 35. Traveling

❑ 36. Trains

❑ 37. Job interviews

❑ 38. Taking medication

❑ 39. Surgery

❑ 40. Elevators

❑ 41. Open spaces

❑ 42. Getting criticized

❑ 43. Using a public restroom

❑ 44. Racing heartbeat

❑ 45. Eating in public

❑ 46. Doing something foolish

❑ 47. Darkness

❑ 48. The sight of blood

❑ 49. Open spaces

❑ 50. Ice cream (okay, not a very common fear!)

If you didn't recognize any fears in the list above, you may be able to just skip this chapter and move on. However, it's possible that you have a few fears we didn't think of. If that's the case, write down your fears in Worksheet 9-2 and keep reading.

List your top five fears in Worksheet 9-2.

Worksheet 9-2	**My Top Five Fears**
1.	
2.	
3.	
4.	
5.	

If a few of your top fears don't seriously interfere with your life, you may decide simply to live with them — and that's okay! For example, Laura (co-author of this book) has no intention of doing anything about her silly fear of bugs. It doesn't prevent her from enjoying the outdoors or life in general, and she always has Charles (the other co-author) around to get rid of them if they appear. If all else fails, 15 tissues provide enough of a barrier between her and any bugs as to enable her to muster the courage to eliminate them.

Building a Staircase of Fear

Pick a fear, any fear. Well, maybe not *any* fear — it should be one that bothers you and that you'd like to do something about (it's probably from your Top Five Fears list; see Worksheet 9-2). The best way to overcome fear is to face it dead-on. Not all at once, mind you, but in steps.

The exposure technique for facing and overcoming fear involves breaking your fear into manageable steps and gradually confronting each one. You don't proceed to the next step until you've conquered the one you started with. You'll know you've mastered a given step when you can repeat the step without getting overly anxious.

Exposure can be carried out both in real life and in your imagination. Some fearful events aren't easy to arrange, such as fear of being laughed at or humiliated, but they're easily imagined. Typically, imagining such events doesn't involve quite as much anxiety as actually experiencing them; however, most people can reduce their anxiety by repeatedly imagining fearful events.

Identifying your fears

The first stage of the exposure technique involves zeroing in on your fear and where it comes from. You construct a staircase that takes you from fear and anxiety to a better place. Your staircase consists of all the situations and activities that evoke your fear. Tackling your fear involves climbing this staircase, starting with the easiest steps and progressively getting a little more difficult. When constructing your staircase, it's important not to make your steps too far apart or you may end up scaring yourself.

You get a pretty nice view from the top, but don't be surprised if the climb challenges you. Just take your time, and use the following example as a guide.

Jason is painfully shy, especially when it comes to women and dating. He has a number of good male friends but trembles at the thought of asking someone out. He tries online match-making and finds that engaging in conversations via e-mail is pretty easy. But he stops short of setting up a face-to-face meeting for fear of rejection. Jason vows to overcome this fear on his 30th birthday. His first step is to work through the Gathering Materials for the Staircase of Fear (see Worksheet 9-3).

Worksheet 9-3   Gathering Materials for Jason's Staircase of Fear

---

1. **How does your anxiety or fear begin?**

   The mere image of picking up the phone to ask someone out scares me to death. Even when I'm conversing with women, my anxiety can get triggered. Gosh, I get nervous when I talk to a good-looking clerk at the grocery store.

2. **What activities do you avoid?**

   Obviously, I haven't had a date in a long time. I avoid going to parties. I avoid talking to available women. I avoid calling them on the phone. I even avoid the staff lunchroom with the excuse that I have too much work to do. My shyness seems to be getting worse, and lately I'm avoiding meeting and talking with new people, even guys.

3. **What other situations or activities could your fear conceivably involve?**

The whole relationship thing worries me. If I did get a date, I wouldn't know what to do or what to say. And I wouldn't know when to make an advance — that's really scary. The one brief relationship I had in college really hurt me, so I worry that if I were to find someone, she'd just reject me, too. Heck, I can hardly even ask for directions from a woman.

4. **Do you use any "crutches" or aids to get through what makes you anxious, such as drugs or alcohol? Do you lean on other people to do what's too hard for you to do? Do you try to distract yourself with songs, rituals, or chants?**

I have a prescription for a tranquilizer. I take one of those sometimes before I have to talk with a woman. At work I avoid committees and meetings and let my co-workers cover for me.

5. **What bad outcomes do you envision occuring if you were to face your fear? In other words, what are the worst imaginable scenarios?**

If I try to ask someone out, I imagine my voice shaking and not being able to speak. I would look like a fool. My stomach would churn, and I'd sweat like a pig. And if I did go out on a date, she'd probably laugh in my face or walk away before the evening was over. If someone was dumb enough to go out with me more than once, she'd no doubt break my heart.

After Jason completes the questions for Gathering Materials for the Staircase of Fear, he moves on to the next step, which helps him arrange his materials according to how much fear they cause (see Worksheet 9-4). He reviews what he wrote in Worksheet 9-3 and uses that information to identify specific activities that he fears carrying out. He rates each activity on a scale of 0 (no fear) to 100 (worst imaginable fear). Jason takes care to come up with items that cover the full range of fear, from little fear to overwhelming fear and everything in between.

Worksheet 9-4 Arranging Materials for Jason's Staircase of Fear

Fearful Activity	Fear Rating (0–100)
Asking someone out on a date in person.	85 (terrifying)
Calling someone on the phone for a date.	75 (pretty darn scary)
Having a conversation with a woman I don't know.	65 (tough, but manageable)
Eating lunch in the staff lunchroom and talking with the people there.	35 (I can handle this)
Picking up someone I've asked out on a date.	90 (Almost unimaginable!)
Asking for help from a female sales clerk.	25 (piece of cake, but there's some tension)

(continued)

Worksheet 9-4 *(continued)*

Fearful Activity	Fear Rating (0–100)
Going to a party.	70 (very tough)
Imagining asking someone for a date and being turned down rudely.	45 (If it really happened, it would be harder than imagining it. But even imagining this scares me.)
Going to the singles' hiking club.	75 (I get nervous thinking about it.)
Volunteering at the food bank and talking with female volunteers there.	60 (not easy)
Taking a public speaking class at the Adult Continuing Education Center and talking with as many of the students as I can.	80 (I hate talking in front of others, but it's part of my problem, I think.)
Volunteering to be on the social committee at work and going to the meetings.	55 (not my idea of fun, but I can do it)

Jason next arranges the items with those that arouse the least anxiety at the bottom and those that cause the most fear at the top, thus creating a staircase for climbing out of his fear (see Worksheet 9-5).

Worksheet 9-5   **Jason's Staircase of Fear**

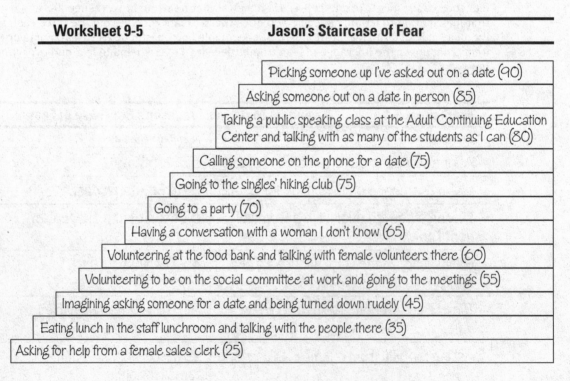

Picking someone up I've asked out on a date (90)

Asking someone out on a date in person (85)

Taking a public speaking class at the Adult Continuing Education Center and talking with as many of the students as I can (80)

Calling someone on the phone for a date (75)

Going to the singles' hiking club (75)

Going to a party (70)

Having a conversation with a woman I don't know (65)

Volunteering at the food bank and talking with female volunteers there (60)

Volunteering to be on the social committee at work and going to the meetings (55)

Imagining asking someone for a date and being turned down rudely (45)

Eating lunch in the staff lunchroom and talking with the people there (35)

Asking for help from a female sales clerk (25)

In Worksheet 9-6, think about the fear you identified at the beginning of this section and answer the following questions. They'll enable you to construct a Staircase of Fear.

Worksheet 9-6	**Gathering Materials for My Staircase of Fear**

1. How does your anxiety or fear begin?

_____

_____

_____

_____

2. What activities do you avoid?

_____

_____

_____

_____

3. What other situations or activities could your fear conceivably involve?

_____

_____

_____

_____

4. Do you use any "crutches" or aids to get through what makes you anxious, such as drugs or alcohol? Do you lean on other people to do what's too hard for you to do? Do you try to distract yourself with songs, rituals, or chants?

_____

_____

_____

_____

5. What bad outcomes do you envision occurring if you were to face your fear? In other words, what are the worst imaginable scenarios?

_____

_____

_____

_____

After you examine your fear, you can move on to breaking it down and rating the fear associated with each activity.

1. Review your answers in Worksheet 9-6.

2. In Worksheet 9-7, list six to twenty items or activities that you fear carrying out or even imagining.

3. Rank each item on a scale of 0 (no fear) to 100 (worst imaginable fear).

4. If you find that your items have large gaps in difficulty (such as no items ranked between 25 and 55), try to think of some more items to fill in the gaps — you don't want to make too large of a step all at once.

Worksheet 9-7	Arranging Materials for My Staircase of Fear
Fearful Activity	*Fear Rating (0–100)*

You can obtain extra copies of these forms at www.dummies.com/go/adwbfd.

Surveying sample staircases of fear

Everyone's fears and worries are a little different, but they frequently have much in common as well. Therefore, it may help you to see a variety of staircases that are typical of many of the clients we've seen. These samples cover many of the major types of anxiety. They can help you get started, but remember that your own staircase is unique to you.

Lydia worries all the time. She frets about her family, friends, finances, and even her figure. She particularly worries about traveling and having enough money saved. So when she has a trip planned, she packs weeks in advance and repeatedly calls for reservation reconfirmation. She also balks at making reasonable purchases that are well within her means. Furthermore, she worries about her husband's love. Thus, anxiety drains enjoyment from Lydia's life. Worksheet 9-8 shows her Staircase of Fear.

Worksheet 9-8	Lydia's Staircase of Fear

Planning a trip to Europe for the family (90)

Allowing my son to take the trip with his senior class (85)

Making myself go buy new bedroom furniture (80)

Going for a day without asking my husband if he loves me (70)

Going for a day without asking my husband if I look okay (60)

Putting off packing for a trip until the day before (50)

Going two days without calling my mother to check on her (45)

Reconfirming my travel plans once instead of my usual ten times (40)

Stopping asking my son about his homework every day (30)

Inviting my friend Rebecca to lunch (20)

Imagining having a check bounce (15)

Leaving the dishes in the sink overnight (10)

Larry is scared to death of flying. Forced to fly for business, he's so anxious that he has three drinks at the airport bar before he boards. After he's on the plane, he has three more drinks and can barely walk off the plane when it lands. Watching the bags go around and around on the baggage claim belt makes him nauseous.

The next morning, Larry suffers through a board meeting with his head pounding and his stomach churning. A fistful of aspirin and frequent trips to the bathroom convince him that he has a problem. He vows to find a better way to deal with his flying phobia. Worksheet 9-9 shows his Staircase of Fear.

Christopher suffers from panic attacks and a fear of crowds. His panic attacks consist of sweating, rapid heartbeat, and a horrible tightness in his chest. When an attack occurs, Christopher feels like he may be dying. Christopher stays away from crowded places. He shops for groceries late at night when few people are around, and he makes all other purchases on the Internet so that he can avoid shopping malls. He feels worst in places in which he thinks he may have trouble escaping, such as crowded movie theaters. Worksheet 9-10 shows Christopher's Staircase of Fear.

If your anxiety includes significant physical symptoms such as difficulty breathing and changes in heart rate, you should consult with your medical doctor prior to treating the anxiety on your own or even with a counselor or therapist.

Worksheet 9-9	Larry's Staircase of Fear

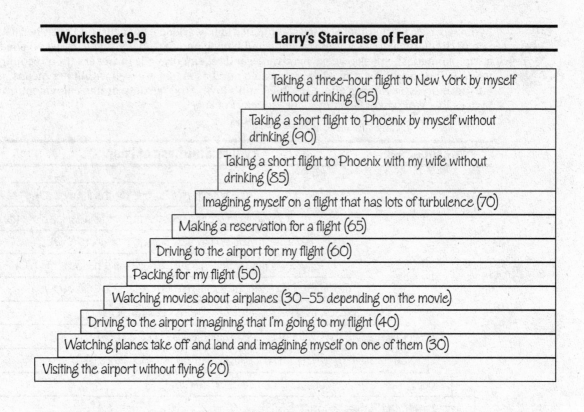

Taking a three-hour flight to New York by myself without drinking (95)

Taking a short flight to Phoenix by myself without drinking (90)

Taking a short flight to Phoenix with my wife without drinking (85)

Imagining myself on a flight that has lots of turbulence (70)

Making a reservation for a flight (65)

Driving to the airport for my flight (60)

Packing for my flight (50)

Watching movies about airplanes (30–55 depending on the movie)

Driving to the airport imagining that I'm going to my flight (40)

Watching planes take off and land and imagining myself on one of them (30)

Visiting the airport without flying (20)

Worksheet 9-10	Christopher's Staircase of Fear

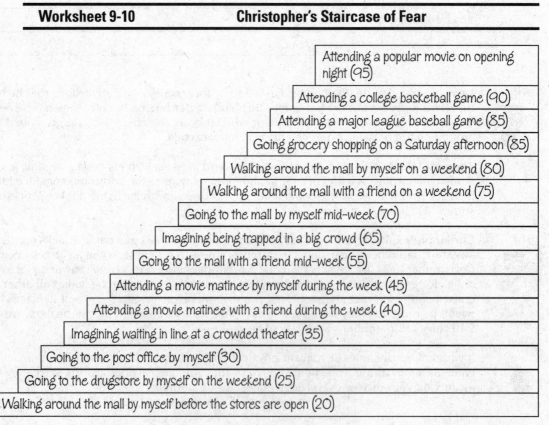

Attending a popular movie on opening night (95)

Attending a college basketball game (90)

Attending a major league baseball game (85)

Going grocery shopping on a Saturday afternoon (85)

Walking around the mall by myself on a weekend (80)

Walking around the mall with a friend on a weekend (75)

Going to the mall by myself mid-week (70)

Imagining being trapped in a big crowd (65)

Going to the mall with a friend mid-week (55)

Attending a movie matinee by myself during the week (45)

Attending a movie matinee with a friend during the week (40)

Imagining waiting in line at a crowded theater (35)

Going to the post office by myself (30)

Going to the drugstore by myself on the weekend (25)

Walking around the mall by myself before the stores are open (20)

Creating your own Staircase of Fear

Now comes the fun part . . . well, maybe not fun, but eye-opening for sure. Using the information you've recorded and the samples in the previous section as a guide, you can build your Staircase of Fear.

1. **Review the fearful activities you listed in Worksheet 9-7.**

2. **Pick the least feared item and write it in the bottom step of Worksheet 9-11.**

3. **Continue filling in Worksheet 9-11, writing activities in the order of the degree of fear they carry.**

Try to make your steps reasonably evenly spaced in terms of the amount of fear involved. Thus, if you rate one step a 25, your next step ideally should have a ranking of 30 to 35. If you don't have such a step, try to think of one.

Some of your steps may involve using your imagination. For example, if your fear involves getting ill, we don't particularly advise you expose yourself to deadly viruses. But you certainly can conjure up an image of getting ill in your mind.

Worksheet 9-11	**My Staircase of Fear**

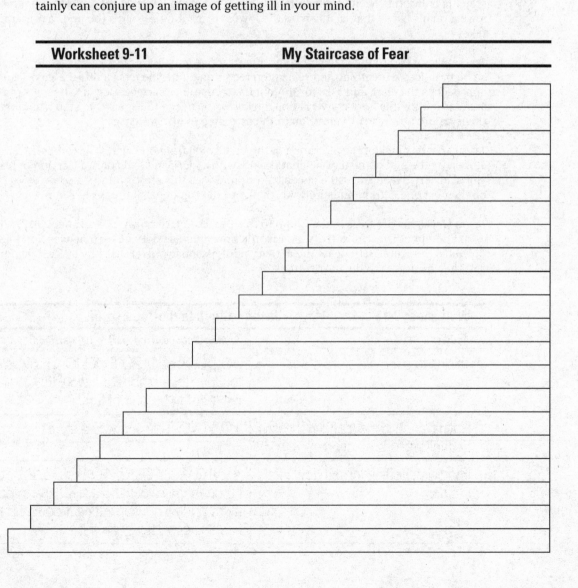

If you find that developing or climbing a Staircase of Fear is so difficult that you just can't make progress on your own, consult a mental health professional.

For extra copies of this form, visit www.dummies.com/go/adwbfd.

Climbing Your Staircase

After you develop your first Staircase of Fear (see the previous section), it's time to face your fear directly. Oh my gosh! This could be kind of hard, huh? It *will* be hard, but if you take care to focus on each step as it comes and climb slowly, you're likely to succeed.

Take the steps as slowly as you need to. Remember, if you find the process too difficult, consult a mental health professional. You don't have to go this alone.

Jump back up to the section "Identifying your fears" and review **Jason**'s story. He's afraid to talk to or date women. After constructing his Staircase of Fear, Jason's ready for the first step in confronting his fear, which requires him to talk to a female sales clerk. (That task is lowest on his list — that is, it carries the lowest fear rating — so it's the first task Jason takes on.)

Jason takes a trip to the mall and spots an attractive female sales clerk. His anxiety rockets, so he practices a breathing and relaxation technique. After he feels a little calmer, Jason approaches the clerk and asks for directions to customer service. Because he feels pretty anxious during this brief conversation, he knows he needs to repeat this step a number of times before he's ready to move on to the next step in his staircase.

Jason spends much of the afternoon in the mall going from one clerk to another in various stores. By the end of the day, he chats easily with a clerk and feels only a fraction of his previous anxiety. Jason knows he needs to continue with this step, but he's also ready to take on the next one. Slowly but surely, he climbs to the top of his Staircase of Fear.

Jason tracks his progress in the Climb to the Top Exercise shown in Worksheet 9-12. After each attempt at a fearful activity, he records how much anxiety he experiences and jots down his thoughts. He repeats the activity until his anxiety decreases by at least 50 percent, and then he moves to the next step.

Worksheet 9-12	Jason's Climb to the Top Exercise
Activity	*Anxiety Ratings: 0 (no fear) to 100 (terrified)*
Talking to a female store clerk	30, 30, 25, 20, 20, 15, 10, 10: This was tougher than I thought it would be at first, but it got to be kind of fun.
Eating lunch in the staff lunchroom and talking to co-workers	20, 20, 15: This one was a snap.
Imagining getting turned down for a date	45, 40, 40, 40, 35, 40, 30, 35, 25, 20: I thought this would be a silly thing to do. I didn't realize how upsetting it could be to imagine something like this.

Activity	Anxiety Ratings: 0 (no fear) to 100 (terrified)
Volunteering to be on the social committee at work and going to the meetings	65, 70, 70, 60, 30, 30: This started out a lot harder than I thought it would be, but it didn't take too long to come down.
Having a conversation with a woman I don't know	70, 70, 65, 65, 55, 70, 55, 40, 65, 35, 35: This is still pretty hard for me. I know I need to keep on practicing, but I think I can handle the next step in the meantime.

As you can see, the first time Jason carried out an activity, his anxiety wasn't always at the level he had expected on his Staircase of Fear (see Worksheet 9-5). As he repeated the activities, his anxiety went up and down but generally tended downward.

Before you begin exposure, or what we call *climbing the staircase,* it's a good idea to start out in a reasonably relaxed state. To help you achieve this state, here's a brief breathing exercise. Practicing this breathing technique gives you a quick way of managing anxiety if it crops up and climbs excessively. (If you want more instructions on learning to relax, see Chapter 13.)

1. **Take a slow, deep breath in through your nose.**

2. **Hold your breath for a few seconds.**

3. **Breathe out very slowly through your mouth.**

4. **As you breathe out, make a slight hissing sound.**

5. **Repeat ten times.**

Now, the hard part — climbing your Staircase of Fear.

1. **In the left-hand column of Worksheet 9-13, write down the activities from your Staircase of Fear (see Worksheet 9-11) in order of difficulty, with the easiest, least fearful items listed first.**

2. **Do the first activity listed, and carefully observe how you feel.** If the item involves an imaginary scene, find a comfortable place to sit and relax. Lie back, close your eyes, and picture the feared item as though it were occurring. Stay with the image as long as it takes for your fear to diminish at least 50 percent.

3. **In the right-hand column of Worksheet 9-13, rate how anxious the activity or imagery makes you feel on a scale of 0 (no anxiety) to 100 (terrifying). Include any interesting reactions or observations.**

4. **Repeat each activity and rate each repetition until your anxiety has dropped by around 50 percent.** If your anxiety remains high, try the breathing technique for a minute or two. If the breathing technique doesn't calm you down, consider backing away from the activity and try to break it down into more manageable steps.

5. **Move on to the next, more difficult activity when your anxiety has dropped and you feel you have mastered the preceding item.**

6. **When you complete the climb of your Staircase of Fear, take a few moments to reflect on the experience and what it's meant to you in Worksheet 9-14.**

Worksheet 9-13	My Climb to the Top Exercise
Activity	*Anxiety Ratings: 0 (no fear) to 100 (terrified)*

You can download as many copies of this form as you want at www.dummies.com/go/adwbfd.

If you find the task of climbing your staircase daunting, turn to the following helpful suggestions for making your climb successful.

- ✔ Consider asking a trusted friend or family member to accompany you on your first attempt at difficult activities. Just be sure to carry out the task by yourself later.

- ✔ Don't give in to mind chatter such as, "I can't do this," "This is stupid," "I'll look like a fool," or "This exercise won't help!" Thoughts like these are merely thoughts, nothing more. Notice how interesting this mind chatter is, but don't be seduced into believing it. (See Chapter 8 for more about dealing with mind chatter.)

- ✔ Consider rewarding yourself for the successful completion of any difficult steps. Treat yourself to something special — you deserve it!

- ✔ Allow yourself to feel some discomfort. After all, this work is difficult. It's okay to feel anxious at times — that shows you're making progress. Just don't forget, "no pain, no gain."

✔ Tell yourself that you can overcome your fears. Be positive. Beating your fears may take some time, but you can do it.

✔ Don't use crutches such as alcohol or excessive medication to get through steps. Crutches diminish the effectiveness of exposure. Try not to distract yourself with chants, songs, or other rituals, either.

✔ Climb those stairs slowly. Exposure takes time, and this isn't a race!

Worksheet 9-14	**My Reflections**

If you find yourself avoiding this exposure part of the program, we suggest you flip back to Chapter 3, which discusses ways of identifying and overcoming roadblocks to change.

Exposing Obsessive-Compulsive Disorder

Obsessive-compulsive disorder (OCD) poses a somewhat greater challenge than the anxieties we discuss earlier in this chapter. OCD frustrates and challenges those afflicted as well as their loved ones. Not only does OCD cause considerable emotional discomfort, it also consumes a considerable amount of time.

Essentially, *obsessions* are unwanted images, impulses, or thoughts that flood the mind. These thoughts may take the form of excessive worry about contamination by germs, chemicals, radiation, and so on. Other obsessions include concerns about whether doors were left unlocked or appliances were turned off. Additional obsessions common to OCD include impulses to hurt someone you love, engage in shameful sexual behaviors, violate your personal religious beliefs, or act in socially unacceptable or highly strange ways.

Compulsions are undesired actions that people find themselves doing over and over in order to temporarily reduce anxiety. Common compulsions include excessive hand washing, over-cleaning, hoarding objects, arranging objects in a particularly rigid manner, checking and rechecking things (such as locks), and creating strict rituals such as counting stairs or putting on clothing in the exact same order every day.

Lots of people experience a few minor obsessions or compulsions, and that's no problem. You don't have a problem with OCD unless your repetitive thoughts and actions begin to seriously infringe on your relationships, your work, or your sense of freedom. You can find considerably more information about this particular problem in *Overcoming Anxiety For Dummies* (Wiley).

Obsessive-compulsive disorder can be a serious, debilitating problem, and most people who suffer from OCD require professional help. You should only attempt the strategies that follow if your problems are fairly mild; consider using this book in collaboration with your therapist or counselor.

The approach for treating OCD is quite similar to the treatments for anxiety and fear reviewed earlier in this chapter. However, as you can see in the following sections, there are a few minor differences.

Beating obsessions

Because obsessions consist of thoughts or mental images, exposure for obsessions typically takes place in the imagination. Also, imagination is the best approach because many obsessions really couldn't or shouldn't be acted out. For example, if your obsession involves strange sexual perversions, we don't recommend that you "expose" yourself to them!

In fact, if you have obsessions that involve unacceptable sexual activities or physically hurting yourself or others, you should consult a mental health professional rather than attempt imaginal or real exposure techniques.

Most obsessions are focused on a single idea, so you may not have a Staircase of Fear to climb. However, you can still utilize exposure to help you deal with many different obsessions. Proceed by answering the questions posed in Worksheet 9-15.

Worksheet 9-15   **Obsessional Exposure**

---

1. **Write down your distressing, obsessional thought or image.**

   _____

   _____

   _____

2. **Rank how upsetting the thought or image is to you on a scale of 0 (no upset) to 100.**

   _____

3. **Find a comfortable, private place to sit and work through this procedure.**

4. **Repeat the thought or image over and over and over and over and over and over and over and over and over and over and over (oops, we're getting a tad compulsive here aren't we?).**

5. **Continue repeating the thought or image for 20 to 30 minutes or as long as it takes to reduce your level of upset (in Step 2) by at least 10 to 20 points.**

6. **Re-rate your thought or image on the same scale (0 [no upset] to 100 [totally disturbing]).** _____

The act of exposing oneself to obsessional thoughts and images is quite the opposite of what people with OCD usually try to do. They often try to immediately expunge obsessive thoughts and images from their minds when they occur. The problem with that approach is that attempting to suppress thoughts only makes them surface more frequently.

For example, try not thinking about purple elephants. Don't even begin to let an image of a purple elephant come into your mind! We may even pay you $1 million if you can keep even a momentary image of a PURPLE ELEPHANT from coming into your mind. See, it's not so easy, is it?

Treating compulsions

Treating compulsions, like the treatment of other anxieties and fears, involves exposure as the first step. You gather materials for a Staircase of Fear, arrange your materials into an actual staircase, and start your climb. The only difference in the treatment of compulsions is that you have to do one extra thing: Not only do you expose yourself to the problematic activities or items, but you also must stop yourself from engaging in the compulsive behavior. The technical name for this procedure is *exposure and response prevention*. The following example shows you how this treatment procedure works for a particular compulsion.

Gina has a common compulsion — washing her hands . . . a lot. In fact, altogether, she spends about three hours a day washing her hands. She does this because she fears coming in contact with germs and becoming ill. However, the compulsion is ruining her life by unnecessarily taking up huge amounts of time. Not to mention that her hands are raw and oozing.

Gina gathers and arranges materials as well as constructs her Staircase of Fear. In Worksheet 9-16, you see the partial results of her Climb to the Top Exercise, her repeated exposures to problematic events and activities *while not washing her hands*. In fact, Gina makes a concerted effort not to wash for at least an hour after the exposure.

Worksheet 9-16	**Gina's Climb to the Top Exercise**
Activity (Exposure without the compulsion)	*Anxiety Ratings: 0 (no fear) to 100 (terrified)*
Handling garments at a clothing store	30, 20, 15, 10: This was sort of gross at first because I kept thinking about all the other people who touched them before me. But it got to be pretty easy.
Handling money with my bare hands	35, 30, 40, 25, 25, 30, 20, 15: This was tough because I usually wear gloves to handle money. It's so disgusting to think about how many hands have been on that money.
Touching doorknobs with my bare hands	55, 55, 60, 60, 50, 40, 30, 30, 35, 25, 25: I hated doing this. I hope I don't get sick from all those germs. I know I have to keep practicing this one, but I'm ready for the next step, I think. . . .
Touching the handrails on the escalator and keeping them there all the way up or down	75, 75, 80, 60, 60, 55, 55, 45, 35, 35, 35: Whew, that was hard! Yuck. But I'm ready to keep climbing. I know I can do this.
Gardening without gloves	80, 80, 75, 70, 60, 55, 45, 55, 45, 35, 35, 35: Wow, it wasn't easy to not wash those disgusting hands. But my hand washing overall is down to almost "normal." I'm getting somewhere, and my garden looks great.

In addition to climbing your Staircase of Fear while preventing the compulsive behavior, consider

✔ Delaying your urges by 30 minutes each time you have them. Later, you can delay for 45 minutes.

✔ Changing your compulsion in various ways. You may use different soap, arrange things a little differently, or make a slight change in your routine.

Now, take a few minutes to ponder what progress you have made after dealing with your OCD problems. In Worksheet 9-17, record your thoughts and insights.

Worksheet 9-17	My Reflections

Chapter 10

Lifting Mood Through Exercise

. . . .

In This Chapter

▶ Figuring out how much physical activity you need

▶ Giving yourself reasons to exercise

▶ Coming up with an exercise strategy

▶ Finding motivation to stick with the program

. . . .

Why devote a whole chapter to exercise in a book that deals with anxiety and depression? Well, because getting up and moving increases the naturally occurring feel-good *endorphins* in the human body. When endorphins, substances occurring naturally in the brain that are chemically similar to morphine, spread through your brain, you get a sense of well-being and pleasure. And it's hard to be depressed or anxious when you feel good inside.

In this chapter, we tell you how much exercise you need to get those endorphins going, and we tell you about all the known benefits of exercise. You pick your top ten reasons for beginning or sticking with an exercise program and then figure out an exercise plan that fits your lifestyle. We also offer some tips for finding the motivation to keep exercise going in your life.

How Much Is Enough?

The best time to get into an exercise habit is when you're young because exercise helps to keep you healthy throughout your life. However, it's *never* too late to start — even 90-year-olds benefit from regular exercise!

If you're in good health, it's okay to start an exercise program on your own. However, for men over 40, women over 50, and anyone with a chronic disease or other health concerns, it's best to check with a physician before beginning a vigorous exercise regimen.

Every five years, the United States government updates its guidelines for nutrition and exercise. The 2005 recommendations significantly increased the recommended amount of time for healthy people to engage in vigorous physical activity. So what do the current guidelines recommend? Take a deep breath and relax. Here they are:

✔ Children should be physically active about an hour a day on most days. Activities can include vigorous play, dance, or organized sports.

✔ Adolescents should engage in at least 60 minutes of exercise every day, most days of the week.

✔ Healthy adults should be physically active for at least 30 minutes per day.

✔ If you're trying to prevent the gradual weight gain associated with normal aging, exercise should be increased to an hour of vigorous activity per day most days of the week.

✔ If you want to lose weight, you should exercise between 60 and 90 minutes on most days.

✔ Most pregnant women should be exercising 30 minutes per day. (Check with your doctor to make sure this recommendation's right for you.)

Write down here how many minutes a day you should be exercising: _____

The point of exercise is to improve physical fitness. Fitness consists of the following:

✔ **Cardiorespiratory endurance:** Your body's ability to pump blood and circulate oxygen, which is improved by elevating your heart rate safely for increasing periods of time.

✔ **Body composition:** Your body's ratio of fat and lean mass, which is improved by all types of exercise.

✔ **Flexibility:** Your body's ability to move fluidly and with good range, which is improved by stretching or activities such as swimming.

✔ **Muscular strength:** Your body's ability to lift and push, which is improved largely through weight training.

✔ **Muscular endurance:** Your body's ability to sustain effort without getting tired, which is also improved by all kinds of exercise.

The Case for Health Improvement

Hold on. The U.S. government gives you guidelines about what you should do exercise-wise, but what's with all the shoulds? In Chapter 5, we told you to stop "shoulding" on yourself. Now, we're telling you that you should exercise. Are we just trying to make you feel guilty? No, not really. In fact, we'd be defeating our own purpose if you started feeling guilty!

However, we believe that exercise has so many benefits that everyone physically capable of moving around would feel better if they just did it. So this section covers the many good things that can happen — as well as the bad things that can be prevented — when you exercise. You may find a few of these items surprising, but they're all 100 percent true and well documented.

You didn't think you'd get away with just reading a list of reasons for exercise, did you? Follow the instructions here in order to identify the ten reasons you should be exercising.

1. **Read through the items in Worksheet 10-1. If the item is something that you're concerned about, check it off.** Some items may be relevant to just about everyone; others may be particularly important to you. For example, if you have a family history of diabetes or colon cancer, those items may be especially important and make it on your top ten list.

2. **When you finish checking off the items that pertain to you, spend a few moments deciding which ones are the most important and relevant to you.**

3. **Pick your top ten reasons for exercising, and record them in Worksheet 10-2.**

Worksheet 10-1	Reasons for Exercising

❑ For fun

❑ Improves energy

❑ Decreases risk of heart disease

❑ Relieves stress

❑ Improves immune system

❑ Decreases depression

❑ Decreases blood pressure

❑ Boosts self-confidence

❑ Decreases risk of diabetes

❑ Decreases risk of breast cancer

❑ Improves lung capacity

❑ Reduces triglycerides

❑ Aids weight loss

❑ Decreases risk of colon cancer

❑ Improves appearance

❑ Decreases risk of falls in the elderly

❑ Improves flexibility

❑ Improves strength

❑ Decreases risk of osteoporosis

❑ Improves sleep

❑ Improves ratio of bad to good cholesterol

❑ Increases mental sharpness

❑ Decreases risk of gallstones in women

❑ Decreases risk of enlarged prostate in men

❑ Improves balance

❑ Improves quality of life

❑ Relieves symptoms of PMS

❑ Reduces breast cancer risk

❑ Improves complexion

❑ Reduces medical and healthcare expenses

❑ Reduces varicose veins

❑ Allows you to eat more without gaining weight

❑ Reduces addictive cravings

❑ Reduces tension and anxiety

❑ Aids digestion

❑ Decreases back pain

❑ Makes you taller and more intelligent — okay, maybe not!

Worksheet 10-2	My Top Ten Reasons for Exercising
1.	
2.	
3.	
4.	
5.	
6.	
7.	
8.	
9.	
10.	

Fitting Exercise into Your Life

You may have some pretty good reasons for exercising now, but wow, 30 to 90 minutes — where will you find the time? You're probably way too busy as it is. We know, we know — we can almost hear those thoughts running through your head.

First of all, you don't have to find one big window of time for exercise. The government guidelines state that it's just as useful to do your exercise in 10- or 15-minute segments. What matters is the total accumulation per day. And it may help you to know that exercise consists of just about any type of activity that occurs at a *moderate level of intensity.* Moderate intensity means that you're increasing your breathing and heart rate, which you can do by mowing the lawn, dancing, swimming, bike riding, jogging, or even walking at a rapid pace.

Thus, if your job is physically demanding, you may already be getting sufficient exercise every day. On the other hand, if you religiously take your dogs on a leisurely walk every morning for 45 minutes, that probably won't do the trick — you need to pick up your pace because anything done leisurely just doesn't cut it.

Everyone is different. People have different schedules, habits, preferences, and lifestyles. Therefore, an exercise program that works for one person may not work for another. The following instructions and checklist in Worksheet 10-3 are designed to help you choose exercise that will work into your life.

1. **Read through Worksheet 10-3, checking off all the exercise ideas that could conceivably become part of your routine.**

2. **Add a few possibilities of your own at the bottom of the list.**

3. **Try each and every activity you select at least a couple of times.**

4. **Jot down your feelings and reactions under My Reflections (see Worksheet 10-4). Include comments on how you think you can work these activities into your daily life.**

Worksheet 10-3   **Exercise Checklist**

❏ Get up 15 minutes early each day and take a brisk walk — take the dogs if you have any!

❏ Leave a little early for work and park your car a good 15 or 20 minutes away from your workplace. Walk quickly.

❏ Take the stairs rather than the elevator.

❏ Take a walk at lunchtime.

❏ Exercise during work breaks.

❏ Join a gym and go three or four times per week.

❏ Find an active sport you like, such as tennis, racquetball, basketball, rollerblading, swimming, and so on.

❏ Jog when you get home from work.

❏ Walk around the mall four or five times per week.

❏ Walk briskly when talking on your cell phone.

❏ Get a personal trainer.

❏ Take dance lessons.

❏ Ride the bike that's been gathering cobwebs in your garage.

❏ Buy an exercise video and work out at home regularly.

❏ Go to a yoga class.

❏ Take other classes such as spinning, kickboxing, or step aerobics.

❏ Buy a treadmill, stationary bike, or elliptical trainer. (Try them out at a gym first to make sure you want to make the investment.)

❏ Exercise while watching television.

❏

❏

❏

❏

❏ Watch sports on TV. Nope! Sorry, that one doesn't count!

Worksheet 10-4   **My Reflections**

_____

_____

_____

_____

_____

What to Do When Willpower Wilts

Working through the preceding section gives you some pretty good reasons for exercising (ten, in fact!). And hopefully you've found a few types of exercise that just may fit into your life and have tried them out. Your intentions may be good, but what happens when your initial enthusiasm and commitment to do something positive for yourself fade? Or, how do you get started if you haven't found that initial enthusiasm?

Fighting de-motivating thoughts

The problem with finding and maintaining motivation to exercise lies in distorted, de-motivating thinking (see Chapters 5, 6, and 7 for more on distorted thinking). De-motivating thinking keeps you from taking action and puts you in a defeatist frame of mind, where you're doomed to fail. When your thinking is distorted, your mind is full of reasons you can't exercise. It's hard to get moving when demotivating thoughts take control. But we have a strategy for defeating defeatism. The following example gives you an idea of how you can give de-motivating thoughts the one-two punch.

Janine, a busy mother of two, works as a bank teller. She rushes off every morning to drop her kids at day care and tries to fit in her errands during a 45-minute lunch break. By dinnertime, she's usually exhausted. It's no wonder Janine suffers from mild depression. When her doctor suggests she begin exercising to improve her mood and health, Janine laughs and says, "You've got to be kidding; I don't have an extra second in my day."

But fortunately for Janine, she has a copy of the *Anxiety & Depression Workbook For Dummies* and completes the Defeating De-Motivating Thoughts exercise. Worksheet 10-5 shows what she comes up with, and Worksheet 10-6 has her reflections on the exercise.

Worksheet 10-5	Janine's Defeating De-Motivating Thoughts Exercise
De-Motivating Thoughts	*Motivating Thoughts*
I don't have time to exercise.	I could cut 30 minutes off my television watching each evening. And it wouldn't be that hard to get up 15 or 20 minutes earlier either. It's a matter of prioritizing what's important, I guess.
I don't have the money to get a baby sitter so I could exercise.	I could get a videotape from the library or take the kids for a walk. They'd love it if I went bike riding with them more often.
I'm too tired all the time to exercise.	Yeah, well as I think about it, exercise usually helps overcome fatigue.
I'm too depressed to exercise.	From what I've read, exercise actually helps defeat depression. Just because I don't feel like exercising doesn't mean I can't do it.

Worksheet 10-6   **Janine's Reflections**

I guess I can see how my thinking is bogging me down on this exercise thing. Part of the reason I feel so down is because I haven't been able to lose the weight from my last baby. What I need to do is stop listening to all these thoughts and just do it. I think I'll ride my bike with the kids down to the library tonight and check out an exercise tape.

Most folks who struggle to work exercise into their lives have thoughts like Janine's. Just because you think something, though, doesn't mean it's true. Therefore, paying attention to the dialogue about exercise that runs through your head is important because you can argue with these thoughts and in turn increase your willingness and motivation to exercise.

To complete your own Defeating De-Motivating Thoughts Exercise,

1. **Read the de-motivating thoughts in the left-hand column of Worksheet 10-7, and circle those that are relevant to you.** These are the most common thoughts people have that get in the way of exercise.

   If you have thoughts that aren't on the list, feel free to add them in the extra spaces provided.

2. **For each thought that you circle or that you add, develop a *motivating thought* that refutes and debunks the de-motivating one.** Consider the following points in developing motivating thoughts:

   • Is the de-motivating thought exaggerated or illogical in any way?

   • Is the thought just an excuse not to exercise?

   • Is there a better way to think about this de-motivating thought?

   • If a friend of mine told me the thought, would I think it was completely legitimate, or would it sound like an excuse?

   • Is the thought helping me?

   • What would happen if I simply tried acting as though the thought weren't true?

   If you struggle to come up with motivating thoughts, flip back to Chapters 5, 6, and 7 for a myriad of ways to defeat such thinking.

3. **Jot down your reactions to this exercise under My Reflections (see Worksheet 10-8).**

Worksheet 10-7   **My Defeating De-Motivating Thoughts Exercise**

De-Motivating Thoughts	*Motivating Thoughts*
I don't feel like exercising. I'll start doing it when it feels right.	
I'm not someone who exercises; it's just not who I am.	
It's not worth the trouble to exercise.	

(continued)

Worksheet 10-7 *(continued)*

De-Motivating Thoughts	Motivating Thoughts
Exercise is a frivolous pursuit.	
I don't have the time to exercise.	
I'm too tired to exercise.	
I'm too old to exercise.	
I hate exercise.	
I'm too depressed or anxious to exercise; I'll do it when I feel better.	
I'm too out of shape to exercise.	
I have too much pain to exercise.	
Gyms and equipment cost too much; I just don't have enough money to exercise.	
Exercise just isn't worth the effort.	

Worksheet 10-8   My Reflections

Keeping track of your progress

An effective way to boost motivation is to keep an exercise calendar. On this calendar, track the physical activity you do everyday, and write down your reactions to the activity. When you commit yourself to writing something down, you tend to pay more attention to what you do. That's just part of human nature. The following is a brief example of an exercise calendar; read it through before starting your own.

Randy is a unit secretary at a busy hospital. He feels like his life is out of control: He can't save enough money to go to school, his social life seems flat, and his mood is gloomy. On top of that, he notices his belly is beginning to stick out for the first time. His pants are too tight, and he feels hopeless. Randy talks to a friend who urges him to join a gym to get active again. Randy's therapist agrees with the recommendation, so Randy joins a gym and begins tracking his daily physical activity (see Worksheet 10-9).

Worksheet 10-9	Calendar of Physical Activities	
Day	*What I Did*	*How I Felt*
Monday	I walked up and down the stairs at work instead of taking the elevator as usual.	I was surprisingly out of breath, but it felt like a step in the right direction.
Tuesday	I made it to a kickboxing class.	I stayed in the back and felt sort of foolish. But afterward, I was in a pretty good mood.
Wednesday	Nothing at all. I was a total couch potato.	Guilty, guilty, guilty.
Thursday	I went for a long walk with the dogs.	I felt really relaxed afterward. And it did my heart good to see how happy the dogs were.
Friday	Made it to the gym again.	I'm hopeful I can make this a habit. I feel good. Besides, there are some gorgeous women at this gym!
Saturday	I went hiking with some friends.	That felt great. It was good to be outside, and I enjoyed the company a lot.
Sunday	Nothing. Total couch potato.	Hey, it's okay to take a break here and there. Beating myself up won't help.

Use Worksheet 10-10 to track your exercise progress. You'll be surprised at how the act of writing everything down keeps you focused on the goal.

Worksheet 10-10		My Calendar of Physical Activities
Day	**What I Did**	**How I Felt**
Monday		
Tuesday		
Wednesday		
Thursday		
Friday		
Saturday		
Sunday		

You can obtain copies of this form at www.dummies.com/go/adwbfd. Download as many as you need for your own use.

REMEMBER

Beating yourself up when you don't succeed at the task won't help you stay on track. Just acknowledge that you didn't do what you wanted to and re-commit yourself to get moving.

Chapter 11

Entertaining Enjoyment

*I*t's hard to be anxious or depressed when you're having fun. Laughter, enjoyment, and pleasure interfere with feelings of sadness or worry, and pleasure actually causes your body to release *endorphins,* brain chemicals that increase a sense of well-being. Unfortunately, when you suffer from anxiety or depression, you tend to withdraw from pleasurable activities. Thus, we recommend that you bring pleasure back into your life as part of your healing process.

In this chapter, we help you choose from a variety of healthy pleasures — activities, people, and events that are good for you and help combat anxiety and depression.

What's Your Pleasure?

Emotional distress interferes with thinking. If you're sad or worried, you may have difficulty coming up with ideas about what sounds pleasurable. Not to worry. That's why we created The Nifty 50 Checklist of Pleasurable Activities (see Worksheet 11-1). As you can see, this list doesn't consist of spectacular, intense pleasures. Rather, it contains a wide range of simple pleasures — and research has found that simple pleasures actually provide more enjoyment than occasional, spectacular pleasures anyway.

1. **Review the list of pleasurable activities in Worksheet 11-1.**

2. **Check off any items that sound appealing to you now or have been pleasurable to you in the past.**

3. **In Worksheet 11-2, record the items that you believe you can bring into your life.**

Worksheet 11-1	The Nifty 50 Checklist of Pleasurable Activities

- ❏ 1. Eating chocolate
- ❏ 2. Acting in community theater
- ❏ 3. Creating art
- ❏ 4. Traveling
- ❏ 5. Shopping
- ❏ 6. Listening to music
- ❏ 7. Drinking tea
- ❏ 8. Playing a sport
- ❏ 9. Camping
- ❏ 10. Eating spicy foods
- ❏ 11. Taking a hot bath
- ❏ 12. Gardening
- ❏ 13. Exercising
- ❏ 14. Going to the beach (assuming you don't live in New Mexico like us)
- ❏ 15. Reading a good novel
- ❏ 16. Finishing a small task
- ❏ 17. Going to a live sporting event
- ❏ 18. Dancing
- ❏ 19. Going out for a meal
- ❏ 20. Getting a massage
- ❏ 21. Visiting a friend
- ❏ 22. Drinking a glass of wine
- ❏ 23. Having sex
- ❏ 24. Going to a book store
- ❏ 25. Sewing
- ❏ 26. Spending time with family
- ❏ 27. Sitting in the sunshine
- ❏ 28. Cooking something special
- ❏ 29. Hiking
- ❏ 30. Playing with your pets
- ❏ 31. Taking a walk with or without your pets
- ❏ 32. Playing cards or games
- ❏ 33. Smelling fresh flowers
- ❏ 34. Surfing the Internet
- ❏ 35. Taking up a hobby
- ❏ 36. Going to a museum
- ❏ 37. Taking a nap

❑ 38. Putting on your sweats after a tough day

❑ 39. Going to a movie

❑ 40. Going to a concert or play

❑ 41. Going to a comedy club

❑ 42. Taking a yoga class

❑ 43. Flying a kite

❑ 44. Meditating

❑ 45. Taking pictures

❑ 46. Sleeping in

❑ 47. People watching

❑ 48. Taking a scenic drive

❑ 49. Going to a coffee shop and having a cappuccino

❑ 50. Learning how to spell cappuccino!

Worksheet 11-2	**Top Ten Pleasures That Work for Me**
1.	
2.	
3.	
4.	
5.	
6.	
7.	
8.	
9.	
10.	

If this list doesn't provide you with a wide range of intriguing possibilities, you're having trouble accepting pleasure into your life. We help you deal with that issue in the section "Pleasure Busters" later in this chapter.

Assuming you've managed to create your own list of pleasurable activities, it's time to schedule them into your life. Use the following instructions to complete this part of the pleasure process.

1. **In Worksheet 11-3, for each day of the week, write down one or more pleasurable activities that you plan to engage in.** Try to pick different activities across the week. Ideally, choose some that you haven't done in a while.

2. **After you complete the pleasurable activity, circle it in the chart as a marker of your accomplishment.**

3. **Notice how you feel at the end of a week in which you've increased your simple pleasures.**

4. **Jot down your observations under My Reflections in Worksheet 11-4.**

Worksheet 11-3	Simple Pleasures
Day	*Pleasurable Activities*
Monday	
Tuesday	
Wednesday	
Thursday	
Friday	
Saturday	
Sunday	

Getting through depression and anxiety involves more than inserting pleasure into your life, as important as that is. See Chapter 12 for information about increasing your participation in other sorts of important activities that can give you a sense of mastery or accomplishment.

Worksheet 11-4	My Reflections

Poisonous Pleasures

We don't want you taking this pleasure idea too far. Pleasure's great, of course, but some pleasures can get you into instant trouble, and other pleasures, when taken to extremes, can be dangerous or unhealthy. Thus, we'd be remiss if we didn't make note of the dangers some pleasures hold. Watch out for

- Drug abuse
- Prostitution
- Alcohol to excess
- Hanging out with bad company
- Sleeping to excess
- Watching television endlessly
- Overeating
- Sexual promiscuity
- Excessive caffeine consumption
- Compulsive exercise
- Shopping beyond your budget
- Reckless driving
- Gambling
- Thrill-seeking through risky behaviors
- Shoplifting
- Gobbling two gallons of cookie dough ice cream (our personal favorite!)

If you engage in one or more of these poisonous pleasures, please consider seeking professional help. Even healthy activities like exercising or dieting, when taken to the extreme or overdone, can become a problem. Furthermore, these behaviors can greatly complicate the task of overcoming anxiety and depression.

Pleasure Busters

Ideally, you found a nice list of pleasurable activities from our Nifty 50 Checklist (see Worksheet 11-1) and were able to insert them into your regular life without too much trouble. However, we know that many people don't find this task so easy to do.

Emotional distress and especially depression cause distorted thinking (see Chapters 5, 6, and 7 for the lowdown on distorted thinking). In this section, we zero in on the thoughts that are most likely to interfere with your efforts to increase pleasure in your life. Three types of distortions typically get in the way: thoughts of undeservingness and unworthiness, thoughts that pleasure is a frivolous waste of time, and thoughts that deny the effectiveness of pleasurable activities.

Deciding to deserve fun

Depression and anxiety affect your self-esteem — and not for the better. When you're sad or anxious, you probably don't think too highly of yourself. And along with low self-esteem come thoughts such as

- I don't deserve happiness or pleasure.
- I'm not good enough.

    ✔ I'm not getting enough done as it is, so I certainly don't have time for pleasure.

    ✔ I deserve punishment, not pleasure.

    ✔ I've let everyone down. How can I justify having fun?

As you may imagine, these types of thoughts don't exactly result in a strong desire to seek pleasure and fun. They also increase emotional distress in general. Clearly, it's best to rethink those thoughts. The following example illustrates how pleasure-busting thoughts can be turned into pleasure-boosting thoughts.

Theresa suffers from depression. Her therapist suggests that she increase the pleasurable activities in her life. Theresa finds herself resisting the idea, so she and her therapist explore the reasons behind her reluctance. They discover two pleasure-busting thoughts standing in the way: "I don't deserve pleasure," and "I'm not getting enough done in my life as it is."

Theresa and her therapist work together to rethink her pleasure-busting thoughts. Worksheet 11-5 shows what they come up with.

Worksheet 11-5	Rethinking Pleasure Busters
Pleasure-Busting Thought	*Pleasure-Boosting Thought*
I don't deserve pleasure.	No one has to earn pleasure. Reintroducing pleasure into my life is partly how I can get over my depression.
I'm not getting enough done in my life as it is.	Part of the reason I'm not getting enough done is because I'm so depressed. If I get less depressed, I'll be more productive.

If you find that you're resisting increasing pleasure in your life, it's likely you have one or more pleasure-busting thoughts. The following exercise helps you identify the pleasure-busting thoughts you may have and develop more adaptive, pleasure-boosting thoughts.

1. **Read the pleasure-busting thoughts in the left-hand column of Worksheet 11-6. These are the most common thoughts people have that get in the way of increasing pleasure. Circle those relevant to you.**

2. **Add any thoughts that aren't on our list in the extra spaces provided.**

3. **For each thought that you've circled or added, develop a pleasure-boosting thought that refutes the pleasure-busting thought.** Consider the following points in developing motivating thoughts:

    • Is this pleasure-busting thought actually exaggerated or illogical in some way?

    • Is there a better way to think about this pleasure-busting thought?

    • If a friend of mine told me that thought, would I think it was completely legitimate or would it sound merely self-defeating?

    • Is this thought helping me?

If you struggle to come up with pleasure-boosting thoughts, turn to Chapter 3 for ways to defeat the distorted thinking that's standing in your way.

Worksheet 11-6	Rethinking Pleasure Busters
Pleasure-Busting Thought	*Pleasure-Boosting Thought*
I don't deserve happiness or pleasure.	
I'm not getting enough done as it is, so I certainly don't have time for pleasure.	
I'm not good enough.	
I deserve punishment, not pleasure.	
I've let everyone down. How can I justify having fun?	

Finding fun frivolous?

Common thoughts among the pleasure-challenged folks of the world are, "Having a good time is a waste of time," and "Fun is frivolous." These people usually think that work and accomplishments are acceptable activities, but fun, entertainment, or even relaxation are definitely unacceptable. Their leisure activities are typically ones that expand their knowledge or increase their skills.

We're not saying that expanding your horizons is a bad thing, but trashy novels, silly movies, a walk in the park, some time at a comedy club, dancing, or a little karaoke (mind you, you'll never, ever see *us* doing this one!) have many benefits.

Benefits, you ask? Absolutely. Research shows that pleasure forms the backbone of a healthy life. For starters, pleasure decreases anxiety and depression because it releases endorphins that make you feel grrrreat. But it also has other important physical and emotional benefits such as

✔ Improved immune function

✔ Decreased feelings of chronic pain

✔ Decreased risk of heart attack

✔ Decreased stress

✔ Prolonged life expectancy

- ✔ Enhanced sense of well-being
- ✔ Improved overall health
- ✔ Increased productivity

Did you notice that last item, "Increased productivity"? Many people think that non-work related activities are frivolous. Truth is, putting pleasure into your life actually makes you more productive when you're working. You have more enthusiasm for your work and more energy. In other words, you're very likely to get more done if you just take a break every once in a while!

If you've fallen into the "fun is frivolous" mind trap, we'd like you to *seriously* consider the benefits of pleasure. Think about what pleasure and its benefits can mean to you and your life. Jot down your conclusions under My Reflections in Worksheet 11-7.

Worksheet 11-7	My Reflections

Pleasure-pooping predictions

Minds riddled with depression and anxiety do a curious thing: They make predictions about how much you're likely to enjoy various activities. And with amazing consistency, these predictions, such as the following, are negative:

- ✔ I'm not going to enjoy myself at all.
- ✔ That sounds so boring.
- ✔ I'll just look stupid.
- ✔ I'm too down to like anything like that.
- ✔ I'm too anxious to enjoy myself at that party.

Recognize any of these thoughts? Research has demonstrated rather conclusively that, especially when you're depressed or anxious, such predictions are worse than unreliable — they're actually *reliably* wrong! In other words, when you push yourself to engage in a potentially pleasurable activity, you're highly likely to discover that you enjoy it more than you think you will.

But if you believe what your mind tells you and take its negative predictions as the gospel truth, you'll follow the wrong road again and again — you'll avoid pursuing pleasure. Listening to your mind is a little like listening to the radio for the daily traffic report. Each and every day the reporter tells you to avoid taking I-40 because of construction delays. So you choose the surface roads and spend an extra 20 minutes getting to work. The only problem is that the reporter is lying to you, and you'd be much better off not listening to his advice. Think of this conniving reporter as your mind, predicting that activities can't possibly cause you pleasure, and fire the reporter in your mind.

To help you overcome your mind's negative predictions, try our Pessimistic Pleasure-Busting Exercise.

1. **From Worksheet 11-1, choose five potentially pleasurable activities that you'd be willing to try.**

2. **List those activities in the left-hand column of Worksheet 11-8.**

3. **Predict the amount of enjoyment or pleasure each activity may give you on a scale of 0 (no fun at all) to 10 (maximal pleasure). Write that number in the middle column.**

4. **Do the pleasurable activity.**

5. **Rate how much enjoyment you actually felt from each activity on the same scale of 0 (no fun at all) to 10 (maximal pleasure).**

6. **Write about your observations and conclusions under My Reflections in Worksheet 11-9.**

Worksheet 11-8	**Pessimistic Pleasure-Busting Exercise**	
Activity	*Predicted Fun (0–10)*	*Experienced Fun (0–10)*

Can you see a trend in Worksheet 11-8 — that you experienced more pleasure than you expected for most of your activities? If you don't see it, keep trying.

The pleasure you feel will likely increase slowly over time. And it's okay to come back to this exercise again later after you've worked on your depression and anxiety in other ways.

Worksheet 11-9	**My Reflections**

Chapter 12

Getting Moving and Tackling Life's Problems

Depression and anxiety steal energy, hope, and motivation. When negative emotions cloud your mind, it's hard to get moving. Everyday tasks seem overwhelming, simple problems appear complex, and molehills become mountains as a vicious cycle begins. In the end, not getting things done and not solving problems only make you more depressed and anxious.

In this chapter, you discover how to get going again. We warn you about the trap of waiting for motivation, and you get action plans for, well, umm . . . action. We also provide a comprehensive, step-by-step game plan for untangling your problems and coping with your solutions.

The Motivation Myth

Especially if you're depressed, you may find yourself spending a lot of time spinning your wheels. In other words, you're not accomplishing what you want to do, and you aren't even able to take the first step toward reversing your inactivity. You're likely to tell yourself, "I'll do these things when I feel motivated." Ahh, but that thought buys into a common myth that if you wait for motivation to arrive on your doorstep, you'll feel like taking action when it finally comes along. In actuality, action creates motivation — the more you do, the more you want to do. It doesn't work as reliably the other way around. The following example highlights the relationship between action and motivation.

It's Saturday morning and we need to get six pages of writing done today in order to stay on schedule. We're in sunny New Mexico, and — big surprise — we don't feel like writing. In fact, we really don't want to write today. The sky is so blue, the temperature outside is perfect, and the winds are calm. So the thought of writing is more and more dreadful by the minute. Ugh. We're getting kind of depressed ourselves. How about we just put this task off until we're more motivated?

There's two little problems with that plan: Not only will we fall behind, but also we're not entirely sure that the motivation will come along. Ever. If we wait for motivation that never comes, we'll never finish the book, you'll never read it, and our publisher will be really, really unhappy with us. The momentary relief from not writing on this beautiful Saturday morning leads to a whole lot of misery. Not a pretty picture.

What's our alternative? To sit down and write, of course! When we do, something miraculous happens: We actually start to feel like doing it. In fact, we have fun with it by writing about this example of action creating motivation rather than the other way around.

One way to jump-start action is through the creation of an *activity log* (see the following example). An activity log is an action plan that plots out at least one small activity to accomplish each day and includes space to record how the task went and how it felt to complete it. Keeping track of the activities and small tasks you accomplish can give you incentive to keep going. Motivation will slowly but surely rise, and you'll do even more than you expected.

Carmen looks around her house and feels self-loathing and disgust. She sees dishes piled everywhere, magazines tossed haphazardly, and unopened letters — mostly bills — strewn across her kitchen countertop. She hasn't cleaned the house in over a month, and the job of straightening up is totally overwhelming to her.

Carmen manages to drag herself to her women's support group that meets Wednesday evenings. She relates her difficulty in tackling basic, daily chores. One member suggests that Carmen fill out an activity log. Worksheet 12-1 shows Carmen's result.

Worksheet 12-1		Carmen's Activity Log
Day	*Activity*	*Outcome*
Monday	Wash just the few dishes lying in the sink and leave the rest.	Once I got started, I ended up doing them all. That felt great!
Tuesday	Pay a couple of bills.	It took me all day to get around to it, but I did it. It didn't make me feel much better though — probably because I waited so long.
Wednesday	Balance the checkbook.	I just couldn't do it; I got too discouraged.
Thursday	Stop by the grocery store on my way home from work.	I've been eating way too much cold cereal for dinner, so this helped.
Friday	Vacuum the house.	Not my favorite thing to do, but it felt like I did something useful.
Saturday	Clean the kitchen.	I really went to town on this one. I'm starting to feel just a little better.
Sunday	Get my car washed.	This really perked me up. It had not been washed in five months!

Carmen notices that after she gets started doing an activity, she usually feels better. She realizes that procrastinating on paying her bills and balancing her checkbook are problem areas for her. She decides to ask her cousin, a bookkeeper, to come in and help her get started on straightening out her finances. Overall, the activity log helps Carmen get going again.

If you've been feeling stuck lately and overwhelmed by all that you need to do, we recommend you create your own activity log to get back on track.

1. **Think about the various tasks and chores you've been putting off.**

2. **In the middle column of Worksheet 12-2, jot down one task or chore for each day of the week.**

   Start with small tasks, and break big tasks into smaller parts. For example, don't take on cleaning out the entire garage on a single day; instead, tackle one messy shelf at a time. Make tasks doable!

3. **On each day, complete the corresponding task and, in the right-hand column, write down how it went and how it made you feel to do it.** If you don't complete a given task, don't beat yourself up; just move onto the next one.

4. **After you finish a week's worth of tasks, jot down your observations of what you've learned under My Reflections (see Worksheet 12-3).**

If you find this exercise useful, continue it for several weeks. Once you start feeling motivation returning, you probably won't need it. But feel free to take it out whenever motivation starts slipping away from you again.

Worksheet 12-2		My Activity Log
Day	*Activity*	*Outcome*
Monday		
Tuesday		
Wednesday		
Thursday		
Friday		
Saturday		
Sunday		

You can download more copies of this form at www.dummies.com/go/adwbfd.

Worksheet 12-3	My Reflections

Scoring Goals with S.O.C.C.E.R.

When people are emotionally distressed, many situations seem overwhelmingly difficult. Anxiety and depression make even small problems appear insurmountable because emotional pain interferes with clear thinking.

When feeling overwhelmed, most folks avoid the problem at hand as long as they can. This avoidance is unfortunate because problems usually grow rather than fade away. Because avoidance is not the answer, we have a way for breaking problems down and figuring out what to do with them. We call the plan *S.O.C.C.E.R.* so that it's easy to remember. Here's what S.O.C.C.E.R. stands for:

- ✔ **S:** *Situation,* meaning the nature and causes of the problem as well as your beliefs and feelings about the issue.

- ✔ **O:** All possible *options* for addressing the problem.

- ✔ **C:** The *consequences* or results most likely to occur with each option.

- ✔ **C:** *Choosing* which option to go with.

- ✔ **E:** The *emotional plan* for dealing with distress associated with the solution you choose.

- ✔ **R:** *Running* and *reviewing* your plan. Afterward, sit back and evaluate how well it worked; you may be pleased with the outcome, or you may want to revise your plan.

In the following sections, we review each of the S.O.C.C.E.R. steps in detail. To give you a complete picture of how this process works, you follow one example subject, Derrick, who solves a problem about his work. You see how he completes each component of the S.O.C.C.E.R. problem-solving process, and then we tell you how to do the same for yourself.

The S.O.C.C.E.R. system is useful regardless of whether you're feeling emotional distress. Even if you feel great, you can employ this plan for tackling some of life's most vexing issues.

Sizing things up (S)

Rather than bury your head in the sand, take a good, hard look at your problem. Gather information about it, and think about the causes and the relative importance of the problem to your life. Believe it or not, you're not the first person to experience your problem. You can obtain information by talking to others, through books and articles, or by searching the Internet. Finally, reflect on what feelings this problem stirs up in you.

Derrick feels frustrated at work as a mechanical engineer. He hasn't been given the level of responsibilities he feels capable of taking on, and he hasn't received the bonuses or recognition he's expected. His frustration grows as he ruminates about his dilemma in the early morning hours. He realizes that the situation is contributing to his mounting depression. Derrick goes online and researches comparable jobs; he also reads some books about career advancement. Derrick decides the first step in tackling his problem is describing it (see Worksheet 12-4).

Worksheet 12-4   **Derrick's Problematic Situation: S.**

I'm not happy with my job. I want more responsibility and the pay and recognition that go along with it. I've been here for six years, and I'm still doing the same things I was when I got here. I don't think the problem is a lack of skills; I'm pretty confident about my talent. One of the books I've read suggests that maybe I haven't been assertive enough and made myself known around here. This issue keeps me up at night, so it's quite important.

After describing his problem in great detail, Derrick is ready to go on to the next step, figuring out his options.

Using Derrick's description as a guide, take the time to describe your problematic situation.

1. **In Worksheet 12-5, describe your problematic situation.**

2. **Consider reading books and articles or searching the Internet for helpful insights, and record any relevant information you find.**

3. **Include information about possible causes of your problem.**

4. **Include your emotional responses to the problem — does it make you feel depressed, frustrated, anxious, or something else?**

5. **Indicate how important the problem is to you.**

Worksheet 12-5   **My Problematic Situation: S.**

_____

_____

_____

_____

_____

_____

Collecting options (O)

After you lay out your problem, it's time to let the creative juices flow. This step asks you to brainstorm any and all possible ways of tackling your problem. Be sure to list all the ideas you have, even if they sound silly. Put your internal critique on hold and let loose.

If you're stumped for solution ideas, consider reading books — your local librarian will have ideas. And ask trusted people who have gone through similar problems.

Derrick learns more about the job market and continues to read about career advancement in his field. He talks with friends and co-workers in order to brainstorm his options. After a lot of research and thought, he lists his ideas (see Worksheet 12-6).

Worksheet 12-6	Derrick's Situation and Options: S.O.

Situation: I'm not happy with my job. I want more responsibility and the pay and recognition that go along with it. I've been here for six years, and I'm still doing the same things I was when I got here. I don't think the problem is a lack of skills; I'm pretty confident about my talent. One of the books I've read suggests that maybe I haven't been assertive enough and made myself known around here. This issue keeps me up at night, so it's quite important.

Options

I can look for another job.

I can work on my assertiveness skills — maybe take a Dale Carnegie class and go to Toastmasters.

I can ask for a meeting with my supervisor and discuss my concerns.

I can do nothing about work and try to find pleasure in outside pursuits.

I could go into business for myself.

I could tell the boss off.

I could get even more education and training in order to impress the higher-ups.

I could network and politic at work more than I do. I could start by attending all those stupid company picnics and parties.

Derrick feels he's covered all bases with his possible options. He's now ready for the next step in the S.O.C.C.E.R. problem-solving process, recognizing consequences.

Complete your own options step by following these instructions:

1. **In Worksheet 12-7, write down the situation you describe in Worksheet 12-5.**

2. **Gather data from books, the Internet, friends — basically anywhere.**

3. **Develop a list of options for dealing with your problem and write them down in the space provided.** Don't forget — one option is to not solve the problem and deal with the status quo.

Don't censor your ideas; put down anything that's even in the ballpark of helping your situation.

Worksheet 12-7	My Situation and Options: S.O.

Situation:

_____

_____

_____

_____

Options

_____

_____

_____

_____

_____

_____

_____

_____

_____

Considering consequences (C)

After you list all the possible options for solving your problem, you need to contemplate the most likely outcomes for each of those options. We're not asking you to be a fortuneteller. Obviously you can't "know" how your solutions will turn out, but you can make a reasonably good guess. So take your best shot at evaluating what you think is most likely to happen. Worksheet 12-8 shows what Derrick comes up with.

Worksheet 12-8   Derrick's Situation, Options, and Consequences: S.O.C.

Situation: I'm not happy with my job. I want more responsibility and the pay and recognition that go along with it. I've been here for six years, and I'm still doing the same things I was when I got here. I don't think the problem is a lack of skills; I'm pretty confident about my talent. One of the books I've read suggests that maybe I haven't been assertive enough and made myself known around here. This issue keeps me up at night, so it's quite important.

Options	Likely Consequences
I can look for another job.	I could, but the economy sucks, and this is actually a good company. I would lose my seniority here, and I'm not sure I'd find something a lot better.
I can work on my assertiveness skills — maybe take a Dale Carnegie class and go to Toastmasters.	It took me a while to realize this, but learning assertiveness and speaking skills may help a lot. The people who've done well here are a lot more sociable than I am.
I can ask for a meeting with my supervisor and discuss my concerns.	I've done a little of this, and it got me nowhere. Maybe after I learn to be more effective it will work better.
I can do nothing about work and try to find pleasure in outside pursuits.	I spend more time at work than anywhere else, and that's how I like it. I need to solve the work problem first.
I could go into business for myself.	Someday this would be nice, but right now, I'd run a high risk of going bankrupt without better financing.
I could tell the boss off.	Sounds very, very tempting, but this could easily get me fired. Not a smart idea.
I could get even more education and training in order to impress the higher-ups.	I already have a master's degree. I haven't seen evidence of more education getting people that far here.
I could network and politic at work more than I do. I could start by attending all those stupid company picnics and parties.	This fits in with my other idea about assertiveness. I think it actually has a pretty darn good chance of working. I won't particularly like doing it, and I'll feel uncomfortable, but it's likely to pay off.

Fill out your own situation, options, and consequences form.

1. **Write down your problematic situation in Worksheet 12-9.** (This time, feel free to abbreviate your situation — you're probably pretty familiar with it by now.)

2. **Briefly list your options from Worksheet 12-7 in the left-hand column.**

3. **Contemplate what you think are the most likely consequences or outcomes for each option, and write them in the right-hand column.**

Worksheet 12-9   My Situation, Options, and Consequences: S.O.C.

Situation:

Options	*Likely Consequences*

Making a choice (C)

In order to make a choice about how to handle your problem, you need to carefully consider each option and its most likely outcome (see Worksheet 12-9). Reflect on how each option would make you feel — if you were to carry it out. Some options may seem pretty difficult. And some options, you would obviously not select.

When you make your selection, commit to it even it it seems very difficult. You may want to tell others what you plan to do because spreading the word often makes the commitment more firm and makes you think twice before backing out or giving up.

It may not seem so, but deciding to make no choice is really making a choice. Doing nothing has its own set of likely outcomes.

Derrick sizes up his options and their potential consequences and makes the decision to work on his communication, assertiveness, social, and political skills. He decides to sign up for some classes, read books, and start going to company functions.

In order to make your own choices, follow these instructions and use Derrick's example as a guide.

1. **Review your S.O.C. form (see Worksheet 12-9).**

2. **Choose the option or options that really make the most sense to you — the ones most likely to get you what you want.**

3. **Jot down your selection in Worksheet 12-10.**

Worksheet 12-10	My Choice: C.

Working up the courage (E)

Many people make decisions to do something but procrastinate when it comes to carrying out those decisions. Why? Because many actions arouse anxiety, fear, or distress. If your choice of options makes you tremble, consider the following tips:

✔ **Role-play and rehearsal:** Using imagery in your mind, you can rehearse carrying out your solution. Or even better, rehearse it aloud by yourself or with a trusted friend. The more times you repeat your rehearsal, the more you're likely to feel prepared and calm.

✔ **Self-talk:** Think of some positive statements you can repeat to yourself as you carry out your plan. Consider writing them on a card to carry with you as a reminder. Positive statements may include:

- This is the right thing to do.

- I can tolerate the discomfort; it won't last long.

- I worked hard to consider other alternatives; this is the best shot.

- I have the absolute right to carry this out.

✔ **Brief relaxation strategy:** Not only is it quick and simple, but this technique helps calm acute anxiety. (See Chapter 13 for more information and practice with relaxation techniques.)

1. Take a slow, deep breath in through your nose.

2. Hold your breath for a few seconds.

3. Breathe out through your mouth very slowly.

4. As you breathe out, make a slight hissing sound.

5. Repeat ten times.

After you work through these recommendations, write down your personal emotional plan in Worksheet 12-11.

Worksheet 12-11   **My Emotional Plan: E.**

_____

_____

_____

_____

_____

Letting it rip (R)

Running your solution and reviewing its effectiveness are crucial to your success. You've gone through the problem-solving process, and now it's time to turn all that work into action. Decide when would be a good time to execute your plan, and do it! Afterward, evaluate how your plan worked.

Derrick decides to improve his communication and social skills, so he completes the actions he selected earlier in the process. Worksheet 12-12 shows Derrick's reflections on how his solution goes.

Worksheet 12-12   **Derrick's Running and Reviewing: R.**

I think some of these strategies are working for me. Just last week, I was chosen to take the lead on a project. That's a first. And I've noticed that other people are seeking me out for advice more. The talk I gave last week actually went okay; I didn't faint. At this point, I want to improve my presentation skills further by taking a class at the university. This feels like a good start.

As you can see, Derrick's plan works out pretty well. Yours may or may not. If your plan isn't a rousing success, be sure to include in your running and reviewing stage any ideas for either continuing what you're doing or making alterations to your game plan. You can even run through the S.O.C.C.E.R. problem-solving process anew.

Use Worksheet 12-13 to record your reflections on the running and reviewing of your problem solutions.

Worksheet 12-13	My Running and Reviewing: R.

Many people like to lay the S.O.C.C.E.R. problem-solving process all out in a single form, like the one shown in Worksheet 12-14. You can use this type of form after you've already chosen your best option(s).

Worksheet 12-14	My S.O.C.C.E.R. Game Plan
Situation	
Option	
Consequences	
Choice	
Emotional plan	
Run and **R**eview	

Part IV
Phocus on Physical Pheelings

The 5th Wave   By Rich Tennant

"If I'm supposed to be so over the hill, how come it feels like I'm still going up one?"

In this part . . .

Depression and anxiety have an important physical, or biological, component. Emotional problems may be the result of chemical imbalances, illnesses, or chronic stress. And on the flipside, many health problems can be traced to or made worse by emotional factors.

In this part, we instruct you in relaxing your body through breathing, exercise, muscle relaxation, and improved sleep. Then we help you decide whether or not you're a good candidate for medication as part of your treatment. If you do decide to take medication, we give you tips on talking with your prescriber and ways of tracking possible side effects.

Chapter 13

Relaxing the Heart and Soul

You're running late. You dash to the car and drive a little too fast. Your cellphone rings, and you reach for it on the seat next to you. When your eyes return to the road, you see that the car ahead of you has come to a dead stop. You stomp on your brakes and barely avoid an accident — an enormous parking lot looms ahead on the freeway. You feel every muscle in your body tighten up, your heart pounds, and you begin to sweat. Drat! Another rotten start to the day.

Modern life supplies a never-ending string of opportunities for revving up your entire system. Your body prepares you to react to perceived dangers and stressors by orchestrating a complex response:

✔ Your brain sends messages to your nervous system to go into high gear.

✔ Your eyes widen to let in more light.

✔ Your heart beats faster.

✔ Your digestion slows so that energy is available for large muscles, which tighten.

✔ Blood flow increases to the arms and legs so that you can run or fight.

✔ Sweating increases to keep your body cool.

All these responses are pretty handy if you need to physically defend yourself or run away. But typically speaking, most folks don't jump out of their cars to beat up other drivers or abandon their cars and run to work. Well, okay, maybe in L.A. they do.

The costs of chronically revving up your body's fight or flight response include high blood pressure, chronic muscle spasms, tension headaches, suppressed immune system, irritable bowel syndrome, ulcers, and on and on. That's a rather high price for responses you rarely need.

In this chapter, we look at the benefits of relaxation. We give you some quick, effective strategies for teaching your body to chill out, even when you find yourself in stressful situations. Finally, we show you how to enhance the quality of your sleep, which increases your ability to cope with stress.

Relaxation: What's in It for Me?

We know your life is probably hectic and stressed, and time is hard to come by. Learning to relax takes some time, so why in the world would you want to devote precious minutes to the task of relaxation? We can think of a few pretty good reasons:

- ✔ Reduced blood pressure
- ✔ Improved immune response
- ✔ Increased sense of well-being
- ✔ Reduced anger
- ✔ Better sleep
- ✔ Decreased risk of heart disease
- ✔ Decreased risk of chronic diseases
- ✔ Reduced pain
- ✔ Decreased anxiety
- ✔ Improved mood
- ✔ Improved ability to cope
- ✔ Improved productivity

Not a bad deal, is it? Relax for a few minutes of each day, and you'll improve your health and sense of well-being. Not only that, you're likely to make up for the time lost through relaxing by becoming more efficient and productive.

Maybe you're a pretty calm person and don't need to learn to relax. How do you know? Take a few minutes to complete the following exercise which will help you decide whether or not spending a little time learning to relax is a good idea for you.

1. **Think about your days over the last week.**

2. **In Worksheet 13-1, write down all situations and times when you felt truly calm and relaxed.**

3. **Write down all the situations and times you recall feeling tense and stressed.**

4. **Take stock of your life, and reflect on whether you need to do something about your approach to relaxation.**

Worksheet 13-1	**Personal Relaxation Review**

Although rather rare, some people report that relaxation techniques sometimes actually induce a sense of panic and loss of control. If that starts to happen to you, cease practicing the strategies covered in this chapter and consult a mental health professional.

Breathing Tension Away

You may not realize it, but the way you breathe can either increase or decrease your tension. Many people breathe in a manner that's counterproductive in terms of relaxation: They breathe too shallowly, restricting their breathing to the upper chest area, or breathe too fast. Sometimes, people under stress even hold their breath for a while, which further heightens their body's arousal.

Abdominal breathing

You don't get the full benefit from breathing when you breathe into your upper chest. Such shallow breathing fails to fill your lungs properly, and it can lead to stress and hyperventilation. Plus, shallow breathing isn't the body's natural response; watch a baby breathing and you'll see that its tummy rises and falls more than its chest area. Somehow, as people grow older, they forget this inborn style of breathing. Perhaps parents give too many directives to stand up straight and hold that stomach in!

This exercise shows you what it's like to breathe like a baby.

1. **Lie down on your back either on a soft carpet, a mat, or a bed.**
2. **Bend your knees slightly so your back is flat and you feel comfortable.**
3. **Place one hand on your stomach.**
4. **Place one hand on your chest.**
5. **Breathe so that your abdomen rises and falls more than your chest.**
6. **Breathe this way for several minutes.**
7. **Take notice of how you feel, and write your observations in Worksheet 13-2.**

Worksheet 13-2	My Reflections

You can practice abdominal breathing just about anywhere, anytime. For example, take three minutes at work to concentrate on breathing deeply. You don't even have to lie down (if you do, make sure the boss doesn't see you!). Just sit quietly and breathe while making sure to let your stomach rise more than your chest so that you fill up your lungs more fully. And three minutes will refresh you. With practice, abdominal breathing just may become routine for you.

Anti-panic breathing

If you ever experience intense anxiety or panic, your breathing no doubt quickens and becomes more shallow. These changes may increase your heart rate and blood pressure, you may feel dizzy, and your thinking may get confused.

This breathing technique can cut short the effects of panic on your breathing. Practice it now and from time to time when you're not panicked so that you know how to do it when you need to most.

1. **Inhale slowly and deeply through your nose.**

2. **Hold your breath and count to six.**

3. **Slowly breathe out through your mouth while making a very slight hissing noise.**
   This noise helps you slow your breath down. The noise should be subtle because you're the only one who needs to hear it. After all, you don't want people thinking you're nuts!

4. **Repeat this cycle five or ten times, until you feel that you've calmed down a little.**

5. **In Worksheet 13-3, write your observations on how this exercise makes you feel.**

Worksheet 13-3	My Reflections

Gentle breathing

It doesn't get any simpler than this breathing technique, and gentle breathing doesn't take much time either.

1. **Go to a comfortable place and sit down.**

2. **Simply pay attention to your breathing. Be aware of the air as it flows through your nose and into your lungs. Notice how your muscles pull the air gently in and out.**

3. **Allow your breathing to develop a slow, even flow — in and out.**

4. **Imagine bringing a delicate flower with dainty petals up to your nostrils. Soften your breath so that the petals remain still.**

5. **Continue to be aware of the air as it goes through your nose and lungs.**

6. **Note how focusing on your breathing gradually relaxes and calms you.**

7. **Feel how refreshing the air is.**

8. **Continue gentle breathing while focusing on the feel of the passing air.**

9. **In Worksheet 13-4, write your observations on how this exercise makes you feel.**

Consider practicing gentle breathing for five minutes every day for ten days or so. You may discover that you want to continue this or one of the other breathing strategies for the rest of your life. Relaxed breathing is a simple, yet powerful way of teaching your body to relax. Gradually, you'll find yourself able to employ such breathing to reduce stress whenever you encounter it.

Worksheet 13-4	My Reflections

_____

_____

_____

_____

_____

Mellowing Your Muscles

One of the most thoroughly researched methods for teaching your body to relax is called *progressive muscle relaxation.* It sounds scientific and complicated, but you can find easy techniques for muscle relaxation in a variety of books, tapes, CDs, and on the Internet. Flat out: Muscle relaxation works. That's why, in this section, we give you one of our favorite muscle relaxation strategies. In the beginning, this technique will take you about 15 or 20 minutes. As you practice the exercise, you'll be able to accomplish relaxation in a shorter period of time. After a while, some people are able to relax their bodies within just two or three minutes!

To get the most out of this relaxation exercise, find a quiet place where you're unlikely to be disturbed. Turn off phones and pagers. Wear comfortable clothing, take off your shoes, and loosen any tight belts or restrictive clothing.

Feel free to record these instructions on a tape. Following tape-recorded instructions is probably more relaxing than reading and then doing each step. Be sure to speak slowly and calmly.

The following relaxation procedure is excerpted from our book, *Overcoming Anxiety For Dummies* (Wiley). Practice this procedure frequently until you can do it without looking at the instructions. This technique involves systematically tensing various muscle groups and holding that tension for a few moments — perhaps five or ten seconds. Then you release the tension and allow relaxation to take over. The procedure starts with your hands and arms, moves through the neck, back, and face, and progresses down the legs and feet.

1. **Take a deep breath from your abdomen, hold it for a few seconds, and slowly exhale, letting the tension go.**

   Imagine that your whole body is a balloon losing air as you exhale and release tension with the air. Take three more such breaths, and feel your entire body become more limp with each one.

2. **Squeeze your fingers into a fist, and feel the tension. Release your hands and let them go limp, allowing the tension in your hands to flow out.**

3. **Raise your arms until they're almost even with your shoulders, and tighten the muscles. Hold the tension, and then drop your arms as though the string holding them up has been cut.**

   Make sure you tense the muscles on the inside and outside of both the upper and lower arms. If you're not sure you're doing that, use one hand to do a tension check on the opposite arm.

4. **Raise your shoulders up as though you were a turtle trying to get into its shell. Hold the tension, and then let your shoulders drop.**

5. **Pull your shoulders back, bringing your shoulder blades closer together. Hold that tension . . . and let it go.**

6. **Scrunch up your entire face by squeezing your forehead down, bringing your jaws together, tightening your eyes and eyebrows, and contracting your tongue and lips. Feel the tension, and then relax.**

7. **Gently drop your head back, and feel the muscles tighten in the back of your neck. Notice that tension, hold it, let go, and relax.**

8. **Gently move your chin toward your chest. Tighten your neck muscles, and let the tension increase. Maintain the tension, and then relax.**

9. **Tighten the muscles in your stomach and chest. Hold the tension, and then let it go.**

10. **Arch your back (by pressing against a chair or just arching it on your own), hang on to the contraction (but don't push too far), and then relax.**

Be gentle with your lower back, and skip this step entirely if you've ever had trouble with this part of your body.

11. **Contract your buttocks muscles so as to gently lift yourself up in your chair. Hold the tension, and then relax your muscles.**

12. **Squeeze and relax your thigh muscles.**

13. **Contract the muscles in your calves by pulling your toes toward your face. Hold the tension, and then relax your calves.**

If you're prone to muscle cramps, don't overdo this exercise. Only contract your muscles as much as you feel comfortable with.

14. **Gently curl your toes, maintain the tension, and then relax.**

15. **Take time to tour your entire body, noticing if you feel different than when you began.**

If you find any areas of tension, allow the relaxed areas to come in and replace the tense ones. If that doesn't work, repeat the tense-and-relax procedure for the tense area.

16. **Spend a few minutes enjoying the relaxed feelings. Let relaxation spread and penetrate every muscle fiber in your body. You may feel warmth, or you may feel a floating sensation. Perhaps you'll feel a sense of sinking down. When you wish to do so, open your eyes and go on with your day, perhaps feeling like you just returned from a brief vacation.**

Although we recommend you spend 15 or 20 minutes a day on the muscle relaxation procedure at first, you can shorten it considerably. With practice, you'll be able to tense up several muscles groups at once. For example, you may tense hands and arms at the same time. Eventually, you may tense all the muscles in your lower body at once, followed by all the muscles in your upper body. If you carry all your tension in your neck, shoulders, or back, try tensing and relaxing just those muscles. Repeat the tense-and-relax cycle once or twice on especially tight muscles if that helps.

Use Worksheet 13-5 to track your thoughts and observations about using progressive muscle relaxation.

Worksheet 13-5 | **My Reflections**

_____

_____

_____

_____

_____

Getting Your Zzzzzzz's

Depression and anxiety disrupt sleep. Some people have trouble falling asleep, others wake up in the early morning hours and can't get back to sleep, and some people even have both problems. On the other hand, a few people with anxiety or depression sleep too much — way too much — and their sleep isn't refreshing.

If you have trouble sleeping, it probably adds to your emotional distress. And as your emotional distress mounts from lack of sleep, your sleep problems deepen. Talk about a vicious cycle.

Serious, chronic sleep disturbances may be a symptom of a major depressive disorder or an undiagnosed physical problem. You should consult your physician if you have major, unremitting problems with your sleep.

In this section, we help you develop good sleep habits. First, jot down a few notes about your particular sleep habits by answering the questions in Worksheet 13-6.

Worksheet 13-6 | **Seven Sleep Situations**

1. What do you eat or drink in the few hours prior to going to bed?

_____

_____

_____

_____

2. What activities do you engage in during the few hours prior to going to bed?

_____

_____

_____

_____

3. Describe the room you sleep in, including the bed, room temperature, and lighting.

_____

_____

_____

_____

4. About how long does it take you to get to sleep? How many hours of sleep do you get each night on average?

_____

_____

_____

_____

5. How often do you wake up in the middle of the night or too early in the morning? Does it take you long to get back to sleep?

_____

_____

_____

_____

6. Do you worry a lot about not getting enough sleep?

_____

_____

_____

_____

7. Do you have nightmares? What are they like? Are they disturbing to you?

_____

_____

_____

_____

Your answers to these questions should give you a good picture of your sleep patterns. If it doesn't appear that you have a sleep problem, feel free to skip the rest of this chapter! But if you clearly struggle with sleep, read on. The following sections tell you what you should know about each of the seven sleep situations in Worksheet 13-6 and what you can do about each one.

Sleep situation #1: Watching what you eat and drink

You probably know that caffeine is a stimulant and, as such, keeps many people awake. Some folks don't seem to be all that affected by caffeine, but others may lie awake for hours after a single cup of java. Coffee isn't the only culprit though; other sources of caffeine include tea, many soft drinks, chocolate, and some pain relievers. Read the labels of what you're consuming or you may be wide awake all night!

You may think that alcohol is the opposite of caffeine, so it should do the trick and put you right to sleep, right? Well, not exactly. Some people find a glass or two of wine relaxing and a helpful inducement of sleep. However, too much alcohol interferes with restful sleep. For that matter, too much of anything — such as rich foods or an especially late dinner — before bed can mess with your sleep.

When it comes to eating and drinking before bed, if you just have to have something, try an herbal tea without caffeine, such as chamomile or valerian. Or have a small glass of milk or a light snack. And we probably don't have to tell you not to drink gallons of fluids before you go to bed or you'll be up all night for different reasons.

Sleep situation #2: Watching what you do

One key to restful sleep is going to bed somewhat relaxed. Strenuous and aerobic activities tend to stimulate the body, so avoid any such activities for at least an hour before you hit the sack. Also, don't call your mother and have a big argument. While you're at it, don't call your ex-spouse or anyone who's likely to get you worked up.

Instead, develop a regular winding-down routine that you can go through prior to bed. A warm bath (not overly hot, which can be stimulative for some), quiet music, a good book (probably not a horror novel), or a little television can all help you wind down.

Experiment with what you personally can or can't do prior to bed. For some, the horrors on the evening news don't have any stressful effects. Others find a murder mystery quite calming. Still others aren't bothered by aerobic exercise. Go figure.

Sleep situation #3: The sleep setting

The environment you sleep in plays a major part in determining the quality of your sleep. For most people, sleep comes more easily when it's dark. But what if your work shift requires that you sleep in the daytime? Consider getting blackout curtains or wearing a sleep mask because darkness tells your brain it's time to sleep.

How about that mattress you've had for 20 years? Is it comfortable? For some, the floor or couch is good enough. For most of us, however, a really comfortable mattress is worth every dime. You may want to invest in some high quality sheets as well to make your sleep setting even more inviting.

When it comes to your sleep setting, noise matters, too. Find a way to keep your environment relatively silent. If you can't do that, you can mask noises with a sound machine. For example, a dog lives next door to us . . . an annoying dog . . . a really annoying dog. He barks for hours at a time. Our dogs, of course, are perfect and only bark when dangerous people, cats, birds, hot air balloons, and delivery trucks threaten our home. Because of the neighbors' chatty four-legged friend, we leave an overhead fan on and the windows closed at night. Works pretty well.

Finally, temperature matters. For most people, cool is better, and they can always pile on the blankets. Sleep researchers have found that core body temperature tends to decrease during good sleep.

Sleep situation #4: How long is too long?

How long does it take you to get to sleep? If you lie restless in bed for more than 30 minutes or so, we recommend that you get up. What? Get up when you want to sleep? Getting up may sound counterproductive, but it's important for your brain to associate your bed with sleep. So if you lie in bed too long without actually sleeping, your brain will only get more mixed up. Furthermore, when you get up and do something boring such as pay bills, your brain will associate unpleasantness with getting up. Just don't do something stimulating. And if you do pay your bills in the middle of the night, please check your addition in the morning.

How many hours of sleep do you rack up on a typical night? Although people differ in their sleep needs, most folks function pretty well on six to eight hours of sleep a night. The bottom line, however, is that if you feel rested, you're getting enough sleep. If you don't feel rested, you may be getting too much or too little.

If you don't feel rested after six to eight hours of sleep, you may have a serious sleep problem known as *sleep apnea*. Sleep apnea involves a series of episodes in which your breathing stops while you sleep. You awaken momentarily to gasp for air, and then you fall back asleep, only to have your breathing cease yet again. Sleep apnea results in very poor quality sleep and frequently leads to nodding off in the daytime. Snoring can be a sign of sleep apnea, but that's not always the case. If you think you may have sleep apnea, your physician can refer you to a sleep clinic where the condition can be accurately diagnosed.

Sleep situation #5: Waking up too much?

Waking up once on most nights is pretty typical and not a problem to be concerned about. However, waking up frequently or being unable to get back to sleep after waking is a problem. This problem should be checked out with your physician because it may indicate

- Prostate problems (that is, if you're a guy).
- Hormonal problems (typically, if you're female).
- Restless leg syndrome, a condition in which you feel an uncomfortable feeling in your legs or feet and an urge to keep moving them.
- Medication issues.
- A major depressive disorder (for which this workbook can help, but you need a professional's opinion, too).
- Other physical conditions of various sorts.
- Other serious emotional disorders (again, this workbook can help, but you should still seek consultation).

If you've eliminated the possible problems listed above and continue to awaken or be unable to get back to sleep, follow the advice under all six other sleep situations in this chapter. In particular, don't lie awake for more than 30 minutes without going back to sleep — get up and do something and give sleep another shot later.

Even with a good amount of sleep each night, some people feel they don't sleep as many hours as they really do. If you feel rested during the day, you're getting enough sleep. If you don't feel rested, something's amiss.

Sleep situation #6: When worries keep you awake

Sleep is very important, right? It's so important that if you don't get enough, your day will be utterly ruined. If you don't sleep enough, you may make terrible mistakes and even get sick. You MUST get enough sleep!

Well, hold the phone. That kind of thinking will *surely* keep you awake at night and make the next day more miserable to boot. When you find yourself thinking such thoughts, turn to Worksheet 13-7 for some more reasonable ways of looking at your situation:

Worksheet 13-7	Sleep-Sabotaging Thoughts & Sleep-Inducing Thoughts
Sleep-Sabotaging Thoughts	*Sleep-Inducing Thoughts*
If I don't get enough sleep, my day will be utterly ruined.	I've survived hundreds of days after not getting enough sleep. I don't like it, but some of those days were downright okay.
It's horrible when I don't fall asleep right away.	I don't like not sleeping, but it's not the worst thing that's ever happened to me. Maybe I can use my relaxation skills and at least rest a little better. This isn't the end of the world.
It's dangerous not to get enough sleep.	I suppose there's a slight danger in driving too far without enough sleep, but I can monitor my fatigue and pull over if I have to. People don't generally die from insufficient sleep.
I can't stand not sleeping.	I'm just catastrophizing here. I simply don't like not sleeping, and there are many worse things. Worrying about it will only worsen the problem. I just need to accept whatever happens and read Chapter 8 of my *Anxiety & Depression Workbook For Dummies* if I have trouble doing that.

Worries about things other than sleep can also mess with your ability to get a good night's sleep. If you're a worrier in general, we recommend you read and carefully work through the exercises in Chapters 5, 6, and 7.

Sleep situation #7: Dream demons

Do nightmares invade your sleep on a regular basis? Everyone has the occasional nightmare, but if they routinely plague your nights and leave you feeling upset or unable to get
back to sleep, try the strategy in Worksheet 13-8, which was developed by sleep specialists
Drs. Krakow and Neidhardt.

Worksheet 13-8	Nightmare Elimination Exercise

1. Write down your nightmare. Dreams tend to fade quickly from memory, so keep a
   pen and paper ready at your bedside.

   _____

   _____

   _____

   _____

2. Write down your thoughts and feelings about your nightmare.

   _____

   _____

   _____

   _____

3. Rewrite your nightmare with a happier, better outcome.

   _____

   _____

   _____

   _____

4. Rehearse your new dream in your mind several times before you go to bed the next
   night. Record how your night goes.

   _____

   _____

   _____

   _____

Your sleep action plan

Review the seven sleep situations covered earlier in this chapter in relation to your personal sleep problems. Ponder which of our recommendations may enhance your sleep. In Worksheet 13-8, write out a personal sleep plan for how to change your sleep behaviors, and record your observations as you carry out the new plan.

Worksheet 13-8	My Personal Sleep Plan

_____

_____

_____

_____

_____

Chapter 14

Making the Medication Decision

Today, we know more about the brain and its relationship to emotional problems than ever before; we understand that chemical imbalances in the brain accompany both anxiety and depression. Because of this growing knowledge, some television commercials would lead you to believe that making some simple corrections to your brain chemistry with the advertised drug will cure your problem. Voila!

If it were that simple, we'd be first in line to recommend medication for whatever emotions disturb you. And we probably wouldn't be writing this book because there'd be no need for it.

Alas, for the vast majority, medication alone doesn't eliminate emotional distress, and rare is the case when medication's the only strategy that one would want to employ. But medication does have an important role to play, so in this chapter, we help you make a good decision about medications and whether you may want to consider this option. We also prepare you for discussing medications with your doctor. If you and your doctor decide that medication is right for you, we then help you track any side effects so that you can keep your doctor accurately informed about your condition.

Because this is a *workbook* and space is limited, we don't review the myriad of medications available for the treatment of anxiety and depression. If you'd like more information on specific medications, look to *Overcoming Anxiety For Dummies* and *Depression For Dummies* (Wiley). And of course, talk the issue over with your doctor.

Whether or not you take medication to alleviate your emotional distress, is a decision that you will make in collaboration with your healthcare provider. One purpose of this chapter is to make you an informed consumer. Ultimately, your doctor will determine if you have a condition that is treatable with medication. And ultimately, you will have to agree to take the medication or not. The more information you and your doctor have, the better informed your decision will be.

To Take or Not to Take

One question we frequently encounter is, "What works best, medications or therapies?" The answer is both. For depression, research tends to suggest that medication and therapy work just about equally well. But for some types of anxiety cognitive behavior, therapies such as the ones covered in this book may hold a slight edge. Some folks see a somewhat better outcome when they combine medication with therapy.

Studies show that cognitive behavior therapy helps prevent relapse, so it's strongly recommended that you don't rely on medications as your sole approach to treatment. (Much of what you're reading in this workbook is based upon the principles of cognitive behavior therapy.)

How do you make the medication decision? First you need to understand that some situations or experiences support taking medication. Worksheet 14-1 lists the reasons for considering medication. All the items suggest a need for professional evaluation. Check off the situations or items that pertain to you; each additional statement that you select increases the likelihood that medication will be part of your treatment plan.

Worksheet 14-1   **Indications for Medications**

❑   1. I seriously think about or plan to hurt myself or others.

❑   2. I feel out of touch with reality. I hear or see things that aren't there.

❑   3. I have severe mood swings from high to low.

❑   4. I feel totally hopeless that things could ever improve.

❑   5. My thoughts are constantly racing and feel out of control.

❑   6. I've experienced a sudden, severely traumatic event.

❑   7. My emotional distress is causing severe disruptions in my life.

❑   8. I've tried therapy for six months or more and feel no improvement at all.

❑   9. My doctor says that medical conditions are primarily causing my depression.

❑   10. I've been depressed or seriously anxious most of my life.

❑   11. I just can't stand the thought of talking with someone about my problems.

❑   12. I feel totally overwhelmed by my emotional problems.

❑   13. I have a problem with alcohol/drug use in addition to depression or anxiety.

❑   14. I feel highly suspicious or paranoid.

❑   15. Lately, I've made really terrible, outrageous decisions.

Now use Worksheet 14-2 to reflect on the items you've checked off. In the space below, elaborate on the statements that apply to you. Use specifics to describe how these problems appear in your life. Include your thoughts, feelings, and observations.

Worksheet 14-2   **My Summary of Medication Indications**

_____

_____

_____

_____

_____

Every coin has two sides. Worksheet 14-1 reveals the possible reasons for considering medication, but there are also reasons you may not wish to take that route. Consider the following reasons some people decide to opt out of taking medications:

✔ **Side effect concerns:** Different medications have various side effects. We review side effects in detail in the section "Sizing Up Side Effects" later in this chapter, but common ones include dry mouth, gastro-intestinal problems, sexual difficulties, weight gain, and headaches. Some people suffer side effects more than others, and although your doctor can usually find ways around the worst of them, side effects are a real concern.

✔ **Worries about long-term effects:** Most medications for emotional problems appear to have relatively little short-term risk. However, some medications haven't been around long enough for doctors to know for sure if problems may show up after many years of use. And because medications often must be taken for a lifetime, long-term effects are a serious concern.

✔ **Addiction:** Some medications for anxiety, such as benzodiazepines, are rather addictive. That means, if you take them for more than a few months, you could become highly dependent on them and experience withdrawal symptoms if and when you discontinue them. However, most antidepressants don't appear to be addictive in the usual sense, and, good, nonaddictive alternatives for the treatment of anxiety are available.

✔ **Pregnancy and breastfeeding:** Under careful medical review, some medications for emotional distress appear relatively safe for pregnant or breastfeeding mothers. However, the safety data isn't comprehensive, and controversy exists around their use in this special case.

Postpartum depression, depression that accompanies giving birth, is relatively common but can become quite serious if left untreated. If you experience symptoms of depression following the birth of a baby, you should get an evaluation.

✔ **Personal preference:** Because of religious reasons, philosophical viewpoints, or strong personal preferences, some people simply choose not to take medication. If that's the case for you, please get treatment for your problems through self-help exercises or through a qualified mental health professional.

Although valid reasons exist for choosing to not take medications for anxiety or depression, if your distress is extremely severe or involves serious suicidal or homicidal thoughts, we hope you'll reconsider your treatment decision and consult with your doctor.

1. **Review your reasons for and against taking medication.**

2. **Consider talking about your concerns with close friends, family, your physician, and/or a mental health professional.**

3. **Make a decision about how you want medication to factor into your treatment, and write out your reasoning process in Worksheet 14-3. Include your thoughts, feelings, and observations.**

Worksheet 14-3	**My Medication Decision**

_____

_____

_____

_____

_____

Preparing Your Prescriber

If you decide to take medication (hopefully you're planning to do so only in conjunction with therapy or self-help exercises), it's important to give your healthcare provider the complete and truthful information so that he or she can make an accurate recommendation for your treatment. We don't know about you, but we often forget what we want to say to our doctors during hurried visits. So, we've created a questionnaire for you to fill out and give to your provider during your visit. Your healthcare provider may need additional information, but the questions in Worksheet 14-4 are a good start to expressing the particulars of your condition.

Worksheet 14-4	Important Information for My Healthcare Provider

1. Describe your emotional symptoms (see Chapter 1 for ideas).

_____

_____

_____

_____

2. About how long have these symptoms been occurring, and how frequently do they appear? Have you had these feelings in the past?

_____

_____

_____

_____

3. Describe how severe your symptoms have been and how they have impacted your life. Be sure to discuss if you've had thoughts about harming yourself or others.

_____

_____

_____

_____

4. Describe any significant changes that have recently occurred in your life. Include deaths, job changes, divorces, injuries, retirement, or financial upheaval.

_____

_____

_____

_____

5. Describe any physical symptoms you've been experiencing (see Chapter 1 for ideas).

_____

_____

_____

_____

6. Describe the frequency and severity of your physical symptoms and how long you've experienced them.

_____

_____

_____

_____

7. List illnesses you've had recently and any medications (and their dosages) that you're currently taking. Include any chronic conditions you're being treated for, including high blood pressure, diabetes, kidney or liver disease, or asthma. Don't forget to mention birth control pills.

_____

_____

_____

_____

8. Do you have a family history of significant emotional problems? Include mental health information for any close relatives.

_____

_____

_____

_____

9. List any herbs, supplements, vitamins, or over-the-counter medications that you take.

_____

_____

_____

_____

10. **Write down your current and past use of cigarettes, alcohol, and drugs. Include frequency and amounts.**

_____

_____

_____

_____

11. **List your allergies. Have you had any bad reactions to any medications, herbs, or foods in the past?**

_____

_____

_____

_____

12. **Are you pregnant, planning to get pregnant, or breastfeeding?**

_____

_____

_____

_____

If you don't want to tear this questionnaire out of this book or lug the whole book to your healthcare provider's office (we don't blame you), you can download extra copies at www.dummies.com/go/adwbfd.

Sizing Up Side Effects

Close to half the number of people who take medications for anxiety or depression stop because of disagreeable side effects and/or because they don't feel they're benefiting from the drug. These people may not be aware that

✔ Many medications can take a number of weeks to achieve a good effect.

✔ Side effects often decrease or go away over time.

✔ The prescriber probably knows of alternative medications with fewer side effects.

✔ Another medication may be added to reduce side effects.

Stopping any medication for emotional difficulties needs to be carefully supervised because even medications that are not addictive in the usual sense can cause troublesome reactions if stopped abruptly. Please do not stop taking prescribed medication without consulting your physicians.

If you're experiencing problems with your medication, the decision to continue with medication, try an alternative medication, or add another drug to the regimen to reduce side effects is best made in tandem with your healthcare provider. You guessed it — that means you must communicate with your prescriber on a regular basis about the specific side effects you're experiencing.

Because it's so important for your healthcare provider to know about your experience with side effects, we created the Side Effect Tracking Form, shown in Worksheet 14-5, for you to fill out and take to your consultations (or use it as a guide during your telephone conversations). We recommend you complete this form at the very least for one month after you start a new medication for depression or anxiety. (You can download additional copies of the worksheet at www.dummies.com/go/adwbfd.)

1. **For each day of the week, place a check mark next to each symptom you experience to a noticeable degree.**

2. **For each symptom checked, rate its intensity on a scale of 1 (minimal) to 10 (maximal).**

Worksheet 14-5			My Side Effect Tracking Form				
Symptom	*Monday*	*Tuesday*	*Wednesday*	*Thursday*	*Friday*	*Saturday*	*Sunday*
Restlessness							
Fatigue							
Euphoria for no reason							
Vision problems							
Constipation							
Sleeplessness (or even feeling little need for sleep)							
Trembling							
Diarrhea							
Sharp decrease in mood for no reason							
Increase in anxiety							
Dry mouth							
Headaches							
Sexual problems							
Nausea or stomach upset							

(continued)

Worksheet 14-5 *(continued)*

Symptom	Monday	Tuesday	Wednesday	Thursday	Friday	Saturday	Sunday
Overwhelming apathy							
Memory problems							
Weight changes (rate once a week)							
Changes in appetite (up or down)							
Racing heartbeat							
Skin rash							
Sweating							
Dizziness							
Feeling revved up							
Problems urinating (too much or too little)							
Muscle spasms or twitching							
Nightmares							
Swelling of feet or hands							
Numbness							
Any other bodily or unexpected emotional changes (list them)							

You always have the option of a few alternative treatments for depression and anxiety. Many people take herbs and supplements for minor emotional distress, and your healthcare provider can tell you about options for especially severe depression. For more information about alternatives to medication, see *Overcoming Anxiety For Dummies* and *Depression For Dummies* (Wiley).

Part V
Relationship Therapy

The 5th Wave By Rich Tennant

"My wife and I were drifting apart. We decided to go back to doing what we used to do when we were first married. So we called her parents and asked to borrow money."

In this part . . .

Your relationships may suffer when you feel significant amounts of anxiety or depression. And when your relationships suffer, you no doubt feel more anxious or depressed. It's a rather vicious cycle.

In this part, we give you techniques to enhance relationships and improve communication. We also help you deal with loss and conflict.

Chapter 15

Restoring Relationships

. . . .

In This Chapter

▶ Discovering the connection between emotions and relationships

▶ Examining your relationship

▶ Enhancing your relationship with positive actions

▶ Dealing with endings

. . . .

Supportive relationships provide a buffer against all types of emotional distress. Numerous studies indicate that good relationships and social support improve both mental and physical health. Humans apparently are social animals that are biologically programmed to function better when in supportive relationships. Like gorillas, birds, and ants, we thrive in close-knit colonies. Therefore, working to improve your relationships can help boost your moods, increase your ability to handle stress, and create a sense of well-being.

Yet, distressing emotions can get in the way of your attempts to improve your relationships. Such emotions can harm friendships, intimate relationships, and even relationships with co-workers or relative strangers. So, along with the obvious ways of working to alleviate your anxiety or depression, shoring up your relationships will also improve your moods.

In this chapter, we review strengthening strategies that you can apply to almost any type of relationship. However, we emphasize intimate relationships because disruptions in these types of relationships cause the most harm and because repairing them is enormously beneficial to your mental health. In addition, we help you cope with the loss of a relationship because such an event can be quite traumatic and trigger intense feelings of anxiety and/or despair.

Revealing the Emotion-Relationship Connection

Whether you like it or not, when you're anxious or depressed, you become more self-absorbed. We don't mean that you become conceited, but your attention becomes focused on your problems and concerns. Although the shift in your focus is quite understandable, your relationships are likely to suffer when your problems lay claim to your energy. Because you're mentally and emotionally drained, you don't pay much attention to nurturing your relationships — and relationships need nurturing.

In addition, when you're anxious and depressed, those who care about you are likely to make attempts to cheer you up or help you. When their efforts fall short, they often feel frustrated and helpless. Eventually, they feel exhausted, too, and may pull away from you. Frankly, after a prolonged time, it's a downer to be around someone who's constantly bummed out.

The following example shows you how depression can easily erode a good relationship.

John slips in and out of depression with the seasons. When daylight diminishes in the winter, his moods darken (see *Depression For Dummies* [Wiley] for more about Seasonal Affective Disorder). After a whirlwind romance last summer, John marries Gia, the woman of his dreams, in a beautiful fall wedding. He's never been so happy.

John warns Gia about his winter blues. However, both hope that their love and her presence in his life will help him ward off depression during the dark months. Unfortunately, depression overtakes John as the days become shorter. John withdraws from Gia, who tries to understand but becomes hurt and frustrated with her inability to cheer him up. John feels guilty that he's hurting his wife but feels powerless to do anything about his predicament. The relationship suffers.

In Worksheet 15-1, answer the questions about an important relationship in your life in order to see if depression or anxiety have been inflicting harm.

Worksheet 15-1   The Relationship Impact Questionnaire

1. **Have I withdrawn or pulled back from my relationship? If so, in what ways?**

   _____

   _____

   _____

   _____

2. **Am I less affectionate than I used to be? If so, in what ways?**

   _____

   _____

   _____

   _____

3. **Am I more irritable or critical than I used to be? If so, in what ways?**

   _____

   _____

   _____

   _____

4. **Am I being less caring, giving fewer compliments, or being less empathetic? If so, in what ways?**

   _____

   _____

   _____

   _____

Although depression and anxiety often cause problems in relationships, they're not the only culprits. Some relationships deteriorate in the presence of severe emotional problems, and some relationships are simply unhealthy. If you wonder why your relationship isn't doing well, or if you suspect you're being abused, check with a mental health professional who specializes in couples work.

Enhancing Your Relationship

Have you ever received or given flowers at the start of a new relationship? Ideally, relationships continue to provide "flowers" of many varieties — compliments, companionship, good times, caring, affection, laughter, and more. Most good relationships start out with enthusiasm and a bouquet of good feelings. But too often, complacency sets in, and life interferes. After a while, it's easy to forget to send flowers.

When you stop cultivating a garden, ugly weeds choke out the flowers. The same is true of a relationship, which wilts as a result of inattention. You can fertilize your relationship by increasing:

- ✔ Positive talk
- ✔ Positive actions

Whether your relationship is really suffering or is doing pretty well but isn't quite what you'd like it to be, the strategies in this section can help you make it better.

Talking together

Communication is the foundation of a good relationship. Everyone benefits from having safe people to express their thoughts and feelings to. In order to help you create the right climate for such positive communication, we introduce two exercises: the Daily News and the Top 12 Things I Appreciate About My Partner.

If your communication with your partner is conflictual, jump to Chapter 16 for a fix. And if the following exercises don't go over well, we recommend you see a therapist for couples counseling.

Perusing the Daily News

The *Daily News* is a way of making sure that you and your partner spend time talking and listening to one another. The purpose of this exercise is to enhance intimacy. We recommend that you make this exercise a high priority and perform it often.

Worksheet 15-2 **The Daily News**

---

1. **Work with your partner to decide on a time when you will sit and talk about the day's events for 20 minutes.** You may choose to chat at the same time every day, or you may want to vary it. Daily is best (that's why we call it the "Daily News," but you'll benefit from talking this way at least three or four times a week.

2. Commit to your meeting times and write them down here.

_____

_____

_____

3. Let your partner begin and speak for ten minutes.

4. Show interest by:

- **Asking a few questions for greater understanding**

- **Nodding your head**

- **Making brief comments**

- **Expressing empathy or understanding for how your partner feels**

Don't give advice or solve your partner's problem at this time. And avoid criticism or stirring up conflict!

5. After your partner shares the events of his or her day, try to summarize what he or she said in a positive manner.

6. Ask your partner if your understanding of what he or she said is basically correct. If not, ask for clarification.

7. Take your turn to talk about your day, asking your partner to follow these same rules.

After you work through the Daily News exercise a few times, reflect on how it went and record your thoughts in Worksheet 15-3. How did you feel before and after the exercise? Do you know more about your partner now, and does your partner know more about you? Do you feel closer?

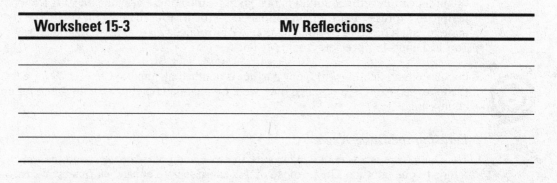

Worksheet 15-3	**My Reflections**

_____

_____

_____

_____

_____

Putting compliments to good use

Compliments, when sincerely offered, enhance communication and positive feelings. When you feel anxious or depressed, you may not think about all the things you appreciate about your partner. But when you don't express what you cherish and admire, your partner is likely to feel unappreciated. We recommend you work through the following exercise, the *Top 12 Things I Appreciate About My Partner,* to get back on track when it comes to complimenting your partner.

1. In Worksheet 15-4, write down all the things you appreciate, value, admire, and cherish about your partner. Include attributes such as intelligence, caring, warmth, attractiveness, talents, help with daily life (such as cooking, cleaning, finances, and so on), sense of humor, and anything else you can think of. Only include items you feel sincerely apply.

Be specific in your assessment of your partner. For example, rather than saying, "You're the best person in the whole world," consider narrowing it down and saying, "I love the way you play with the baby." Also, avoid "buts"; for example, don't say, "I really like your hair, but it would look better shorter." That's really just a backhanded compliment — it could go either way.

2. **Compliment your partner at least once a day from your list (or you may come up with something new).**

3. **Create a strategy for remembering to make these compliments.** For example, you may make a note in your calendar or put sticky notes in various places around the house.

Get into the habit of handing out genuine compliments to everyone, not just your partner. Doing so will improve your popularity by making people notice you, and it may even get you a raise!

Worksheet 15-4	The Top 12 Things I Appreciate About My Partner
1.	
2.	
3.	
4.	
5.	
6.	
7.	
8.	
9.	
10.	
11.	
12.	

Some people dismiss compliments by saying, "Oh, you don't mean that," or "That isn't really true." If your partner responds in this way, keep complimenting. People dismiss compliments not because they don't want to hear them but because they have trouble accepting them.

After you spend a couple of weeks increasing the compliments you give your partner, reflect on any changes in your relationship (see Worksheet 15-5). Do you notice any increased warmth, affection, or communication? Are you or your partner in a better mood?

Worksheet 15-5	My Reflections

If you can't think of anything to genuinely appreciate about your partner, your relationship is in serious trouble. Seek help from a professional trained in couples counseling, or consider moving on to a new relationship.

Delightful doings

If communication is the foundation of a good relationship (see the "Talking together" section), sharing pleasurable activities is the house that sits on top. In this section, we review an important technique for increasing positive times with your partner: the Positive Behavioral Exchange System.

The *Positive Behavioral Exchange System* is designed to give you an easy way of showing your partner that you care. The system involves making a list of small caring actions that you and your partner can do for each other frequently. After making a list, each person keeps track of what the other has done. We recommend that you review this strategy with your partner and that you both participate in the exercise. Although this technique may look simplistic, research shows that it works and builds surprisingly positive feelings. (We've taken the essence of this idea from our friend and colleague, Dr. Richard B. Stuart.) Before you get started on your own Positive Behavioral Exchange System, consider the following example.

Trisha and **Michael** decide to try the Positive Behavioral Exchange System because they've noticed that their relationship has been getting stale. Trisha and Michael discuss specific actions they can take to increase the pleasure they get from one another. Michael asks Trisha to stop complaining about their finances, but in talking, they realize that his request is both negative and focused on something they frequently argue about. So, they think of other, more positive actions to take to increase pleasure. For example, Trisha asks Michael to be nicer to her mother. But upon reflection, she realizes that her request is too vague, so she asks him to spend one or two minutes speaking to her mother on the phone when she calls. Worksheet 15-6 shows what they finally settle on and the results of their first week of taking the decided actions.

Worksheet 15-6   Trisha's and Michael's Positive Behavioral Exchange System

Desired Actions	Dates Carried Out
Michael brings in morning newspaper.	7/16, 7/20, 7/21
Trisha rubs Michael's back.	7/16
Michael rubs Trisha's back.	7/16
Trisha starts dinner before Michael gets home.	7/17, 7/18, 7/21, 7/22
Michael buys Trisha a small gift.	7/22
Trisha calls Michael at work just to chat.	7/16, 7/18, 7/19
Michael talks to Trisha's mother when she calls.	7/21
Trisha helps the kids with homework while Michael watches the news.	7/16, 7/20
Michael puts gas in Trisha's car.	7/22

Desired Actions	Dates Carried Out
Trisha mows the front yard.	7/18
Michael makes coffee in the morning.	7/16, 7/17, 7/19, 7/20, 7/22
Trisha pays the bills.	7/20

Trisha and Michael discover that, to their surprise, this strategy actually leads them to feel closer and warmer to each other, and they aren't arguing as much. In fact, they enjoy the results so much that the following week, they add several more items to their list. Both notice an increased desire to please the other.

1. **Talk with your partner and develop a list of small actions that either of you interpret as an indication of caring or affection.** These actions must be

   - Stated positively.

   - Clear and specific (so you will know for sure if it happens).

   - Easily carried out.

   - Able to be frequently carried out.

   - Not something you've been fighting about.

2. **List these actions in the left-hand column of Worksheet 15-7.**

3. **Each day, in the right-hand column, write the date when you notice your partner doing one of the items for you, and your partner should do the same.**

4. **At the end of each day, briefly discuss the progress of your exercise with your partner.**

5. **Commit to doing at least three to five of these actions every day, whether your partner does the same or not.** Don't feel obligated to do any particular item, but try to carry out a variety of them.

Consider taping this list to your refrigerator or some other obvious place in the house so that it's easy for you and your partner to keep track of each other's actions and see the progress you're making.

Worksheet 15-7	Our Positive Behavioral Exchange System
Desired Actions	**Dates Carried Out**

(continued)

Worksheet 15-7 *(continued)*

Desired Actions	Dates Carried Out

You can download as many copies of this form as you need at www.dummies.com/go/adwbfd.

When you and your partner work on this exercise, one of you will inevitably slip from time to time by forgetting about the positive behavioral exchange exercise. Simply recommit yourself each time that happens. Resist the temptation to be critical when that occurs.

After you carry out the Positive Behavioral Exchange System for a week, reflect on its effects on your relationship and record your thoughts in Worksheet 15-8.

Worksheet 15-8 **My Reflections**

_____

_____

_____

_____

_____

Dealing with Relationship Loss

It would be nice if people lived forever and relationships always endured. But life isn't a fairy tale — everyone doesn't live "happily ever after." Relationships break up, marriages dissolve, circumstances cause prolonged separations, and people die. And loss, whether from death or happenstance, causes great distress.

In fact, loss sometimes causes depression. When you lose someone, it's natural to grieve and feel sad. However, grief isn't quite the same thing as depression. The main difference is that depression includes feelings of inadequacy and low self-esteem, whereas grief centers around feelings of loss and loneliness. Also, most people find that grief decreases with time, unlike depression. Loss or fear of loss can also create anxiety. You may think you can't handle life without your loved one; you may feel dependent and overwhelmed.

If you've lost someone, first and foremost, take care of yourself. Be sure to eat healthy, stay away from abusing drugs and alcohol, and exercise regularly, whether you feel like it or not — even if you just take a 30-minute brisk walk each day. And be sure to get enough sleep. Grieving takes a physical and mental toll, and you need all your resources to get through it.

In addition, you may want to turn to other sources of support. Don't be afraid to ask for help! Such sources can include

- ✔ Religious or spiritual resources
- ✔ Grief support groups
- ✔ Friends and family
- ✔ Mental health professionals

If you lose someone and feel like you can't go on, or if you have thoughts of hopelessness or suicide, please seek professional help promptly.

Moving on

When you're grieving, it's natural to feel like staying in bed and pulling the covers over your head. And there's a tendency to try and avoid thinking about the lost person or relationship. Some folks even turn to drugs or alcohol in order to blunt their pain. However, all those strategies merely make things worse.

A better approach is to explore your thoughts and feelings about the lost person. Yes, you should actually spend some active time reviewing and reconstructing the relationship and what the person meant to you. This process facilitates moving on.

In order to get the most out of this Grief Exploration Questionnaire (see Worksheet 15-9), set aside at least an hour to answer the questions. Don't rush the process. Also, you should expect to feel some intense sadness or grief; in fact, you're likely to cry. But if you feel over-whelmed or feel that you can't handle this exercise, please seek professional help.

Worksheet 15-9	**Grief Exploration Questionnaire**

1. What was my life like when I was with this person?

_____

_____

_____

_____

2. What did I value about this person?

_____

_____

_____

_____

3. What was difficult about this person?

_____

_____

_____

_____

4. What lessons did I learn from this relationship, both positive and negative?

_____

_____

_____

_____

5. What is different about my life now?

_____

_____

_____

_____

6. What am I most angry or resentful about?

_____

_____

_____

_____

7. What aspects of this relationship am I most grateful for?

_____

_____

_____

_____

8. **What did I enjoy about this relationship?**

_____

_____

_____

_____

9. **Compose a letter to the person you've lost. The purpose of this letter is to provide you with closure. Review questions 1-7 for material you may wish to include in your letter, and feel free to be emotional and express anything that's on your mind.**

_____

_____

_____

_____

_____

_____

_____

_____

_____

_____

_____

Becoming active

You'll never fully replace someone you've lost because people and relationships are all unique and, in one sense, irreplaceable. Nonetheless, you can pick up the pieces, move on, and refill your life with meaningful relationships and activities. We suggest you explore the following after you begin to recover:

✔ **Volunteer work:** A great way to regain a sense of meaning in your life is to help others. Plus, volunteer work often leads to friendships and a new social circle.

✔ **Pleasurable activities:** Even if you feel sad and unenthusiastic, putting pleasure back into your life is possible (see Chapter 11 for more about healthy pleasures). You won't feel like you "should" indulge in pleasure, but after you start to recover from your loss, allowing yourself to enjoy things can accelerate your healing.

✔ **Socializing:** Whether it's visiting with friends and family or starting to date again, being with other people helps you get through tough times. Sometimes starting to date or making new friends can feel frightening at first. However, both are steps in learning to love and establish new connections. Venturing back into the world is part of the healing process.

Chapter 16

Smoothing Out Conflict

. . . .

. . . .

Conflict with someone you care about hurts, and when you're depressed or anxious, you tend to be more irritable, which leads to more conflict. Like so many other problems related to depression and anxiety, a vicious cycle ensues.

In this chapter, we help you break the negative cycle of conflict. We explain how what we call the *malicious assumption* leads to defensiveness and counterattacks. Then we show you how to track the malicious assumption and defensiveness in your relationships. You see how identifying and understanding your hot buttons and those of your partner can help you depersonalize what you previously considered criticism. Finally, we provide some tips for dealing with conflict constructively.

Overriding Defensiveness

When people feel emotionally vulnerable, whether from depression, anxiety, or conflict in a relationship, they all too easily start making the *malicious assumption* in response to something their partners say or do. The malicious assumption refers to the tendency to automatically interpret communications or actions in the most negative, critical way possible. More often than not, the malicious assumption grossly misinterprets the true meaning of the message.

Here's a common, concrete example of the malicious assumption in everyday life. Suppose you're driving on the freeway, and someone cuts you off. You can interpret the driver's motive in one of two ways: as the result of careless inattentiveness or as a hostile action aimed at you directly. Which is the malicious assumption? The belief that the driver cut you off deliberately and with hostility. Thus, if you make this assumption, you may respond by opening your car window and giving the other driver a good look at one of your fingers (and we're guessing you know which one). This action, in turn, may lead to a dangerous escalation of violent action, also known as road rage.

Defensiveness occurs when the malicious assumption causes you to perceive a communication or behavior as an attack. In a defensive response, you say that you aren't to blame in any way for the problem, or you counterattack. Saying that something's not your fault assumes that your partner had hostile intentions. And when you counterattack, all you accomplish is an escalation of conflict. Either reaction is likely to provide fuel for an argument.

Sarcasm usually indicates defensiveness. Pay particular attention when you hear yourself being sarcastic, and try to reign yourself in with reasonability.

The examples in Worksheet 16-1 help you see how the insidious process of assumption and defensiveness works.

Worksheet 16-1	Malicious Assumptions and Defensive Responses	
Initial Communication or Action	*Malicious Assumption*	*Defensive Response*
"You look tired today."	She's saying I look horrible.	"You don't look so great either."
"Where's the checkbook?"	He's saying I didn't put it back where it should be.	"Hey, I didn't lose it; you had it last!"
"Did you fill the car up with gas?"	She's criticizing me for not getting gas.	"No, but why can't you get gas sometimes?"
Your partner forgets your birthday.	Obviously, she doesn't care about me anymore.	That's just fine; I'll get back at her.
Your partner tells you to change some wording in a book you're writing together.	He must think I'm stupid.	"It's not like everything *you* write reads like Hemingway!"
"The house is a mess."	He's saying I don't keep the place clean like I should.	"So, what am I, your maid? Clean it up if you don't like it."

Notice that in Worksheet 16-1, all the initial communications and actions are at least somewhat ambiguous. In other words, you can't tell with certainty whether the person had hostile intentions. Besides, whether a message or behavior is clearly hostile, it doesn't do much good to respond defensively — unless, of course, all you want is a good fight.

Shining the light on your defensive behavior

Before you can stop making the malicious assumption and following it with defensive responses, you need to see how these behaviors play out in your life. Therefore, we suggest you track events in which these behaviors crop up. Use the following instructions as your guide. (After you identify your own defensive behaviors, we give you an alternative to defensiveness and explain a method for dealing with truly hostile criticism in a way that may lead to better outcomes.)

1. **Whenever your partner says or does something that you feel may have been intended as hostile, write it down in the left-hand column of Worksheet 16-2.**

2. **In the middle column, write down how you interpret what happened.** Try to be honest; don't clean up your reaction (or your language!). Say how you really feel about what your partner said or did.

3. In the right-hand column, jot down how you respond, and analyze your response for defensiveness: Did you try to absolve yourself of all blame, or did you counterattack in some way?

Worksheet 16-2   My Malicious Assumptions and Defensive Responses

Initial Communication or Action	*Malicious Assumption*	*Defensive Response*

Review your malicious assumptions and defensive responses. In Worksheet 16-3, reflect on how they may be causing problems in your relationship.

Worksheet 16-3   My Reflections

_____

_____

_____

_____

_____

Check, please

Hopefully the exercise in the preceding section has made you more aware of when you get defensive. But what's an alternative when you perceive your partner's actions or words as hostile or malicious? We recommend something called *checking it out*.

Checking it out involves first catching the urge to be defensive. Then, when you're ready, you make a gentle inquiry about your partner's true intentions.

Max promises to pick up **Teva** for dinner and a movie at 6:30. He arrives breathless at 6:50 saying, "Sorry, traffic was horrible." Teva immediately makes a malicious assumption, believing that Max was purposely late, which proves that Max is losing interest in her. She almost says, "That's what you said last time, you jerk," but she decides to check it out. She stops herself and takes a deep breath or two. After she calms down a little, she asks, "Max, I'm a little worried that you might be losing interest. Is that possible?" Max is quite surprised by the question and says, "Gosh, no. I'm really sorry if it seemed that way to you. There really was a terrible accident. I really care about you and enjoy every second that I'm with you."

When you find yourself in a potentially hostile situation, take a moment and practice the checking it out technique by following these instructions:

1. **The moment you feel attacked or criticized, close your mouth!**

2. **Take a slow, deep breath in, and exhale very slowly. Repeat once or twice until you feel a little calmer.**

   While you're breathing, remind yourself that if you speak while you're upset, the odds of saying something useful or productive have been precisely calculated at 1 in 5.86 billion.

3. **When you feel calmer, inquire about your partner's actual intentions. Gently explain what your worry or concern is about, but don't accuse or attack.**

4. **Keep track of your exchange so that you can work through it with less emotion involved. In Worksheet 16-4, record the initial communication or action in the left-hand column.**

5. **Write down your malicious assumption in the middle column.**

6. **In the right-hand column, jot down how you checked out your assumption.**

Worksheet 16-4   My Malicious Assumptions and Checking It Out Responses

Initial Communication or Action	Malicious Assumption	Checking It Out

Initial Communication or Action	Malicious Assumption	Checking It Out

Don't refuse to defuse

Another alternative to defensiveness or counterattacking is *defusing*. You use this technique when your partner clearly is engaging in criticism. Basically, defusing consists of saying something downright counterintuitive — finding at least a sliver of truth in your partner's statement. When you acknowledge part (or sometimes all) of your partner's concerns, you keep the dialogue going and take the emotional charge out of the interaction. We're not suggesting that you completely capitulate or lie to your partner but rather that you genuinely work hard to discover your partner's perspective on the problem at hand. Usually, you and your partner can find at least something to agree upon.

This technique doesn't work for dealing with flat-out verbal abuse. For that kind of situation, you need to get help. But sometimes it's difficult to know if you're being emotionally abused. So, if you're not sure if your partner is being abusive, consult with a mental health professional.

Worksheet 16-5 contains examples of criticisms with corresponding defusing responses. In each defusing response, a section appears in italics to show you which part of the criticism is valid and acknowledged by the person being criticized. For the last three criticisms in the worksheet, fill in the defusing responses that you think would be most effective.

Worksheet 16-5	Defusing Criticism
Criticism	*Defusing Response*
You spend too much money.	*Sometimes I probably do,* but I'm not sure what you're referring to right now.
You yell at the kids too much.	*You may have a point.* I'll try to be more aware of when I yell.
The house is a mess; you never clean it.	*I understand how you might feel that way,* but I don't think I value a pristine house as much as you do. Can we figure out a compromise here?
You're always telling me what to do. You're way too controlling.	*I can agree that I sometimes fall into that habit,* although I think I let you have your way on a lot of things. What is your specific complaint?

(continued)

Worksheet 16-5 (continued)

Criticism	Defusing Response
I don't want to spend so much time over at your mother's place.	
You're a mouse; you let your boss walk all over you.	
You need to lose weight.	

Practice defusing whenever you can. It's not the type of reaction that comes naturally, but all your relationships will go more smoothly if you master the technique.

After you put the defusing technique as well as the checking it out technique (see the preceding section) to the test in your own relationships, reflect on how these alternatives to defensiveness and counterattacking have worked for you. Did you find that checking it out revealed that your partner indeed was being hostile? Or did you discover that your partner wasn't intending to inflict hurt or criticism? In either case, did checking it out keep things from escalating like they usually do? When you tried to defuse your partner's comments, did the potential conflict seem to deflate? Record your reflections in Worksheet 16-5.

Worksheet 16-5   My Reflections

_____

_____

_____

_____

_____

Discovering the Problem Isn't All About You

When someone you care about is angry or distraught, you may think that the upset relates to you in some way. This assumption is natural but not always correct. When you wrongly take responsibility for your partner's emotions, you engage in *personalizing*. And when you personalize, you're likely to feel distressed and just may become defensive or counterattack (see "Overriding Defensiveness" for more on those reactions).

It's often the case that when people get upset, it has very little to do with you — even if they say it does! What? How can that be? Truth is, most of the time, people have intense emotions about events because one or more of their personal hot buttons have been pushed. These hot buttons are what we call *problematic life-lenses* (check out Chapter 7 for a full explanation). They're the core beliefs that people have about themselves and the world, and they arouse a lot of emotion.

If you can identify what your partner's hot buttons are, you can understand what triggers his or her anger and other heightened emotions. It also helps to know that your partner's upset has more to do with problematic life-lenses than with you. Understanding problematic life-lenses allows you to *depersonalize* the event, which in turn leads you to feel a little empathy rather than defensiveness.

If you haven't done so already, we recommend that you flip to Chapter 7 and get to the bottom of your own problematic life-lenses. If you already worked through Chapter 7, we suggest you go back and review it now. Understanding your own issues is as important as understanding your partner's.

It's time to figure out which of the problematic life-lenses listed in Worksheet 16-6 apply to your partner.

1. **Read over the problematic life-lenses in Worksheet 16-6.**

2. **Think about your partner and how he or she reacts to life events.**

3. **Rate each lens based on how it describes your partner's behavior and reactions to life events.** Use a scale of 1 to 5 for your frequency rating: 1 for almost never, 2 for occasionally, 3 for sometimes, 4 for usually, and 5 for almost always.

   You may discover that your partner has seemingly contradictory life-lenses, such as feeling both perfectionistic and at times inadequate. Don't worry; combinations are fairly common.

Worksheet 16-6   My Partner's Problematic Life-Lenses Questionnaire

Lens	*Opposite Lens*
____ *Unworthy:* I don't feel like I deserve to have good things happen to me. I feel uncomfortable whenever someone does something nice for me.	____ *Entitled:* I deserve the best of everything. I should have almost anything I want. If my needs unexpectedly go unmet, I feel threatened, sad, or angry.
____ *Abandonment-fearful:* I need lots of reassurance to feel loved. I feel lost without someone in my life, and I worry about losing those I care about. I feel jealous and cling to my loved ones because of my fear.	____ *Intimacy-avoidant:* I don't like to get close to anyone. I'd just as soon stay away from any emotional involvement. I don't really want anybody in my life.
____ *Inadequate:* I feel like I'm not as talented or skillful as most other people. I just don't measure up. I don't like taking on things I've never done before if they look difficult.	____ *Perfectionistic:* I feel like I must do everything perfectly. I feel like there's a right way and a wrong way to do things, and I want to do things the right way.
____ *Guilty and blameworthy:* I feel like everything that goes wrong is my fault. I worry about whether I've done the wrong thing. I can't stand hurting anyone else.	____ *Guiltless:* I don't let stupid things like morality and conscience stand in my way if I want something bad enough. I never care about what other people think.
____ *Vulnerable:* Bad things happen all the time. I worry a lot about the future. I'm scared. The world feels very dangerous.	____ *Invulnerable:* I'm invincible — nothing can ever hurt me. The world treats me extremely well. I always have great luck, and I never worry about taking precautions.
____ *Help-seeking:* I depend on others a lot, and I feel better when other people take care of me. I can't handle life by myself.	____ *Help-avoidant:* I hate asking for favors, and I don't like it when other people try to help me.

(continued)

Worksheet 16-6 *(continued)*

Lens	Opposite Lens
____ *Under-control:* If I want to do something, I follow my impulses. It's hard for me to set limits with people, so I tend to get walked on. I'd rather express my emotions than control them.	____ *Over-control:* Nothing is worse than losing control. I never let anyone see how I feel. I like to keep my fingers in everything. I don't like working for someone else, and I can't stand leaving my fate in the control of others.

If you rated your partner as having a 3 or above on any of the problematic life-lenses in this table, you've found a hot button. Life happenings that tie into those life-lenses are likely to produce strong emotions — and the intensity of those emotions probably has more to do with your partner's life-lens than with you. Keeping track of when your partner becomes upset and figuring out which problematic life-lens is involved is always a good move because knowing this connection may not make you feel good about your partner's upset, but at least you can understand what's going on and perhaps let it go with more ease.

Isabelle has a hot temper. She gets angry about almost anything that goes wrong, and even small stuff gets her really worked up. Isabelle's partner, Lisa, blames herself when Isabelle goes off on one of her tirades. Lisa completes the problematic life-lens questionnaire on Isabelle's behaviors (see Worksheet 16-6) and discovers that Isabelle appears to look through the lenses *perfectionistic, help-avoidant,* and *vulnerable.* It's no wonder she gets upset so easily! With that information in hand, Lisa tracks Isabelle's life-lenses over a variety of life events (see Worksheet 16-7), and reflects on her findings (see Worksheet 16-8).

Worksheet 16-7	**Isabelle's Life-Lens Tracking Sheet**	
Event	*Emotion & Reaction*	*Life-Lens*
I forgot to pay a bill on time.	Isabelle exploded with anger and called me stupid. She said she should never have counted on me to pay the bill in the first place.	Perfectionistic, Help-avoidant
I left the house door unlocked.	Isabelle was shaking with anger. She said we're really lucky we didn't get robbed.	Vulnerable
I got a painter to repaint the outside trim while Isabelle was out of town on business.	When she saw what I'd done, she said I was throwing money away. She said she could have done the work even though I know she doesn't have the time.	Help-avoidant
Isabelle forgot to put the milk away.	Isabelle swore and hit her fist into the wall, and I felt like it was my fault.	Perfectionistic

Worksheet 16-8	Lisa's Reflections

I really see now that I've been beating myself up over what are really Isabelle's problems. I can tell that she gets really pissed off when she's afraid, and she turns it all on me. Her perfectionism drives her nuts whenever the slightest thing goes wrong. And she hates asking for help on anything. I don't much like her tirades, but at least I can depersonalize them a little. I understand now that her anger isn't all about me. I don't deserve to be treated like this. I'm going to work up the courage to tell Isabelle that she needs some help with these issues, and I may suggest we go to couples counseling as well.

Use the following instructions to understand and depersonalize your partner's hot button reactions.

1. **After you figure out your partner's problematic life-lenses (see Worksheet 16-6), observe him or her in action over the next few weeks.**

2. **When you notice your partner expressing strong, negative emotions, write down the event that appeared to trigger the reaction in the left-hand column of Worksheet 16-9.**

3. **In the middle column, record your partner's emotions and overall reactions.**

4. **In the right-hand column, write down your partner's problematic life-lens that relates to his or her emotions and reactions to that particular event.**

5. **Use Worksheet 16-10 to reflect on your observations. Try to depersonalize your partner's behavior and let some of your own upset go.**

Worksheet 16-9	My Partner's Life-Lens Tracking Sheet	
Event	*Emotion & Reaction*	*Life-Lens*

Worksheet 16-10	My Reflections

Talking About the Tough Stuff

As we explain in Chapter 15, communication is the foundation of any good relationship. In that chapter, we give you tools for sharing experiences and positive feelings. In this chapter, we tell you how to talk about dicier issues, such as concerns, disagreements, and dissatisfactions. After all, sometimes people just need to discuss this stuff. Unfortunately, most people don't know how to do that very well. Our two strategies for helping you express the tough stuff are *I Messages* and *buffering*.

Shifting the focus with I Messages

When you want to communicate concerns or dissatisfaction, the language you use makes a big difference in how heated your communication becomes. If you're critical or blaming, you're likely to produce defensiveness or a counterattack in your partner. *I Messages* state your concerns in terms of how they affect you and don't blame or accuse your partner of anything. To use this technique, you clearly state how *you* feel about an issue; you know you're giving an I Message when you start your communication with the word "I" instead of "you."

Don't expect to master the I Message technique quickly or easily because the natural, perhaps instinctive response is to lash out. Thus, I Messages take lots of rehearsal and practice.

 Worksheet 16-11 lays out several examples of blaming messages accompanied by alternative I Messages. Read through the examples, and then come up with your own I Messages for the blaming messages at the bottom of the list.

Worksheet 16-11	The I Message Technique
Blaming Messages	*I Messages*
You don't love me anymore.	I'm feeling a little insecure. I'd sure like a little more affection.
You never cut the grass unless I bug you about it over and over again.	I don't like being a nag about the grass. I would like it if you could find a way to do it more regularly so I wouldn't feel a need to bug you.
You complain about everything.	I worry sometimes that you're not happy because you have so many complaints.

Blaming Messages	I Messages
You really tick me off.	I'm feeling a little annoyed with you.
You charge way too much on the credit cards.	
You never put your dishes in the dishwasher!	
You're always late.	
You don't appreciate all the things I do around here.	

Of course it is possible that I Messages could lead to a negative response by your partner. They simply improve your odds as compared to blaming and complaining "You Messages."

You can make your I Messages even more effective by not only expressing what you feel but also stating your concern gently.

Softening the blow through buffering

When you communicate negative or critical concerns, you have basically two choices: You can smash your partner over the head, or you can soften the blow. Guess which one works best?

Like buffered aspirin, *buffering* reduces the acidity in your communications. To buffer, you add a phrase that conveys the possibility that your position may not be entirely correct or that your reaction may be a little excessive. We know, we know — you may feel you're undoubtedly 100 percent correct, but it never hurts to cover your confidence a bit. Even if you're totally in the right, buffering can help.

Take a look at buffered and unbuffered concern examples in Worksheet 16-12, and decide for yourself which approach is more likely to lead to a *productive exchange* — that's one in which you have possible compromise and useful conversation. After reading through the examples, fill in your own buffered alternatives for the unbuffered concerns at the end of the list.

Combining your buffering with an I Message (see "Shifting the focus with I Messages" earlier in the chapter) can convey your point even more effectively. The Buffering Strategy below includes I Messages in addition to using buffered phrases that suggest your position may not be entirely 100-percent correct.

Worksheet 16-12	The Buffering Strategy
Unbuffered Concerns	Buffered Concerns
You're messing up the checkbook.	I probably overreact to the checkbook problem, but I'd like us to come up with a better system.
You were rude to our neighbors.	I may be seeing this wrong, but it felt like you were a little rude to the neighbors.

(continued)

Worksheet 16-12 *(continued)*

Unbuffered Concerns	*Buffered Concerns*
You were flirting with that woman at the party.	I could be off on this, but I felt like you were flirting with that woman at the party, and I felt hurt.
You're working way too many hours at the office lately. Your priorities are out of whack.	Help me understand what's keeping you at the job so many hours. I miss you when you're not around.
You're spending way too much on clothes.	
You're always screaming and yelling at the kids — they can't stand to be around you.	
You spoil the kids. They're becoming brats because of you.	
You're always signing us up to write another *For Dummies* book. We never have enough time for vacations. Just stop! (Just kidding folks; we love writing.)	

Part VI
Looking Beyond Anxiety and Depression

The 5th Wave   By Rich Tennant

"This position is good for reaching inner calm, mental clarity, and things that roll behind the refrigerator."

In this part . . .

We take you beyond getting better and help you prepare for possible difficulties in the road ahead. Relapse of anxiety or depression is disturbingly common, but you don't have to sit back and let it happen. We tell you what you can do to prevent relapse or at least head it off early on.

Finally, we turn our focus to what makes people happy. After all, we don't want you to just get over your emotional distress; we want you to feel true joy from your life. That's why we provide exercises that focus your efforts on finding meaning, purpose, and fulfillment.

Chapter 17

Reining In Relapse

• •

In This Chapter

▶ Determining the risk of relapse

▶ Looking out for relapse signs

▶ Taking steps to catch and deal with relapse early on

• •

The good news about anxiety and depression is that they're both highly treatable disorders. Typically, you can expect treatment efforts, either on your own or in conjunction with professional help, to improve your moods and emotions considerably. The bad news is that relapse is common. But there's a lot you can do to prevent relapse and get better quickly should it occur.

If you've made a substantial improvement in your anxiety or depression and you want to hold onto your gains, this is the chapter for you. In this chapter, we help you figure out if you're at risk for relapse. Watching for relapse signs allows you to nip problems in the bud before they overwhelm you. We also give you a couple of strategies for preventing relapse from occurring in the first place.

If you've worked (*really* worked, that is) through the rest of this book and your moods remain anxious or depressed, this is not the chapter for you. Seek professional help if you haven't improved or you're struggling more than you'd like. However, if you've improved but not gotten to the point of recovery you'd like to be at, keep doing more of what you've been doing.

Sizing Up Your Risk of Relapse

If your main problem is depression, your risk of relapse is particularly high. In fact, if you treated your depression only with medication, your risk of relapse exceeds 50 percent over the next couple of years. Anxiety poses a somewhat lower relapse risk.

Studies indicate that cognitive behavior therapies (those that focus on changes in thinking and behaving), which are the basis for most of this book, work. Not only do these therapies work, they appear to significantly reduce relapse risk. So the bottom line is that if all you've tried is medication, we recommend you embrace the skills we give you throughout this book and/or see a therapist trained in cognitive behavior therapy.

You're probably wondering how much risk you actually have for relapse. To figure out your risk, check off the items in Worksheet 17-1 that pertain to you.

Worksheet 17-1	Relapse Risk Quiz

❏ 1. I am completely over my anxiety or depression. I have no fear it will return.

❏ 2. I have been previously depressed more than once in my life.

❏ 3. I have had bouts of anxiety off and on for years.

❏ 4. I have only taken medication for my problems.

❏ 5. I suffer from a chronic illness.

❏ 6. I have had some big financial problems lately.

❏ 7. I recently lost someone I care deeply about through breakup or death.

❏ 8. I recently experienced a traumatic event.

❏ 9. I lost my job not long ago.

❏ 10. I just retired.

❏ 11. There's been an increase in family conflict lately.

❏ 12. I just graduated from high school or college.

❏ 13. When I get depressed or anxious, I know it's entirely my fault.

❏ 14. I can't control my moods at all.

❏ 15. I need people to like me in order to be happy.

You may think that checking off the first statement in the list reduces your risk of relapse. Wrong. Surprisingly, overconfidence has been found to be a risk factor for relapse. In other words, a little optimism is a good thing, but you need to temper that optimism with realism. Knowing that you have some risk of relapse is vital to helping you deal with early signs.

If you checked any statements at all in the Relapse Risk Quiz, you're at increased risk for the return of emotional distress. Checking more than two or three statements puts you at extremely high risk.

Depression and anxiety should be treated until symptoms almost completely subside. Therapy should extend for at least six or eight weeks after you experience a return to full energy, appetite, sleep, and pleasure levels. Medication should be continued even longer — six to twelve months after full remission of symptoms.

If you work through the exercises in this chapter and a relapse still occurs, don't catastrophize. You're not starting at square one. You have some skills, and you can apply them anew. Or you can try one of the exercises that you haven't gotten around to. If you can't get out of your funk on your own, you can always turn to professional help. You *can* feel better; don't just sit around and feel miserable.

Not Letting Relapse Sneak Up on You

With relapse, subtle signs may start to appear and go unnoticed. Then, suddenly, you find your problems have returned, possibly even worse than before.

We don't want relapse to get the best of you, so we recommend that, after you've recovered from anxiety or depression, you conduct a review of your emotions and feelings on a weekly basis. Over time, you can reduce the frequency of these reviews to once every month or two as your risk of relapse becomes less and less.

To review your emotions and feelings, complete the Early Warning Signs: Emotion Relapse Review in Worksheet 17-2. Take your time to think about each question regarding specific warning signs and describe in writing what's been going on with you.

Worksheet 17-2   Early Warning Signs: Emotion Relapse Review

1. Have I started avoiding people lately? If so, who, what, when, where, and why?

_____

_____

_____

_____

2. Have my thoughts been dark and pessimistic? If so, what are they, and how intense are they?

_____

_____

_____

_____

3. Have I noticed any changes in my appetite? If so, how long has it lasted, and have I lost or gained any weight?

_____

_____

_____

_____

4. Have I been avoiding activities or places lately? If so, what, where, when, and why?

_____

_____

_____

_____

5. Have I noticed any changes in my sleeping patterns? If so, what are the changes, and how often do they occur?

_____

_____

_____

_____

6. **Have I been more irritable than usual? If so, when, and under what circumstances?**

_____

_____

_____

_____

7. **Has someone close to me said that I've been out of sorts in any way? If so, what was said?**

_____

_____

_____

_____

8. **Have I noticed changes in my memory, concentration, or energy? If so, what are these changes?**

_____

_____

_____

_____

9. **Have I been feeling excessively guilty or down on myself about anything? If so, what's that been about?**

_____

_____

_____

_____

10. **Have I been sad or worried about anything recently? If so, what, where, when, and why?**

_____

_____

_____

_____

Visit www.dummies.com/go/adwbfd to download and print as many of these forms as you need for your own use.

If you fill out our Emotional Relapse Review form regularly, relapse isn't very likely to overtake you unexpectedly. The moment you spot significant signs of relapse (as described in Worksheet 17-2), please read and work through the next two sections of this chapter. In addition, we recommend that you go back and do more of whatever it was that reduced your emotional distress previously.

Changes in energy, appetite, or sleep may be due to a physical problem. If you're experiencing these types of changes in your normal behavior, check things out with your primary care physician.

Having a Fire Extinguisher Ready

Hopefully, you don't wait for a fire to start before you make a plan for dealing with it. Fire drills save lives, as do rehearsals of how you'll deal with relapse. Approaching the potential of relapse as you would the potential for fire can save you a lot of grief and prevent relapse.

Worksheet 17-2 lays out the early warning signs you should look out for. In Worksheet 17-3, we list a few of the common events that trigger emotional distress. Read through the list, thinking about which events you fear may cause you trouble at some point in the future. For each item, jot down the specifics of your concern. (At the end of the list, add any likely future events that you worry about encountering.)

Worksheet 17-3	Fuel for Emotional Fires Questionnaire

1. Loss of someone important to me

_____

_____

_____

2. Getting rejected

_____

_____

_____

3. Getting sick or hurt

_____

_____

_____

4. Money problems

_____

_____

_____

5. **Major political changes**

_____

_____

_____

6. **Humiliation, shame, or embarrassment**

_____

_____

_____

7. **My additional concerns**

_____

_____

_____

So, are we trying to get you to worry about all the bad things that may happen to you? What about our advice in Chapter 8 about the value of staying centered in the present? Well, you raise a good point! Staying in the present is a good idea, but so is being reasonably prepared for the future.

In order to be prepared, we suggest the Fire Drill Strategy. Take each event that you list as worrisome in Worksheet 17-3 and figure out how you would cope if that event occurred. First, review this example of the Fire Drill Strategy.

David recovered from a combination of anxiety and depression about two months ago. He's preparing to stop seeing his professional counselor from the past six months. Before ending their sessions, David's therapist suggests that David prepare for possible fire, or the flare-up of one of his fears. The therapist has David fill out the Fire Drill Strategy (see Worksheet 17-4) on one of David's worries. David's father and uncle both died of colon cancer in their 50s, and David's now 51, so the fear of developing colon cancer is very real for him.

Worksheet 17-4	**David's Fire Drill Strategy**

Situation: Fear of colon cancer

1. **How would someone else cope with this situation?**

   I can't deny that it would be incredibly tough. However, my father used the last years of his life to get his affairs in order and spend time with his family. He also was very helpful to many people in his cancer support group. I could do that. I remember my uncle was very angry and seemed to suffer a lot more. I'd rather be like my father.

2. Have I dealt with something like this in the past? How did I do it?

When I was in college I came down with meningitis. I was really sick, and everyone was very worried. I don't remember being terrified, though. I think I could use the same acceptance I had then.

3. How much will this event affect my life a year after it occurs?

Actually, given that I get regular screenings, the odds are pretty good that it won't be affecting me much a year after diagnosis. I just may be catastrophizing about this issue.

4. Is this event as awful as I'm making it out to be?

Obviously not. There have been so many advances both in terms of catching it early as well as treatment that I think I'd be okay. As for the slim chance that I'd die, I guess I could deal with that, too. I'd have to.

5. Are there any intriguing, creative ways of dealing with this challenge?

I've been meaning to participate in the cancer walk-a-thon. Maybe I'll get off my behind (so to speak) and just do it. If I do get diagnosed, I'll join the support group like my Dad did. He seemed to really benefit and help others at the same time.

After completing this exercise, David realizes that he can cope with even his worst fears. Seeing the benefit of the exercise, he also fills out a Fire Drill Strategy on several other problems that he may encounter down the road.

Using Worksheet 17-5, complete your own Fire Drill Strategy. Simply list your specific fear at the top and answer the questions that follow. Fill out a questionnaire for each problematic concern you identified in the Fuel for Emotional Fires Questionnaire (see Worksheet 17-3).

Worksheet 17-5   **My Fire Drill Strategy**

Situation: _____

1. How would someone else cope with this situation?

_____

_____

_____

_____

2. Have I dealt with something like this in the past? How did I do it?

_____

_____

_____

_____

3. How much will this event affect my life a year after it occurs?

_____

_____

_____

_____

4. Is this event as awful as I'm making it out to be?

_____

_____

_____

_____

5. Are there any intriguing, creative ways of dealing with this challenge?

_____

_____

_____

_____

Visit www.dummies.com/go/adwbfd to download as many copies of this form as you need for your personal use.

How did you feel before you filled out your Fire Drill Strategy? Did answering the questions reveal anything about your fear? Take a few moments to reflect on what you've learned about preparing for future difficulties, and record your thoughts in Worksheet 17-6.

Worksheet 17-6 **My Reflections**
___

_____

_____

_____

_____

_____

Keeping the Ball Rolling

If you work hard and conquer your depression or anxiety, that's great! But you still probably experience minor bumps in the road. And some people fail to appreciate the things that are going well for them. Are you one of those folks? Do you notice the activities that increase your feelings of satisfaction and well-being?

Doing the right things

The technique we explain in this section, the Satisfaction Tracker, is designed to track satisfying activities. Paying close attention to satisfying activities highlights what's going right in your life, and increasing your focus on your well-being improves your odds of preventing relapse.

Cindy has had a tough year. She broke up with her boyfriend and was diagnosed with breast cancer. Her physical recovery was excellent and rapid by most standards. However, as is common with breast cancer survivors, Cindy suffered from depression off and on during her ordeal. Now a year later, her depression has thoroughly abated. Cindy tracks her satisfying activities as a way of solidifying her gains and preventing relapse (see Worksheet 17-7).

Worksheet 17-7	Cindy's Satisfaction Tracker	
Situation	*Satisfying Thoughts*	*Satisfaction Intensity (0–100)*
I took pictures at a wedding.	My hobby has turned into a second career. That was my dream!	80
I was chosen to teach a continuing education class in digital photography.	I love teaching. I must be getting pretty good at what I do.	70
I went on a cruise with friends.	This was great. I was never able to treat myself like this before.	85
I took a long walk in my neighborhood and noticed the scenery.	I appreciate things like this more than ever.	60
I paid my bills.	I'd been putting that off for too long. It wasn't a major high, but felt nice.	40
I went to my first party since my recovery.	I felt a little on-stage, but it was nice to see my friends there.	65

Using Cindy's Satisfaction Tracker as a guide, complete your own Tracker in Worksheet 17-8 in order to keep track of the good stuff going on in your life. Remember to include major as well as minor events.

1. **Note a particular event in the left-hand column.**

2. **In the middle column, write down your thoughts and feelings about the event.**

3. **In the right-hand column, rate the sense of satisfaction you experienced from that event on a scale of 0 (no satisfaction) to 100 (total ecstasy).**

4. **Following the exercise, use Worksheet 17-9 to reflect on what you've discovered about your recovery and current well-being.**

Worksheet 17-8	My Satisfaction Tracker	
Situation	*Satisfying Thoughts*	*Satisfaction Intensity (0–100)*

At www.dummies.com/go/adwbfd, you can download as many copies of this form as you need.

Worksheet 17-9	My Reflections

_____

_____

_____

_____

Disrupting satisfaction interrupters

Sometimes, activities that you anticipate being wonderful turn out to be just okay, blah, or downright downers. This kind of outcome may indicate that your satisfaction was sabotaged by a *satisfaction interrupter*. The culprit is usually a thought that steals your initial or planned enjoyment of an activity. To understand satisfaction interrupters and their effects on your experiences, check out the following example.

Austin loves golf and looks forward to playing in a weekend charity game. It's a crisp, clear day, and the course is beautiful. Austin is clearly the best player of his foursome. He expects to have a really a great time. But as he plays, he finds himself having thoughts that interrupt his good feelings. Therefore, after he's finished his round of golf, Austin fills out a Satisfaction

Interrupter (see Worksheet 17-10) in order to get a better handle on what his thoughts have been doing to him. After completing the exercise, he realizes that he needs to do something about his satisfaction-interrupting thoughts and completes the Satisfaction-Interrupter Disrupter shown in Worksheet 17-11.

Worksheet 17-10	Austin's Satisfaction Interrupter	
Event	*Satisfying Thought*	*Satisfaction-Interrupting Thought*
On the first tee, I drove the ball straight down the middle of the fairway.	Nice beginning; I could take this tournament.	The last time I started like this, I ended up getting a double bogey.
Nate said, "You're really on today!"	He's right; I am!	He's jinxed me. I feel like I'm going to start slipping.
I'm in the lead at the end of the first round.	My game is really improving. I should think about getting on the circuit.	Every time I have thoughts like this, I can hear my mother telling me that I'll never amount to anything.

Notice how Austin's initial, satisfying thoughts were zapped by his satisfaction-interrupting thoughts. These satisfaction-interrupting thoughts didn't make Austin feel depressed (like the thoughts discussed in Chapters 5, 6, and 7), but they robbed him of his good feelings. When the joy in your life gets stolen in this manner, you're be more susceptible to relapse.

So what can you do to hold onto your joy? Well, we have a strategy for dealing with satisfaction interrupters. Check out Worksheet 17-11 to see how Austin uses the Satisfaction-Interrupter Disrupter.

Worksheet 17-11	Austin's Satisfaction-Interrupter Disrupter

Satisfaction-Interrupting Thought: Every time I have thoughts like this, I can hear my mother telling me that I'll never amount to anything.

1. **What evidence do I have that either supports or refutes my satisfaction-interrupting thought?**

   I'm doing fine. I have a good job with lots of potential for advancement. My mother has been wrong about so many things in my life that it's almost funny.

2. **If a friend of mine told me that he or she had this thought, would I think it sounded reasonable or self-defeating?**

   I've had friends who are good golfers, and I've encouraged them to compete. If my friend told me that he felt like a failure because of something his mother said, I'd tell him to grow up and get over it.

3. **Do I have experiences in my life that could refute this thought?**

I've won several local golf tournaments. I can't be that much of a loser. I don't have to be the world's best golfer to get somewhere in life, but hey, I'm darn good.

4. **Is this satisfaction-interrupting thought distorted, and can I come up with a more accurate replacement thought? (See Chapter 6 for more information on thought distortions.)**

Clearly, thinking that my mother's view has anything to do with reality is pretty darn distorted. I'm overgeneralizing and dismissing evidence that shows I'm doing great. I can replace my satisfaction-interrupting thought with, "I'm doing great with my golf game. I don't need to listen to my mother's voice anymore."

After Austin answers the Satisfaction-Interrupter Disrupter questions, he realizes that he has been allowing distorted thinking to interfere with his pleasure.

Now that you've seen how it's done, track your satisfaction-interrupting thoughts in Worksheet 17-12.

1. **In the left-hand column, use a few words to capture what should have been a satisfying event.**

2. **If you initially had satisfying thoughts about that event, record those in the middle column. If you didn't have such thoughts, leave this column blank.**

3. **Record your satisfaction-interrupting thoughts in the right-hand column.** Remember, these are any thoughts that somehow took away the pleasure you may have otherwise felt.

Some people almost automatically sabotage their satisfaction with general beliefs such as, "Fun is frivolous," "I don't deserve to have a good time," or "I should be working." These thoughts stop satisfaction before it even begins. Look out for such beliefs in your own thinking, and read more about them in Chapters 7 and 11.

Worksheet 17-12	My Satisfaction Interrupter	
Event	*Satisfying Thought*	*Satisfaction-Interrupting Thought*

Download as many of these forms as you need at www.dummies.com/go/adwbfd.

One at a time, subject your thoughts from Worksheet 7-12 to the Satisfaction-Interrupter Disrupter questions in Worksheet 17-13.

1. **Choose one of your satisfaction-interrupting thoughts and write it in the space provided at the top of the questionnaire.**

2. **Answer each of the questions that follow in relation to that thought.** If you have trouble answering these questions, please review Chapters 5 and 6.

3. **In Worksheet 17-14, reflect on what these exercises have shown you. Can you see how your satisfaction interrupter thoughts are robbing you of joy? Can you see that replacement thoughts make a difference in the way you feel?**

Worksheet 17-13	**My Satisfaction-Interrupter Disrupter**

Satisfaction-Interrupting Thought: _____

1. **What evidence do I have that either supports or refutes my satisfaction-interrupting thought?**

    _____

    _____

    _____

    _____

2. **If a friend of mine told me that he or she had this thought, would I think it sounded reasonable or self-defeating?**

    _____

    _____

    _____

    _____

3. **Do I have experiences in my life that could refute this thought?**

    _____

    _____

    _____

    _____

4. **Is this satisfaction-interrupting thought distorted, and can I come up with a more accurate replacement thought? (See Chapter 6 for more information on thought distortions.)**

    _____

    _____

    _____

    _____

Worksheet 17-14	My Reflections

Chapter 18

Promoting Positives

● ●

In This Chapter

▶ Being thankful

▶ Reaching out to help others

▶ Forgiving and moving past your anger

▶ Finding meaning in everyday life

● ●

Throughout this book, we focus on ways to help you overcome depression and defeat anxiety. We know that working through the exercises we lay out and trying the strategies presented will improve your moods. You deserve to feel better, and if you already feel pretty good, this chapter is for you.

In this chapter, we go beyond depression and anxiety and reach for true happiness. Why? Because science tell us that happiness doesn't just feel good — happy people have better immune systems, live longer, have lower blood pressure, and have more empathy for others. Happy people are also more productive and make more money. That's a pretty good argument for finding happiness.

If happiness is such a good thing, you may wonder what exactly makes people happy. Although happy people usually make a little more money, research shows that money alone doesn't lead to more happiness. Unless you're in extreme poverty and struggling to put food on the table, studies indicate that even winning a big lottery payout doesn't increase happiness for very long. And, surprisingly, power, youth, and good looks don't seem to contribute much at all to people's reported happiness.

As psychologists, we see firsthand how often those with money, looks, and power suffer from depression and anxiety. Basically rich, gorgeous, young, and powerful people are as likely to be just as miserable as anyone else. That's not to say you should give away all your money, neglect your appearance, and quit your job! It's just that having all those things doesn't lead to happiness.

So what does lead to happiness? In Chapter 11, we talk about the value of seeking what we call *healthy pleasures*. Simple healthy pleasures are very helpful for kick-starting better moods, but they're somewhat transitory. In this chapter, we present ideas for finding deeper, longer-lasting satisfaction and well-being.

Focusing on Gratitude

You may have a grandmother or mother who suggests that you think about good things and put aside the bad. That's pretty good advice. The common-sense advice of our elders usually has more than a grain of truth to it. Truth is, concentrating on the good things in your life and whatever fills you with a sense of gratitude can be surprisingly helpful to developing your sense of well-being.

Keeping track of the things that make you grateful

Studies show that keeping track of what you appreciate or are thankful for improves mood, sleep, and health. What's really amazing is how easy it is to enhance your life-satisfaction in this manner.

Janet had a bout of depression and recovered a few months ago. She carefully monitors herself for signs of relapse and feels grateful that she seems to have beaten the blues. Before terminating therapy, her therapist suggests that Janet count her blessings for a while. So Janet fills out a Gratitude Diary; Worksheet 18-1 shows her first week's efforts.

Worksheet 18-1	Janet's Gratitude Diary
Day	*What I Feel Grateful For*
Monday	1) I found a great parking space this morning. 2) I lost two pounds. 3) Work went well today. 4) I love my dog! 5) My kids are terrific.
Tuesday	1) The same parking space was there today! 2) The weather is wonderful. 3) The kids did their homework without me nagging. 4) I'm so glad I have good health. 5) The traffic wasn't too bad today. 6) I don't have any money problems right now.
Wednesday	1) I like this town. 2) Nothing bad happened at work. 3) I went for a great walk. 4) I'm not depressed. 5) I like my car.
Thursday	1) The kids got off to school without their usual whining. 2) Traffic was pretty darn good today. 3) I got by that speed trap without getting caught! 4) I had fun in my aerobics class. 5) I had a good talk with my friend, Lisa.
Friday	1) It's Friday! 2) It looks like I may get a raise. 3) I had a delicious lunch with my friend. 4) I'm not depressed. 5) I rented a good movie.
Saturday	1) I enjoyed watching my daughter's soccer game. 2) I helped out a neighbor by watching her kids and felt great that I could do that. 3) The repair bill for the air conditioner wasn't as bad as I feared. 4) I'm not depressed! 5) I went out for dinner with my boyfriend. We had a nice time.
Sunday	1) I planted tomatoes. 2) I took the kids over to their friend's house and had a few hours to myself. 3) I talked to my mother, and she seemed in good spirits. 4) I lost another pound. 5) I felt a little down about starting the week again, but I pulled myself out of a bad mood. I couldn't do that before.

Janet is surprised at how good it feels to track what makes her feel grateful for a few weeks. She starts to exercise more than before, and she feels a deeper sense of satisfaction with her life.

Using Janet's Gratitude Diary as a guide, fill out your own Diary in Worksheet 18-2.

1. **On each day of the week, think of five things you feel grateful for that day.** These items can be very small, such as finding a great parking space, or more substantial, such as your good health.

2. **Write each item in the diary on its corresponding day, and reflect on how appreciative you feel that day.**

3. **At the end of the week, use Worksheet 18-3 to reflect on what you've learned as a result of keeping tabs on what makes you feel grateful.**

Consider continuing this exercise every week for a month and from time to time in the future.

Worksheet 18-2	My Gratitude Diary
Day	**What I Feel Grateful For**
Monday	
Tuesday	
Wednesday	
Thursday	
Friday	
Saturday	
Sunday	

Download as many copies of this exercise as you need for your personal use at www.dummies.com/go/adwbfd.

Worksheet 18-3	My Reflections

_____

_____

_____

_____

_____

Writing testimonials

One strategy for bringing gratitude into your life by writing testimonials was developed by Dr. Martin Seligman, and we think it's a great idea. Dr. Seligman conducted some research on this technique and found that participants felt great after completing it.

Dustin has a lot to be grateful for. He conquered his social anxiety more than a year ago. His college roommate, Jack, was instrumental in helping Dustin overcome his anxiety. Now, a junior in college, Dustin is taking an upper-level psychology class. His professor suggests a project called the Testimonial Exercise. The students are instructed to choose someone from their lives who made a real difference and write out a testimonial to that individual. The students are told to deliver the testimonial and read it to their selected person. In Worksheet 18-4, you can read what Dustin writes about his roommate.

Worksheet 18-4	Testimonial Exercise

Dear Jack,

I was given the assignment of writing a testimonial to someone who has made a difference in my life, and guess what? You're it. I felt pretty weird about this at first, but the more I thought about it, the more I liked the idea. I don't think I've ever told you how much I appreciate what you did for me in helping me overcome my social anxiety. That first year of college was brutal for me. Your friendship saved me from utter misery.

You took me under your wing and pushed me to do things I didn't think I could. And you were a role model for me. You taught me how to talk with women. We had some pretty good times, didn't we? But sometimes I would get pretty down about my problems, and you'd kick me in the butt. You told me I needed to get counseling. Oh how I didn't want to hear that! But you were right. The whole first-year experience changed my life. I give you credit for so much.

My hat's off to you, buddy. They don't come any better than you. Your friendship is incredibly valuable to me. And now before I make myself totally sick, I'd better end this thing! But seriously, I appreciate all you did.

Your buddy,

Dustin

Use Worksheet 18-5 and the following instructions to complete your own Testimonial Exercise.

1. **Choose someone from your life who has made a real positive difference in your life.** Ideally, the person you choose shouldn't be someone you're romantically involved with.

2. **Write at least two or three paragraphs expressing your gratitude and telling the person what he or she did for you.** Write out your testimonial in longhand — it's more personal that way.

3. **Arrange a time to meet with the person to whom you wrote, and read your testimonial out loud to him or her.**

4. **Spend some time talking with your chosen person.**

5. **In Worksheet 18-6, reflect on this exercise and what it's taught you about the good people and things in your life.**

Worksheet 18-5	Testimonial Exercise

Dear   ,

Worksheet 18-6	My Reflections

_____

_____

_____

_____

_____

Making the World a Bit Nicer

A powerful way of achieving happiness is through helping others. Being kind to others helps you in two ways: First, you're likely to enjoy the feeling you get from giving service or kindness to others. Second, doing something nice for another person takes your mind off your own problems.

To get you started, Worksheet 18-7 lists some possible good things you can do to help others. It's good to come up with your own list of things that are important to you, but for more ideas, consider checking out www.actsofkindness.org.

Worksheet 18-7	Nice Ideas

❑ Walk dogs at your local Humane Society

❑ Offer to take someone else's shopping cart back to the store

❑ Volunteer to tutor someone

❑ Volunteer to drive for a Senior Center

❑ Offer to run an errand for a neighbor

❑ Pick up litter in your neighborhood

❑ Let another driver merge into your lane

❑ Donate blood

❑ Donate food or clothing to a homeless shelter

❑ Write a thank-you note to someone

This exercise helps you discover the personal benefits of small acts of kindness. Even in small ways, you make the world a better place while simultaneously enhancing your own well-being.

1. **Brainstorm a list of at least 20 small acts of kindness — things you could do almost anytime. Write them in the left-hand column of Worksheet 18-8.** The key is to think of ideas that are truly gifts — in other words, you shouldn't expect something in return. If you want to include a few more substantial acts, that's fine; remember, the frequency of your actions is what really makes the difference.

2. **After you develop your list, start doing the things you've listed!**

3. Track each act of kindness in the right-hand column by recording the date when you complete the act.

4. In Worksheet 18-9, reflect on how this exercise affects you.

Worksheet 18-8	My Nice Ideas
Acts of Kindness	*When I Did It*

Worksheet 18-9	My Reflections

Letting Go

One way people ruin their chances for happiness is by holding on to resentments, anger, and rage. When you've been wronged, it's natural to feel upset, and anger can be useful, at least for a while. Anger helps you defend yourself when attacked because it revs up your body to right a wrong.

However, anger that's held for too long begins to poison your body and soul. Chronic anger leads to high blood pressure, emotional disturbance, and a decrease in common sense. Thus, when you're angry, you simply can't be happy.

But ridding yourself of chronic anger isn't an especially easy task. You must do something that feels rather counterintuitive: Somehow find forgiveness for those who have wronged you.

There may be certain wrongs that you probably can't realistically forgive. For example, you may find yourself unable to forgive acts of severe violence or abuse. In that case, an alternative approach is to let go of the anger and rage by finding acceptance. See Chapter 8 for ideas on acquiring acceptance.

In Worksheet 18-10, we guide you through a series of steps for finding forgiveness and the serenity that comes along with it.

Worksheet 18-10	**Finding Forgiveness**

1. **Write down what has happened to you to make you angry. Be specific. Try to avoid using words of rage and retribution; instead, describe the person and event in dispassionate terms. Review what you've written over and over until your feelings about it begin to lessen.**

   _____

   _____

   _____

   _____

2. **Try to put yourself in the offender's shoes. Search for some understanding as to why he or she may have carried out the offense against you. Was the offender or perpetrator afraid, misguided, depressed, defensive, lacking judgment, or purposefully hurtful? Write down your ideas.**

   _____

   _____

   _____

   _____

3. **Think of yourself as a forgiving person, not a victim. Describe how your life may be different when you learn to let go of your anger and forgive.**

   _____

   _____

   _____

   _____

4. **When thoughts of revenge come into your mind, write down reasons for letting them go. Remember that anger and rage harm you more than the perpetrator.**

_____

_____

_____

_____

5. **Consider writing a letter of forgiveness in the space below. You don't have to send it to the perpetrator, but you may find comfort in discussing it with others.**

_____

_____

_____

_____

 Forgiving isn't the same as saying that the wrong was okay. Forgiveness gives back the peace that you had before the event occurred. And letting go of your anger allows you to regain your previous happiness.

Exercising Self-Control

In pursuing happiness, avoiding the *quick fix* is very important. Quick fixes come in all shapes and sizes — alcohol, drugs, chocolate, a new car, a better house, more clothes, blah, blah, blah. Such things are fine in moderation, of course, but they don't create lasting happiness.

In fact, numerous studies demonstrate that in the long run, self-control and the ability to delay gratification lead to better adjustment and greater satisfaction with life. Yet we live in a world that promises and encourages instant gratification and suggests that you should be happy at all times. Those expectations can easily set you up for disappointment. The truth is that

✔ People aren't always happy.

✔ Meaningful goals require effort and patience.

✔ Overindulgence leads to satiation and depleted pleasure.

✔ People who expect instant gratification are inevitably frustrated and disappointed.

 Worksheet 18-11 starts you on the path to achieving greater self-control. Even small steps in this direction enhance your sense of well-being. Please realize you don't have to make major changes all at once, and most importantly, devote some serious time to this exercise to get the best results.

Worksheet 18-11	Strengthening Self-Control

1. Write a brief description of an area in your life in which you've given in to impulses or expected instant gratification.

_____

_____

_____

_____

2. Write your reflections on how increasing self-control may improve your long-term satisfaction.

_____

_____

_____

_____

3. Based on what you've written, develop a goal for change.

_____

_____

_____

_____

4. Record your reflections on how your life would change for the better if you were to achieve this new goal.

_____

_____

_____

_____

Discovering What's Really Important

What do you value? How much of your time to you devote to activities that are meaningful and consistent with your values? And do you live your life according to those values? If not, you're probably not as happy as you could be.

The following Values Clarification Quiz can help you focus on what's really important to you. After you fill it out, you can use the results to redirect your life plan in a more meaningful way.

1. Read through all the values listed in Worksheet 18-12.

2. Circle the eight items you prize most highly.

3. Of those eight, pick your top three most-prized items and write them in Worksheet 18-13.

Worksheet 18-12	**Values Clarification Quiz**
Money	Donating time or money to others
Pleasure	Cleaning up the environment
Independence	Political activism
Risk-taking and/or excitement	Competition
Creativity	Leisure time
Recognition	Honesty
Achievement	Winning
Variety	Family life
Entertainment	Recreation
Close friends	Status
A loving partner	Expensive possessions
Spirituality	Intellectual pursuits
Health	Looking good
Good food	Satisfying work
Having happy kids	Showing kindness
Art	Mental or physical stimulation
Economic security	Safety
Influencing others	Predictability

Worksheet 18-13	**My Top Three Values**

1.

2.

3.

Ponder how you've spent your time in the past month. Estimate the amount of time you've devoted to activities that are concordant with your top three values (see Worksheet 18-13). If you notice a discrepancy between what you value and what you do, consider re-prioritizing. In Worksheet 18-14, jot down how you plan to re-allocate your schedule and resources to better reflect what you deem as important. Making these changes is likely to improve your long-term life satisfaction.

Worksheet 18-14	My Reflections

_____

_____

_____

_____

_____

Finding Meaning at Your Funeral

You probably think that your funeral would be a rather odd place to find meaning in your life, and you may wonder why a book purporting to provide help with emotional distress is asking you to think about dying. Well, give us a minute here, okay? Let us explain.

Finding meaning and purpose in life is about connecting with ideas and concepts that are larger and deeper than yourself. For many, religion and spirituality are the primary channels for finding such meaning. But regardless of your spiritual beliefs, giving serious consideration to what you want your life to be about, in other words, the legacy you want to leave behind, can be an enlightening exercise.

In this section, we ask you to think about your funeral or memorial service and the thoughts and feelings that those in attendance may experience when contemplating your life. What do you want people to remember about your life? The following exercise helps you discover the traits, characteristics, and values you hold most dearly. By reminding yourself to live the rest of your life accordingly, you'll feel more enriched and fulfilled.

Roland completes the Eulogy in Advance exercise as a way of enhancing the sense of meaning and purpose he gets from his life. As he prepares to write his eulogy, Roland realizes that he hasn't been living his life in a way that justifies how he wants to be remembered. Nevertheless, he writes out how he wants people to think of him and his life after he's gone (see Worksheet 18-15).

Worksheet 18-15	Roland's Eulogy in Advance

We are gathered here today to say goodbye to our friend and family member, Roland. Roland was a wonderful father and husband. He loved and enjoyed spending time with his family. Roland's children grew up to be successful and happy. He loved and cherished his wife throughout their marriage. He was careful to keep the romance alive, even until the end. Roland was a true friend to many of us here today. When someone needed help, Roland was the first to offer. His door was always open. Whether or not people needed his time or even his money, Roland was generous. Roland also gave to his community; he organized members of his congregation to pick up seniors who were unable to drive so that they could attend church services and functions. Truly, he made the world a little better place.

Roland sees a painful contrast between the life he's been living and the one he wants to be remembered for. Thus, he realizes that he spends far too much of his time working and buying unnecessary "stuff." He doesn't want people to recall that he was the first on his block to have a plasma television or that he leased a new car every year. Roland vows that in the future, he'll spend more time with his friends and family, and he makes a plan for contributing more to his community. After all, he cherishes these values far more than all the material prizes in the world.

Use the space in Worksheet 18-16 to write your own Eulogy in Advance. Remember to be honest about how you'd like to be remembered, regardless of your current activities and behaviors.

1. **Sit back and relax for a few minutes.**

2. **Ponder how you would like to be remembered at the end of your life.** Think of loved ones and friends — what do you wish they would say or think about you?

3. **Write down your thoughts.** Your Eulogy in Advance should reflect the things you value most, in other words, what you want the rest of your life to be about.

Worksheet 18-16	**My Eulogy in Advance**

Starting at this moment, right now, you're beginning the rest of your life. Whether you're 15 or 84, it's never too late to start living a life with meaning and purpose.

Part VII
The Part of Tens

The 5th Wave   By Rich Tennant

"I'm looking for someone who will love me for who I think I am."

In this part . . .

We provide you with some very useful quick references in the grand *For Dummies* tradition. First, we offer lists of resources that you can turn to for extra assistance; you're likely to find one or more of these resources helpful. Then, we spend a bit of time on the small stuff; we provide ten quick strategies for successfully combating mild to moderate distressing feelings.

Chapter 19

Ten Resources for Help

In This Chapter

▶ Looking for help in all the right places

▶ Making a personal commitment to find help

*W*e certainly hope and expect that you've found this book useful, but most people benefit from multiple sources of help. This chapter contains our recommended resources for finding additional support if you're facing anxiety or depression. Feel free to pick and choose among the options we list here.

Spending Time with Self-Help Books

Bookstores offer a dizzying array of self-help books. Unfortunately, some of them present strategies that are based on unproven methods or shoddy science, and others claim instant cures or make unrealistic, outlandish claims. The following is a short list of books that give solid help based on well-researched strategies for alleviating emotional distress. Obviously, these aren't the only good books out there; however, these are ones we most frequently recommend.

- *Addiction & Recovery For Dummies* by Brian F. Shaw, Paul Ritvo, Jane Irvine, and M. David Lewis (Wiley, 2004)

- *Authentic Happiness: Using the New Positive Psychology to Realize Your Potential for Lasting Fulfillment,* by Martin E. P. Seligman (Free Press, 2004)

- *Changing For Good: A Revolutionary Six-Stage Program for Overcoming Bad Habits and Moving Your Life Positively Forward* by James O. Prochaska, John C. Norcross, and Carlo C. DiClemente (William Morrow & Co., Inc., 1994)

- *Choosing to Live: How to Defeat Suicide Through Cognitive Therapy,* by Thomas E. Ellis and Cory F. Newman (New Harbinger Publications, 1996)

- *Depression For Dummies*, by Laura L. Smith and Charles H. Elliott (Wiley, 2003)

- *Feeling Better, Getting Better, Staying Better: Profound Self-Help Therapy for Your Emotions,* by Albert Ellis (Impact Publishers, Inc., 2001)

- *Full Catastrophe Living: Using the Wisdom of Your Body and Mind to Face Stress, Pain, and Illness,* by Jon Kabat-Zinn (Delta, 1990)

- *Learn to Relax: Proven Techniques for Reducing Stress, Tension, and Anxiety — and Promoting Peak Performance,* by C. Eugene Walker (Wiley, 2000)

- *Love Is Never Enough: How Couples Can Overcome Misunderstandings, Resolve Conflicts, and Solve Relationship Problems Through Cognitive Therapy,* by Aaron T. Beck (HarperCollins, 1989)

✔ *Mastery of Your Anxiety and Panic,* by David Barlow and Michelle Craske (Oxford University Press, 2005)

✔ *Mind Over Mood: Change How You Feel by Changing the Way You Think,* by Dennis Greenberger and Christine A. Padesky (Guildford Press, 1995)

✔ *Mindful Recovery: A Spiritual Path to Healing from Addiction,* by Thomas Bien and Beverly Bien (Wiley, 2002)

✔ *Overcoming Anxiety For Dummies,* by Charles H. Elliott and Laura L. Smith (Wiley, 2002)

✔ *The Anxiety & Phobia Workbook,* by Edmund J. Bourne (New Harbinger Publications, Inc., 2005)

✔ *The Feeling Good Handbook,* by David D. Burns (Plume, 1999)

✔ *The Seven Principles for Making Marriage Work,* by John M. Gottman and Nan Silver (Three Rivers Press, 2000)

✔ *Why Can't I Get What I Want?: How to Stop Making the Same Old Mistakes and Start Living a Life You Can Love,* by Charles H. Elliott and Maureen Kirby Lassen (Davies-Black Publishing, 1998)

Browsing Helpful Web Sites

The Internet gives you access to incredible amounts of information, good and bad, accurate and inaccurate, so you need to be careful about what you read and put to use in your situation. We can attest to the quality of the information and advice provided by the following sites:

✔ **American Psychiatric Association** (www.psych.org/public_info): Provides information about depression and other mental disorders.

✔ **American Psychological Association** (www.apa.org/pubinfo): Provides information about the treatment of depression and other emotional disorders as well as interesting facts about these topics.

✔ **Anxiety Disorders Association of America** (www.adaa.org): Lists self-help groups across the United States. It also displays a variety of anxiety-screening tools for self-assessment as well as an online newsletter and a message board. Because anxiety sometimes accompanies depression, you may want to check this site out even if you think you're only dealing with depression.

✔ **National Alliance for the Mentally Ill** (www.nami.org): A wonderful organization that serves as an advocate for people and families affected by mental disorders. This site provides information about the causes, prevalence, and treatments of mental disorders that affect children and adults.

✔ **National Institute of Mental Health** (www.nimh.nih.gov): Reports on research concerning a wide variety of mental health issues. This Web site supplies an array of educational materials on depression as well as resources for researchers and practitioners in the field.

✔ **WebMD** (www.webmd.com): Provides a vast array of information on both physical and mental health issues, including information about psychological treatments, drug therapy, and prevention.

Participating in Support Groups

Sometimes it's not a bad idea to seek out support from others who currently experience or have experienced problems similar to your own. Check out your local newspaper for a listing of support groups — you'll probably be surprised at how many different groups you find.

 Be careful when it comes to the many Internet support groups that exist. Sometimes, rather strange and disturbed people go to support group chat rooms and attempt to take advantage of vulnerable people.

Checking In with Primary Care Doctors

Most family practitioners and internists don't have specialized training in the treatment of emotional disorders. However, your anxiety and depression may be caused by physical problems, and your physician can rule that possibility out. Furthermore, your primary care doctor can refer you to the right mental health professionals.

Sharing with Psychiatrists

Psychiatrists have extensive training in diagnosing and treating mental disorders. Most psychiatrists primarily utilize medication in treating these disorders, and they're particularly expert in the management of medications' side effects. (See Chapter 14 for more information about treatment through medication.) Some psychiatrists have specialized training in psychotherapy techniques such as those reviewed in this book, so you should inquire ahead of time if that's the kind of help you're looking for.

Getting a Hand from Psychologists

Psychologists typically have PhDs in psychology, which give them extensive training in the diagnosis and treatment of mental disorders. They primarily utilize *psychotherapy,* which involves individual sessions during which you and your psychologist work together on goals for overcoming your difficulties. For the best results, make sure your psychologist is familiar with scientifically validated therapies such as those covered in this book. In a few states, psychologists with additional, specialized training are allowed to prescribe medication as well.

Talking Things Through with Counselors

Most counselors have master's degrees in counseling or psychology and have been trained in the treatment and diagnosis of emotional disorders. Before you begin a treatment program, make sure that your counselor is familiar with scientifically validated psychotherapeutic techniques.

Getting Extra Help from Social Workers

Social workers typically have master's degrees in social work. They often specialize in helping people access community resources, but many are trained in psychotherapy as well. Before you begin a treatment program, inquire as to your social worker's knowledge about scientifically validated psychotherapies.

Taking Advantage of Community Centers

If your town has a university, medical school, or community mental health center, you may be able to take advantage of any available mental health services, sometimes even at a reduced cost or on a scale based on income. Students may provide the actual services, but they're usually closely supervised by experienced faculty.

Leaning on Family and Friends

Almost everyone turns to friends or family for help from time to time, and we certainly encourage you to do so. Although your friends and family probably don't have the expertise to do more than support and listen to you, such support is invaluable in stressful times.

Avoid making your loved ones feel responsible for your mental health. Doing so may jeopardize your relationship and won't help you in the end. You must take charge of getting better.

Considering the Best Options for You

Take some time to reflect on which of the resources above you wish to pursue. In Worksheet 19-1, jot down a statement of commitment to pursue your chosen resources. You may also record notes here regarding your own investigation of these resources.

Worksheet 19-1	My Resources and Commitment

Chapter 20

Ten Quick Ways Out of Upset

The ideas in this chapter are designed to give you a lift when you're feeling a little down or uptight. Mind you, we're not talking about deep depression or intense anxiety — that's what the rest of the book is about. But if you're feeling not quite yourself, you're likely to find these tips useful.

Just Breathe

Typically, when you're distraught, your breathing quickens and becomes shallow. These changes in breathing are bound to add to your stress and make you more uncomfortable than you already are. You can counter such distress with this quick breathing technique:

1. **Place one hand on your abdomen and the other on your chest.**

2. **Breathe in slowly, concentrating on inflating your abdomen first and then your chest.**

3. **Exhale slowly, quietly saying the word "relax" as the air goes out.**

4. **Repeat Steps 1 through 3 for at least ten breaths.**

Talk It Out

People are social creatures. When you connect with others, you're likely to feel better. If you're feeling down, call a friend and discuss what's bothering you. Or call someone just to chat. Whatever the reason you connect, it's likely to help.

Get Soaked

Sitting in a warm bath or standing in a hot shower can comfort the body by loosening all those muscles that tighten up when you're stressed. (Hot tubs work pretty well, too, as do saunas, but not everyone has one of these handy.) As you feel the water rushing over or around you, think of yourself as wrapped up in a warm blanket. You'll feel safe, soothed, and serene.

Feel the Big Chill

This technique sounds pretty weird, but it works. When your distress feels intense, fill a sink or large bowl with ice water (that's right, ice water), take a deep breath, and immerse your face in the water for 30 seconds or so. Believe us, it's not as terrible as it sounds. This calming technique is believed to work because it elicits what's known as the body's *dive reflex*. When you're in ice-cold water, the body slows its metabolism in order to spare vital organs. A slowed metabolism reduces tension, so when your face is in ice water, your metabolism slows, your tension goes down, and you stop fretting about the things that are bothering you and your negative mind chatter ceases. As we said, it sounds weird, but we urge you to try it!

Take a Quick Thought Challenge

To figure out exactly what's bothering you and consider it in relation to the big picture of your life's events, answer the following questions. *Note:* This quick strategy works best if you first read Part II of this book.

1. **What's bothering me?**

   _____

   _____

   _____

2. **How important will this upset be to me in one year?**

   _____

   _____

   _____

3. **Do I have any evidence that would suggest my thoughts about the event are incorrect?**

   _____

   _____

   _____

4. **Is there a more reasonable way of looking at what happened?**

   _____

   _____

   _____

Exorcise with Exercise

The body responds to upset by producing stress hormones. However, you can quickly burn up those hormones by exercising at least 15 to 20 minutes. Try something aerobic such as running, jogging, or brisk walking. If it's a nice day, going outside gives you the added benefit of sunshine and fresh air. Or if it's more convenient, go to the gym and participate in an exercise class.

Mellow with Music

Sound influences the mind and body. It can jar, startle, upset, or soothe you. When you feel distressed, try listening to music that you find relaxing, whether classical, jazz, or even heavy metal. (For us, listening to heavy metal would send us into a crazed tizzy, but whatever works for you is what you should turn to.) Or you may listen to something pleasant and mellow but nonmusical, such as a fountain or the sounds of nature.

Pacify with Pets

Studies have shown that pets promote better moods and possibly better health. In fact, one study suggests that petting dogs helps reduce blood pressure. Therefore, if you don't have a pet, consider getting one, or at least borrowing a friend's from time to time. Watching animals play is delightful, and petting them seems to soothe the body.

Distract Your Distress

When you're upset, usually the only thing on your mind is your discomfort. And focusing on that discomfort only makes things worse. We're not advocating putting your head in the sand, but for quick relief of minor stress, consider distraction. Try these activities:

- ✔ Reading a good novel.
- ✔ Going to the movies.
- ✔ Watching television.
- ✔ Surfing the Internet.
- ✔ Playing a game.

Stay in the Present

Remember that most of what upsets you has to do with the past or the future. You may feel guilty and depressed about events from the past, and you may feel anxious about events that have not yet occurred and often never will. To snap yourself out of this trap, focus on what's actually happening around you right now. Notice your breathing. Feel your feet on the ground. Notice the firmness of your chair. Pay attention to the temperature. Look around you and observe. Don't judge. Just observe, and breathe.

Figure Out What Works for You

1. Take a few moments to reflect on how the various techniques in this chapter have worked for you.

2. In Worksheet 20-1, jot down the techniques that have helped you and how you felt when you used them.

Worksheet 20-1	My Reflections

Index

Notes

Notes

Notes

Notes

BUSINESS, CAREERS & PERSONAL FINANCE

Grant Writing FOR DUMMIES
0-7645-5307-0

Home Buying FOR DUMMIES
0-7645-5331-3 *†

Also available:
- Accounting For Dummies †
  0-7645-5314-3
- Business Plans Kit For Dummies †
  0-7645-5365-8
- Cover Letters For Dummies
  0-7645-5224-4
- Frugal Living For Dummies
  0-7645-5403-4
- Leadership For Dummies
  0-7645-5176-0
- Managing For Dummies
  0-7645-1771-6

- Marketing For Dummies
  0-7645-5600-2
- Personal Finance For Dummies *
  0-7645-2590-5
- Project Management For Dummies
  0-7645-5283-X
- Resumes For Dummies †
  0-7645-5471-9
- Selling For Dummies
  0-7645-5363-1
- Small Business Kit For Dummies *†
  0-7645-5093-4

HOME & BUSINESS COMPUTER BASICS

Windows XP FOR DUMMIES
0-7645-4074-2

Excel 2003 FOR DUMMIES
0-7645-3758-X

Also available:
- ACT! 6 For Dummies
  0-7645-2645-6
- iLife '04 All-in-One Desk Reference
  For Dummies
  0-7645-7347-0
- iPAQ For Dummies
  0-7645-6769-1
- Mac OS X Panther Timesaving
  Techniques For Dummies
  0-7645-5812-9
- Macs For Dummies
  0-7645-5656-8
- Microsoft Money 2004 For Dummies
  0-7645-4195-1

- Office 2003 All-in-One Desk Reference
  For Dummies
  0-7645-3883-7
- Outlook 2003 For Dummies
  0-7645-3759-8
- PCs For Dummies
  0-7645-4074-2
- TiVo For Dummies
  0-7645-6923-6
- Upgrading and Fixing PCs For Dummies
  0-7645-1665-5
- Windows XP Timesaving Techniques
  For Dummies
  0-7645-3748-2

FOOD, HOME, GARDEN, HOBBIES, MUSIC & PETS

Feng Shui FOR DUMMIES
0-7645-5295-3

Poker FOR DUMMIES
0-7645-5232-5

Also available:
- Bass Guitar For Dummies
  0-7645-2487-9
- Diabetes Cookbook For Dummies
  0-7645-5230-9
- Gardening For Dummies *
  0-7645-5130-2
- Guitar For Dummies
  0-7645-5106-X
- Holiday Decorating For Dummies
  0-7645-2570-0
- Home Improvement All-in-One
  For Dummies
  0-7645-5680-0

- Knitting For Dummies
  0-7645-5395-X
- Piano For Dummies
  0-7645-5105-1
- Puppies For Dummies
  0-7645-5255-4
- Scrapbooking For Dummies
  0-7645-7208-3
- Senior Dogs For Dummies
  0-7645-5818-8
- Singing For Dummies
  0-7645-2475-5
- 30-Minute Meals For Dummies
  0-7645-2589-1

INTERNET & DIGITAL MEDIA

Digital Photography FOR DUMMIES
0-7645-1664-7

Starting an eBay Business FOR DUMMIES
0-7645-6924-4

Also available:
- 2005 Online Shopping Directory
  For Dummies
  0-7645-7495-7
- CD & DVD Recording For Dummies
  0-7645-5956-7
- eBay For Dummies
  0-7645-5654-1
- Fighting Spam For Dummies
  0-7645-5965-6
- Genealogy Online For Dummies
  0-7645-5964-8
- Google For Dummies
  0-7645-4420-9

- Home Recording For Musicians
  For Dummies
  0-7645-1634-5
- The Internet For Dummies
  0-7645-4173-0
- iPod & iTunes For Dummies
  0-7645-7772-7
- Preventing Identity Theft For Dummies
  0-7645-7336-5
- Pro Tools All-in-One Desk Reference
  For Dummies
  0-7645-5714-9
- Roxio Easy Media Creator For Dummies
  0-7645-7131-1

* Separate Canadian edition also available
† Separate U.K. edition also available

SPORTS, FITNESS, PARENTING, RELIGION & SPIRITUALITY

0-7645-5146-9

0-7645-5418-2

Also available:

- Adoption For Dummies
  0-7645-5488-3
- Basketball For Dummies
  0-7645-5248-1
- The Bible For Dummies
  0-7645-5296-1
- Buddhism For Dummies
  0-7645-5359-3
- Catholicism For Dummies
  0-7645-5391-7
- Hockey For Dummies
  0-7645-5228-7

- Judaism For Dummies
  0-7645-5299-6
- Martial Arts For Dummies
  0-7645-5358-5
- Pilates For Dummies
  0-7645-5397-6
- Religion For Dummies
  0-7645-5264-3
- Teaching Kids to Read For Dummies
  0-7645-4043-2
- Weight Training For Dummies
  0-7645-5168-X
- Yoga For Dummies
  0-7645-5117-5

TRAVEL

0-7645-5438-7

0-7645-5453-0

Also available:

- Alaska For Dummies
  0-7645-1761-9
- Arizona For Dummies
  0-7645-6938-4
- Cancún and the Yucatán For Dummies
  0-7645-2437-2
- Cruise Vacations For Dummies
  0-7645-6941-4
- Europe For Dummies
  0-7645-5456-5
- Ireland For Dummies
  0-7645-5455-7

- Las Vegas For Dummies
  0-7645-5448-4
- London For Dummies
  0-7645-4277-X
- New York City For Dummies
  0-7645-6945-7
- Paris For Dummies
  0-7645-5494-8
- RV Vacations For Dummies
  0-7645-5443-3
- Walt Disney World & Orlando For Dummies
  0-7645-6943-0

GRAPHICS, DESIGN & WEB DEVELOPMENT

0-7645-4345-8

0-7645-5589-8

Also available:

- Adobe Acrobat 6 PDF For Dummies
  0-7645-3760-1
- Building a Web Site For Dummies
  0-7645-7144-3
- Dreamweaver MX 2004 For Dummies
  0-7645-4342-3
- FrontPage 2003 For Dummies
  0-7645-3882-9
- HTML 4 For Dummies
  0-7645-1995-6
- Illustrator CS For Dummies
  0-7645-4084-X

- Macromedia Flash MX 2004 For Dummies
  0-7645-4358-X
- Photoshop 7 All-in-One Desk Reference
  For Dummies
  0-7645-1667-1
- Photoshop CS Timesaving Techniques
  For Dummies
  0-7645-6782-9
- PHP 5 For Dummies
  0-7645-4166-8
- PowerPoint 2003 For Dummies
  0-7645-3908-6
- QuarkXPress 6 For Dummies
  0-7645-2593-X

NETWORKING, SECURITY, PROGRAMMING & DATABASES

0-7645-6852-3

0-7645-5784-X

Also available:

- A+ Certification For Dummies
  0-7645-4187-0
- Access 2003 All-in-One Desk Reference
  For Dummies
  0-7645-3988-4
- Beginning Programming For Dummies
  0-7645-4997-9
- C For Dummies
  0-7645-7068-4
- Firewalls For Dummies
  0-7645-4048-3
- Home Networking For Dummies
  0-7645-42796

- Network Security For Dummies
  0-7645-1679-5
- Networking For Dummies
  0-7645-1677-9
- TCP/IP For Dummies
  0-7645-1760-0
- VBA For Dummies
  0-7645-3989-2
- Wireless All In-One Desk Reference
  For Dummies
  0-7645-7496-5
- Wireless Home Networking For Dummies
  0-7645-3910-8

HEALTH & SELF-HELP

0-7645-6820-5 *†

0-7645-2566-2

Also available:

- Alzheimer's For Dummies
  0-7645-3899-3
- Asthma For Dummies
  0-7645-4233-8
- Controlling Cholesterol For Dummies
  0-7645-5440-9
- Depression For Dummies
  0-7645-3900-0
- Dieting For Dummies
  0-7645-4149-8
- Fertility For Dummies
  0-7645-2549-2
- Fibromyalgia For Dummies
  0-7645-5441-7

- Improving Your Memory For Dummies
  0-7645-5435-2
- Pregnancy For Dummies †
  0-7645-4483-7
- Quitting Smoking For Dummies
  0-7645-2629-4
- Relationships For Dummies
  0-7645-5384-4
- Thyroid For Dummies
  0-7645-5385-2

EDUCATION, HISTORY, REFERENCE & TEST PREPARATION

0-7645-5194-9

0-7645-4186-2

Also available:

- Algebra For Dummies
  0-7645-5325-9
- British History For Dummies
  0-7645-7021-8
- Calculus For Dummies
  0-7645-2498-4
- English Grammar For Dummies
  0-7645-5322-4
- Forensics For Dummies
  0-7645-5580-4
- The GMAT For Dummies
  0-7645-5251-1
- Inglés Para Dummies
  0-7645-5427-1

- Italian For Dummies
  0-7645-5196-5
- Latin For Dummies
  0-7645-5431-X
- Lewis & Clark For Dummies
  0-7645-2545-X
- Research Papers For Dummies
  0-7645-5426-3
- The SAT I For Dummies
  0-7645-7193-1
- Science Fair Projects For Dummies
  0-7645-5460-3
- U.S. History For Dummies
  0-7645-5249-X

Get smart @ dummies.com®

- **Find a full list of Dummies titles**
- **Look into loads of FREE on-site articles**
- **Sign up for FREE eTips e-mailed to you weekly**
- **See what other products carry the Dummies name**
- **Shop directly from the Dummies bookstore**
- **Enter to win new prizes every month!**

* Separate Canadian edition also available
† Separate U.K. edition also available

Available wherever books are sold. For more information or to order direct: U.S. customers visit www.dummies.com or call 1-877-762-2974.
U.K. customers visit www.wileyeurope.com or call 0800 243407. Canadian customers visit www.wiley.ca or call 1-800-567-4797.

Notes

Notes

Notes

Notes

Notes

Notes